Contents

About the Editor v

Introduction 1
Peter Afflerbach

Teachers as Evaluation Experts 13
Peter Johnston

Reading Assessment: Time for a Change 18
Sheila W. Valencia and P. David Pearson

Meeting AYP in a High-Need School: A Formative Experiment 24
Douglas Fisher, Nancy Frey, and Diane Lapp

Developing the IRIS: Toward Situated and Valid Assessment Measures in Collaborative Professional Development and School Reform in Literacy 35
Theresa Rogers, Kari Lynn Winters, Gregory Bryan, John Price, Frank McCormick, Liisa House, Dianna Mezzarobba, and Carollyne Sinclaire

A Framework for Authentic Literacy Assessment 46
Scott G. Paris, Robert C. Calfee, Nikola Filby, Elfrieda H. Hiebert, P. David Pearson, Sheila W. Valencia, and Kenneth P. Wolf

Reading Fluency Assessment and Instruction: What, Why, and How? 58
Roxanne F. Hudson, Holly B. Lane, and Paige C. Pullen

QAR: Enhancing Comprehension and Test Taking Across Grades and Content Areas 73
Taffy E. Raphael and Kathryn H. Au

Tile Test: A Hands-On Approach for Assessing Phonics in the Early Grades 89
Kimberly A. Norman and Robert C. Calfee

Assessing Adolescents' Motivation to Read 101
Sharon M. Pitcher, Lettie K. Albright, Carol J. DeLaney, Nancy T. Walker, Krishna Seunarinesingh, Stephen Mogge, Kathy N. Headley, Victoria Gentry Ridgeway, Sharon Peck, Rebecca Hunt, and Pamela J. Dunston

Teacher Questioning as Assessment 119
Peter Afflerbach

Focused Anecdotal Records Assessment: A Tool for Standards-Based, Authentic Assessment 135
Paul Boyd-Batstone

"I'm Not Stupid": How Assessment Drives (In)Appropriate Reading Instruction 146
Danielle V. Dennis

Parents and Children Reading and Reflecting Together:
The Possibilities of Family Retrospective Miscue Analysis 155
Bobbie Kabuto

Assessing English-Language Learners in Mainstream Classrooms 166
Susan Davis Lenski, Fabiola Ehlers-Zavala, Mayra C. Daniel, and Xiaoqin Sun-Irminger

Show Me: Principles for Assessing Students' Visual Literacy 178
Jon Callow

Using Electronic Portfolios to Make Learning Public 190
Kevin Fahey, Joshua Lawrence, and Jeanne Paratore

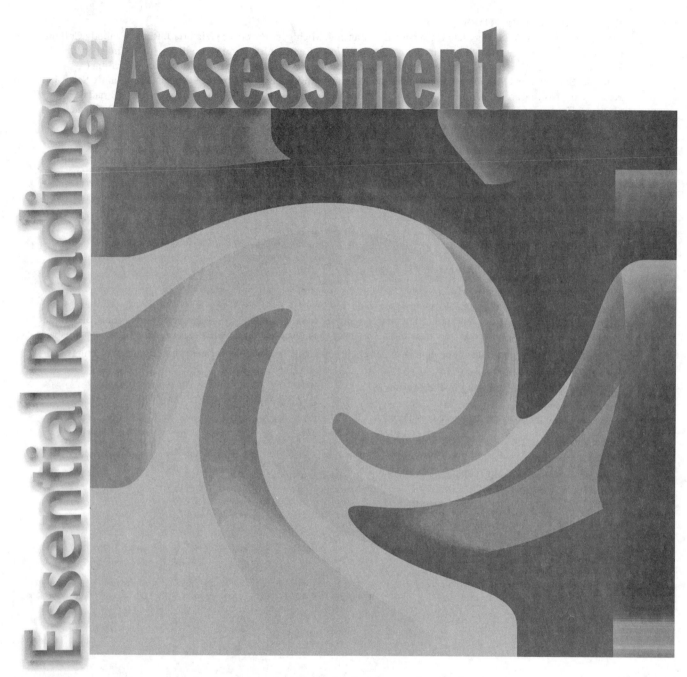

Essential Readings on Assessment

Compiled and introduced by Peter Afflerbach

International Reading Association
800 Barksdale Road, PO Box 8139
Newark, DE 19714-8139, USA
www.reading.org

The International Reading Association attempts, through its publications, to provide a forum for a wide spectrum of opinions on reading. This policy permits divergent viewpoints without implying the endorsement of the Association.

Executive Editor, Books Corinne M. Mooney
Developmental Editor Charlene M. Nichols
Developmental Editor Stacey L. Reid
Editorial Production Manager Shannon T. Fortner
Design and Composition Manager Anette Schuetz

Project Editors Stacey Reid and Wendy L. Logan

Cover Design Linda Steere

The publisher would appreciate notification where errors occur so that they may be corrected in subsequent printings and/or editions.

Library of Congress Cataloging-in-Publication Data
Afflerbach, Peter.
Essential readings on assessment / Peter Afflerbach.
p. cm.
Includes bibliographical references.
ISBN 978-0-87207-812-3
1. Reading--Ability testing. 2. Reading (Secondary) 3. Reading (Middle school) I. Title.
LB1050.46.A35 2010
428.4'076--dc22

2010028953

Suggested APA Reference
Afflerbach, P. (Ed.). (2010). *Essential readings on assessment.* Newark, DE: International Reading Association.

About the Editor

Peter Afflerbach is professor of reading education in the Department of Curriculum and Instruction at the University of Maryland, College Park, USA. He teaches graduate and undergraduate courses in reading assessment, models of reading, and reading comprehension. Peter received his master's degree in reading education and PhD in reading psychology from the University at Albany, State University of New York, USA. Prior to becoming a professor he taught grade K–6 Title 1 reading, middle school remedial reading and writing, and high school English in public schools in New York.

Peter has authored numerous books, most recently *Understanding and Using Reading Assessment, K–12* (2007) and *Adolescent Literacy Inventory, Grades 6–12* (with William Brozo, 2010). His work appears in numerous theoretical and practical journals, including *Reading Research Quarterly, Cognition and Instruction, The Elementary School Journal, Journal of Reading, Journal of Reading Behavior, The Reading Teacher, Journal of Adolescent & Adult Literacy*, and *Language Arts*. He is also the author of *High Stakes Testing and Reading Assessment*, a National Reading Conference policy brief

Peter is a coeditor of the *Handbook of Reading Research* (4th edition, 2011), the Assessment section of the *Handbook of Research on Teaching the English Language Arts* (2011), and the research journal *Metacognition and Learning*. He has served on National Assessment of Educational Progress committees, including the 2009 Reading Framework Committee and the standing Reading Committee, and on review panels for the Common Core Standards for English Language Arts & Literacy in History/Social Studies, Science, and Technical Subjects. Peter chaired the International Reading Association's Issues in Literacy Assessment Committee and served on the IRA–NCTE Joint Task Force on Assessment, which recently produced the *Standards for the Assessment of Reading and Writing* (2010).

Peter was elected to the Reading Hall of Fame in 2009.

Introduction

Peter Afflerbach

Reading assessment informs our understanding of individual students and our related efforts to best teach them, which shapes students' self-concepts, motivations, and attitudes related to reading. It signifies, to many, the success and accountability of our teachers and schools. To serve these important and varied purposes, assessment should be involved in our daily classroom routines, and it should measure students' and teachers' long-term accomplishments. Reading assessment should tell the story of developing readers' learning and mastery of the mechanics of reading and of their ability to construct literal, inferential, and critical understandings. The assessment should also help us understand if, and how, students are developing enthusiasm for reading. It should report on, and support, student reading development. Given the importance of assessment in the lives of readers, this volume offers a collection of readings taken from the archives of the International Reading Association (IRA). These readings focus on different, critical aspects of effective reading assessment.

The Current State of Reading Assessment

What is reading? How do we conceptualize it? How do we foster our students' reading development? Our experiences, and the detailed research base on reading and literacy, best inform the answers to these questions. Over the centuries, ideas about how reading is conceptualized and what qualifies a reader as accomplished have undergone continual revision (Kaestle, 1991). The mark of the good reader has evolved from providing verbatim recall of a recently read text, to effectively identifying details and main ideas, to employing prior knowledge to construct meaning, to critically appraising meaning. Most recently, the conceptualization of reading includes comprehending text and using the constructed meaning of texts, including multimedia texts and those found on the Internet, to conduct related tasks.

As conceptions of reading change so, too, must reading assessment. For example, when the ability to provide verbatim recall was equated with accomplished reading, an effective assessment involved matching the reader's spoken or written recall with the actual text and determining the degree of match. When the epitome of good reading was considered the ability to identify details and main ideas, multiple-choice questions that required readers' correct selection of main idea and details from competing choices was suitable. If, however, the good reader is one who constructs meaning from texts and then uses the constructed meaning in a task, then assessment should describe the reader's achievement in related terms. For our developing student readers, synthesizing information from different texts, combining it with graphic and pictorial information, then using this information to help solve problems could serve as suitable assessment.

Effective assessment demonstrates alignment of four levels: (1) the construct of reading, (2) reading standards and benchmarks, (3) reading curriculum and instruction, and (4) reading assessment. Understandings from research and practice inform our conceptualization of reading and reading development. They describe the *construct of reading*, from which district, state, and national *reading standards and benchmarks* are derived. *Curriculum and instruction* follow; mapped carefully onto standards and benchmarks, curriculum and instruction are the means for helping students approach and meet the goals. *Reading assessment*, derived from curriculum and instruction, reports on the achievement of student readers in relation to curriculum and instruction. Each of the four levels must be aligned, and the direct connection between the construct of reading and reading assessment serves as a test of the construct validity of assessment.

Today our progress in understanding how reading works, and how developing readers grow, is not fully reflected in many current reading assessments. The reasons for this are varied, but they combine to present the ongoing challenge of making sure that how we think about reading and how we think about reading assessment are informed by our most recent and comprehensive understandings of both.

Understanding Reading

We should create and use reading assessment that best reflects our current and robust understandings of what reading is, how it works, and how it is used. We should also be wary of reading assessments and programs that provide only a partial picture of our students' reading challenges and accomplishments. Effective assessment helps us understand both developing readers and established readers. Thus, our assessment programs should focus on the core skills and strategies that developing readers must learn and master, as well as the increasingly complex thinking that we expect of students. For example, effective assessment helps us understand the developing reader's phonemic awareness and use of sound–symbol correspondence knowledge. Such assessment is relatively straightforward—we can determine students' phonics knowledge through examination of their writing, miscue analysis of their oral reading, and matching exercises. Fluency may be examined as students read aloud and we determine rate, accuracy, and prosody (Rasinski, 2006). This information helps us understand how readers establish competence in the mechanics of reading.

Reading assessment currently focuses, almost exclusively, on the reading skills and strategies highlighted by the National Institute of Child Health and Human Development (2000) and related No Child Left Behind (NCLB) legislation. These are the "five pillars" of reading: (1) phonemic awareness, (2) phonics, (3) fluency, (4) vocabulary, and (5) comprehension. These important skills and strategies are but a part of the construct (and related standards and instruction) of reading. Yet, more recent efforts represent the evolving understanding of reading and related curriculum and instruction. Consider the characterization of reading provided in the *Reading Framework for the 2009 National Assessment of Educational Progress* (National Assessment Governing Board, 2008):

> Reading is an active and complex process that involves:
>
> • Understanding written text.
>
> • Developing and interpreting meaning.
>
> • Using meaning as appropriate to type of text, purpose, and situation. (p. iv)

This definition represents reading as both constructing meaning and using that constructed meaning. Thus, assessment should help us understand how students construct meaning from text, the nature of the constructed meaning, and how they use the constructed meaning in related tasks. Assessment of a student's ability to determine a main idea or to make inferences from text remains important information, but it cannot tell the full story of how a student is growing as a reader.

The Common Core State Standards (Common Core Standards Initiative, 2010) propose reading benchmark performances that also push the boundary of how reading is conceptualized. Consider, for example, the following 12th-grade reading standard for informational text: It is expected that students meeting standard will "integrate and evaluate multiple sources of information presented in different media or formats (e.g., visually, quantitatively) as well as in words in order to address a question or solve a problem" (p. 40). This standard reflects our understanding of the strategies and mindsets that are needed when a reader reads two or more texts on a related topic. In such reading, the reader must create single understandings of each text, then combine these understandings to create a constructed meaning that accommodates what may be conflicting information in the different texts.

The preceding portrayals of reading assume that readers have learned and mastered prerequisite skills and strategies and that they possess appropriate prior knowledge and stances toward reading to undertake such reading. These developmental reading achievements are an important focus for reading assessment. In fact, they receive the bulk of attention as students progress through elementary school. Thus, a challenge is to judiciously plan the focus of teaching and assessment, making sure that reading in school fully represents the construct of reading and that reading assessment is best situated to measure and describe reading.

Understanding Assessment

As our understanding of reading evolves so, too, does our knowledge about effective assessment. Pellegrino, Chudowsky, and Glaser (2001) propose a model of assessment that includes *cognition*, *observation*, and *interpretation*. Cognition—the important cognitive skills and strategies that are necessary for successful reading and the content that is learned from reading in school—is the primary focus of reading assessment. Observation includes the specific assessment materials and procedures that are used to gather assessment information. Interpretation involves the inferences that we make from our assessment data. When we have confidence in the alignment of our assessment (*observation*) with the thing(s) to be measured (*cognition*), we can make appropriate inferences (*interpretation*) about student reading achievement (i.e., what a student has accomplished and what remains to be learned).

I have several observations related to Pellegrino et al.'s (2001) model of assessment. First, it focuses exclusively on the cognition component of reading—it applies to the reading skills and strategies that readers develop, as well as the knowledge that is constructed about content through acts of reading. Second, and relatedly, the model does not focus on reader motivation or affect, components of reading that are known to influence both individual acts of reading and lifelong reading behaviors. Third, the model is scalable: It speaks to the important acts of assessing phonemic awareness, as well as fluency and reading comprehension. Last, the model provides strong argument for how valid, effective reading assessment emanates from state-of-the-art knowledge of reading and assessment.

My colleagues and I (Afflerbach, 2007; Leipzig & Afflerbach, 2000) proposed the CURRV model, which focuses on the consequences, usefulness, and roles and responsibilities related to the assessment, as well as the traditional benchmarks of reliability and validity, when we plan our reading assessments. For example, if a school district contemplates adopting a performance assessment program, it must focus on consequences that include the performance assessment's ability to inform instruction, provide ongoing formative assessment information, and help teach students to use rubrics and approach independence in self-assessment. As well, performance assessments demand considerable teacher and student expertise, and how teachers and students are supported as they work toward this expertise in performance assessment is a key consideration. The a priori consideration of any and all consequences of assessment puts us in better position to make judgments and decisions to adopt, support, or question a particular type of assessment. A consequential validity perspective proposes that we consider the consequences of an assessment, or of the use of assessment results, as part of an assessment development or selection process. Are the labels *above average*, *average*, and *below average* appropriate? Whatever an assessment tells us about a student's cognitive skills and strategies and learning of text content, does it make sense to influence students' self-esteem and self-concept as a reader with such words? What are the consequences of being labeled a *below-average reader* throughout one's school career? Words matter (Johnston, 2004), and our consideration of the consequences of the language we use to describe students could not be more important.

The usefulness of the assessment should be given full accounting. Does a reading assessment support students in their efforts to become better readers? Does it provide teachers with regular updates of student growth? Does it mesh well with end of unit, marking period, and year tests? Given the need for assessment to serve diverse audiences well, how assessment is useful must be central to any discussion of possible assessments.

An additional aspect of the CURRV model (Liepzig & Afflerbach, 2000) is consideration of the roles and responsibilities of an assessment. Consider that our most recent understandings of reading and reading assessment suggest that formative assessment is a critical component of successful instruction. Consider also that students who are truly independent readers must be able to self-assess their reading. Each of these insights creates special demands, or responsibilities. In the instance of formative assessment, teachers must be responsible for the regular collection, analysis, and use of classroom-based reading assessment information. They must assume responsibility for becoming assessment experts in such assessment (Johnston, 1987). In terms of self-assessment, students must assume new roles and responsibilities. Most students have a relatively passive approach to assessment: They answer teachers' questions and they take tests, as most assessment is done *to* and *for* students, not *by* and *with* students. Should a school adopt portfolio or performance assessment, students and teachers would be expected to assume more active roles. Support for both teachers and students as they acclimate to these new roles and responsibilities is critical.

The Socially Situated Nature of Reading Assessment

Given the evolving understanding of reading and assessment, the state of reading assessment may be surprising to some. It rarely reflects our robust knowledge. Reading assessment is situated in complex social contexts and influenced by political, economic, and social forces. There is no more compelling proof of this than the continued use of high-stakes testing. The possible negative effects of high-stakes testing are well documented (Afflerbach, 2005; Frederiksen, 1984). That these tests carry such evidentiary weight in claims that schools are thriving or failing, that teachers are accountable or negligent, and that students are succeeding or not is proof of their power. How can such assessments, which provide little or no useful information to classroom teachers (Afflerbach, 2007), be the mainstay of an education system? Clearly, it is not because of their value to the enterprise of day-to-day teaching, learning, and reading. If usefulness to teachers and students is not the primary argument for high-stakes tests, what is? Consider the social, economic, and political forces at work. Many adults believe that standardized, norm-referenced tests are scientific, fair, and efficient (Afflerbach, 2005). The complex statistical data that accompany the tests, and the fact that a child's complex reading performance can be transformed from a raw score to a percentile ranking, give tests a scientific air (Lemann, 1999). Further, many believe that standardized tests are an efficient means of gathering information about students' reading development, mistaking tests' relative ease of administration and machine scoring of multiple-choice items for efficiency. Thus, tests score quite well in terms of social acceptance.

As for economic forces, *opportunity cost* and *path dependency* (McDonnell, 2008) are terms worthy of our consideration. Opportunity cost refers to the ramifications of economic choices that are made, in this case related to assessment. The use of school resources such as time and money is always an important consideration. What are the results of choosing to maintain the practice of high-stakes testing? What is the sum cost of buying, administering, scoring, and reporting high-stakes tests? How might severely limited school resources be otherwise spent? Are opportunities for teachers' professional development in assessment diminished or eliminated because of the amount of money spent on tests? When we consider the opportunity costs involved in using a particular type of assessment, we can determine what is gained and what is lost.

A second concept from economics, one that helps explain the primacy of testing, is *path dependency*. Path dependency suggests that people and organizations that stand to benefit from the status quo (in this case the continuing use of high-stakes testing) develop the means to maintain the status quo to serve their self-interests. A primary example is testing companies, whose wares generate hundreds of millions (if not billions) of dollars of revenue each year. A company that is profitable seeks to maintain aspects of business that are generating profit. Consider the following estimate of costs related to the testing mandated by NCLB:

> Trends indicate that, between 2002 and 2008, states will be spending between $1.9 billion and $5.3 billion to implement tests mandated under No Child Left Behind, says the non-partisan Government Accounting Office. Those GAO figures cover only the direct costs of developing, scoring and reporting the tests. Add in the indirect costs for classroom teachers charged with prepping students and coordinating and administering the tests, and the costs could be 10 to 15 times higher. (Hamilton, 2005, n.p.)

The profits generated from such massive outlays of school dollars result in strong efforts to maintain the profits.

Reading assessment is also influenced by politics. NCLB is intended to improve the teaching and learning of reading, and high-stakes testing (the primary indicator of adequate yearly progress) is the primary lever intended to move schools in this direction. An underlying (and untested) assumption is that all schools and teachers need testing to prod them to move in this direction and that summative tests are the best lever for achieving this goal. Not contemplated is the fact that massive spending on summative tests results in stringent limits on formative assessment. That NCLB was supported by the U.S. Senate with a 91–8 vote is startling—not only in that it was bipartisan support, but that the legislation added the requirement to test every student in reading (and math) in grades 3 through 8 without much apparent thought about the cost and the relatively meager return of assessment information.

The confluence of such powerful forces often results in the selection and use of reading assessment that serves the needs of the most powerful audiences and their purposes. Unfortunately, teachers and students may not be counted in this group of powerful audiences, and the important work of daily reading assessment, assessment that informs and enhances growth, may be assigned second-class citizenship. Part of the challenge of developing and maintaining an effective reading assessment program is honoring all legitimate audiences and their needs for assessment. These audiences include teachers, students, parents, administrators, legislators, and the general public. Thus, the development of assessment should be informed by different audiences and their needs, and an attempt should be made to use assessment materials and procedures that can serve more than one audience well.

What Gets Assessed?

Reading assessment has a predominant focus on cognitive skills and strategies. With this focus, we are able to chart student development in the mechanics of reading and in the constructive acts of meaning making as texts are comprehended. The skills and strategies related to phonics, phonemic awareness, fluency, vocabulary, and reading comprehension are central to the processing of information and the construction of meaning, and the careful assessment of these skills and strategies is critical to reading development. As well, readers must have prior knowledge of the topic(s) of the texts they read, or they will construct, at best, only partial meaning of the text.

While cognitive skills and strategies are required for successful reading, they are not the only aspects of reading worthy of measure. There are affective factors that move students toward (or away from) reading, and these factors operate before, during, and after reading. The student's ability to persevere in the face of difficulty, maintain focus, establish positive self-concept and self-esteem, or attribute reading performance accurately all may be positive outcomes of reading programs. Or they may be preconditions that students bring to reading in school. Given the potential power of the Matthew effect (Stanovich, 1986), in which reading success begets further success (or early reading failure begets diminished future results), assessment of the beginning state of student affect related to reading—and assessment of how reading and reading instruction help develop, maintain, or change affect related to reading—is critical. Motivation is a potentially powerful force in the life of student readers (Guthrie & Wigfield, 2000), because it can steer students toward positive interactions with acts of reading and build positive self-esteem.

Formative and Summative Assessments

Reading assessment can be used in a formative and summative manner. Formative assessment is a key feature of popular models of teaching and learning. It figures in zones of proximal development (Vygotsky, 1978), because formative assessment helps teachers identify a student's current level of learning and achievement and then, combined with pedagogical knowledge, helps the teacher configure a teaching space in which the student participates in an appropriate learning challenge. Formative reading assessment also figures in reflective teaching (Schön, 1987). Reflective practitioners are metacognitive: They use their understanding of themselves and their teaching to maintain or modify instruction in the best interests of the student. Reading assessment information can provide a consistent stream of information—information that is reflected upon by the teacher: Did the student reach the goal of the lesson? What remains to be learned? Should I move ahead with instruction? How can I individualize the lesson to best connect with the student's prior experiences?

Formative assessment is central to the processes and successes of Response to Intervention (RTI), in which detailed information related to individual students' needs and accomplishments helps in the assignment of students to Tier 1, 2, or 3. Most important, reading assessment in RTI must be gauged to the focus and level of preciseness that best informs instructional efforts. Daily formative assessment contributes to regular growth and achievement—and for this reason is clearly one form of high-stakes assessment. Formative assessment is that which is conducted with the purpose of informing our educational thinking and action. The increased attention to (and dependence on) formative assessment demands that teachers play a central role in classroom assessment of reading. Yet, many teachers do not have the opportunity to develop expertise in assessment, because it is not the focus in many teacher preparation programs and is not often the focus of ongoing professional development (Johnston, 1989).

Summative assessment is attended to lavishly in many schools, districts, and states. Such assessment provides valuable information in relation to students' attainment of learning goals and outcomes, but it does so with decidedly product assessment information. Thus, the opportunities for summative assessment to directly inform instruction are relatively constrained when compared with formative assessment. Both formative and summative assessment should function in a complementary manner within a particular reading assessment program. Although summative assessment is used to measure accountability (often by a single test on a single day), formative assessment contributes to accountability, because it informs teaching and learning in a regular, detailed fashion.

The Purpose and Structure of This Volume

Essential Readings on Assessment presents an array of perspectives on the nature and importance of reading assessment. Each of the publications in this collection describes one or more aspects of how reading assessment can contribute to effective instruction and meaningful learning. This volume includes articles that demonstrate the work that has been done to develop systems of assessment and the individual assessment materials and routines that combine in successful systems. There is an exciting catalog of writings on reading assessment, and I have had the pleasure of reading my way through IRA's assessment archives to determine which articles and chapters best fit the purposes of this volume.

I used numerous criteria to select the readings. Given the rich catalog of reading assessment publications and the state of the field, I chose publications that focus on

- The central role that teachers can play in reading assessment
- A historical perspective on reading assessment
- Systemic approaches to reading assessment development
- What is assessed when we assess reading: Assessing key aspects of reading development
- The centrality of formative assessment to student development
- The consequences of assessment
- Reading assessment for all students
- Assessment in relation to our evolving understanding of reading

The Central Role That Teachers Can Play in Reading Assessment

The readings begin with Johnston's "Teachers as Evaluation Experts," which proposes that teachers are capable of expertise in evaluation. This notion is central to the other readings in this volume: Much of the described reading assessment assumes classroom teachers are capable of planning, collecting, interpreting, and using reading assessment on a regular basis. According to Johnston, the greatest resource for timely and detailed reading assessment information is the teacher who is situated in the classroom and professionally prepared to conduct valid, reliable, and useful reading assessment. Through observation, listening, and careful questioning, the expert teacher creates opportunities to gather reading assessment information. As important as the idea of teacher as evaluation expert is the idea that schools, districts, and states should support teachers' professional development in reading assessment. The teacher work described in this volume could not have been undertaken had the teachers not received professional development support for their assessment efforts. Thus, the promise of teachers as evaluation experts is best realized when their professional development is suitably supported.

A Historical Perspective on Reading Assessment

The history of reading assessment reflects many things, including evolving concepts of reading and assessment and the benefits of using our best knowledge about both to design and use effective reading assessment. A historical perspective on reading assessment also educates us about previous concerted efforts to improve assessment, make it a more central feature in the instructional day, and have it provide rich information about students. This perspective reminds us that our best and most recent knowledge of reading and assessment must combine for valid and reliable reading assessment. In large part, the issues of today are yesterday's issues, and there is a seeming disconnect between what we know about reading and assessment and how we assess reading. Consider that Valencia and Pearson's "Reading Assessment: Time for a Change," penned almost a quarter century ago, clearly argues for why change is needed in assessment and how to begin to effect change in reading assessment in schools and classrooms. The article addresses both how our conceptualization of reading and how our understanding of assessment have changed. We have known about the strengths and shortcomings of particular assessments for decades, but we do not always act in relation to this knowledge.

Systemic Approaches to Reading Assessment Development

The most effective evolution of assessment use is tied to a systemic approach to reading assessment development and reform. In "Meeting AYP in a High-Need School: A Formative

Experiment," Fisher, Frey, and Lapp focus on how assessment can, and should, accompany reform efforts related to curriculum and instruction. When schools develop innovative curriculum, assessments must follow suit: Learning related to hands-on science or historical inquiry must be complemented by assessment that honors the complexity of the expected learning. Adequate yearly progress is attained through careful consideration of the needs of all students in the school and not by chasing after higher test scores on a standardized, norm-referenced test.

In "Developing the IRIS: Toward Situated and Valid Assessment Measures in Collaborative Professional Development and School Reform in Literacy," Rogers and colleagues illustrate that effective reading assessment can evolve in concert with schoolwide reform in literacy and the necessary professional development for teachers. When much is given to the planning, development, and use of assessment, much can be expected. In one sense, the described program, IRIS, is a paradigm for those schools and districts that can dedicate resources to the important work of curriculum and assessment development along with teacher development.

Paris and colleagues point out in "A Framework for Authentic Literacy Assessment" that it is rare for schools, districts, and states to focus on reading assessment in a systematic, classroom-based manner. Thus, it is right to question whether a teacher or group of teachers might accomplish much without the outright support of a district's resources and administration. A realistic goal should be doing the best that one (or one group) can—realizing some goals with assessment is better than not realizing any. Setting an evolving reading assessment program in motion, even though it may be years before the vision is realized, is better than not doing anything. To this end, I recommend that readers of this volume consider what they can take from the individual articles and chapters and what may be synthesized across them. Much important and insightful work has been done, and one criterion for inclusion in this volume is that the assessments work.

What Is Assessed When We Assess Reading: Assessing Key Aspects of Reading Development

A fourth focus is the array of assessments available for us to learn about students' developing reading skills, strategies, and motivations. While the last decade has seen intensive focus on several of the general instructional goals of the NCLB five pillars of reading, there is not universal agreement on the best means of assessing them. Early readers must learn, practice, and master a series of skills and strategies that form one of the foundations of reading proficiency. In "Reading Fluency Assessment and Instruction: What, Why, and How?" Hudson, Lane, and Pullen provide an example of how quality reading assessment is produced. They describe, in considerable detail, the nature and construct of fluency and its relation to other important aspects of successful reading and reading development, situating the construct of fluency so that we might more fully consider appropriate assessments. In essence, the article mirrors the idea that we should know what we want to assess before developing or choosing our assessments (see Pellegrino et al., 2001). The opportunity to provide effective instruction based on assessment results follows.

Raphael and Au, in "QAR: Enhancing Comprehension and Test Taking Across Grades and Content Areas," demonstrate that careful planning around the relationship of classroom practice and assessment can boost students' higher order thinking and their reading test scores without the burden of specifically teaching to the test. The authors describe how their proven instructional approach helps prepare students to do well on tests by helping them become better readers and more critical, analytic thinkers.

Norman and Calfee's "Tile Test: A Hands-On Approach for Assessing Phonics in the Early Grades" describes an assessment that provides teachers with detailed information about students' phonics knowledge while providing students with opportunities to develop metalinguistic knowledge about reading and to become mindful about their developing reading ability. This is an excellent example of a seemingly straightforward, value-added assessment of a key reading skill. Examination of the strategic placement of assessment tasks illustrates that assessment can also serve as instruction. One of the keys of thoughtful assessment is dual use: When we assess student reading, we may also be able to teach students about assessment. This, it turns out, is necessary for independent and successful reading.

In "Assessing Adolescents' Motivation to Read," Pitcher and colleagues remind us of the importance of motivation in the development of students' reading and the need for assessing how students' motivations to read grow, maintain, or diminish. Further, the authors focus on adolescent student readers—readers for whom a seemingly endless array of distractions and alternatives to reading are presented daily. If we ignore students' motivations for reading and the development of positive affect in relation to reading, we miss opportunities to build on a developing reader's extant enthusiasm. We may miss the chance to improve a student's generally negative view of reading. This article focuses on motivations for reading, and there are numerous other aspects of reading that can be assessed, including readers' self-concepts, their interests, and the attributions they make for success and failure in reading.

The Centrality of Formative Assessment to Student Development

If the focus of reading assessment is increasingly on students' reading processes and behaviors, formative assessment must be in place to understand students' accomplishments and ongoing challenges. This is no small feat, as considerable effort must be placed into advocating the importance of formative assessment in the face of high-stakes, summative tests. Yet, we know that formative assessment is central to effective teaching and student learning. Effective assessment programs include formative and summative assessments. My own "Teacher Questioning: Understanding and Using Reading Assessment, K–12" examines teacher questioning as a consistent source of formative assessment information. From moment-to-moment questions (e.g., Does that make sense? How do you know?) to more broad questions (e.g., Are you making progress toward your goals for reading?), teacher questioning evokes student responses that help form our understanding of students and their current strengths and challenges. Much as readers construct meaning from text, student responses to carefully posed questions help teachers construct meaning about student achievement.

Boyd-Batstone's "Focused Anecdotal Records Assessment: A Tool for Standards-Based, Authentic Assessment" addresses a perennial tension between formative and summative assessment: How can daily formative assessment be conducted to provide fine-grained, useful information for instruction and also build toward students' meeting rigorous standards? In this article, the author addresses the need to attend to regular, authentic assessments of reading *and* the reading standards of a particular school district or state. We should expect that assessments in classrooms, aligned with curriculum and instruction, would also be aligned with standards and benchmark performances for reading, yet this is more easily proposed than realized. Anecdotal records of students engaged in authentic literacy tasks are used to shape instruction and to examine the links between curriculum and instruction, standards and assessment.

The Consequences of Assessment

The sixth focus, consequences of assessment, allows us to consider the effects of assessment, be they planned or unplanned. In "'I'm Not Stupid': How Assessment Drives (In)Appropriate Reading Instruction," Dennis reminds us that assessment can have consequences that are positive and negative—and that we must be vigilant in examining assessment, realizing both the strengths and weaknesses. We need to know the informative power of each and every assessment that we use; the educated consumer and user of assessment will make the most of the assessment information that is available. Further, Dennis describes a scenario in which many "underachieving" students find themselves—at risk for developing detrimental and permanent negative self-esteem and self-concepts as readers as a consequence of tests that regularly describe them as below average or struggling.

Reading assessment may be encountered by parents as a letter grade, a number, a percentile ranking, or a series of brief, written comments. Here, assessment serves to report on the nature and status of student learning. When we have faith in the information that is collected and represented with reading assessment, we may be able to move beyond the reporting role of assessment to roles that support and teach. Consider Kabuto's use of miscue analysis to help parents learn about both their children's reading development and their own (mis)conceptions of reading, described in "Parents and Children Reading and Reflecting Together: The Possibilities of Family Retrospective Miscue Analysis." In the described program, parents are asked to read and examine their own oral reading behaviors. A result is that parents can learn that perfect word-by-word reading does not always equate with decent comprehension and that almost no one reads perfectly (i.e., without miscues). Like the teacher who examines a student's miscues to gain insight into the student's reading development, parents can examine their own reading to better understand the nature of the process, the aspects of reading that are known to their children, and how to best support ongoing instruction and learning. Here, reading assessment has novel and potentially positive consequence.

Reading Assessment for All Students

It is important that reading assessment works for all students and all teachers. This means that students must be accommodated. English-language learners (ELLs) and learning-disabled students number approximately 20% of the students in U.S. schools (Afflerbach, 2007). Across the globe, the percentage of these students varies, but it is always a significant number. In "Assessing English-Language Learners in Mainstream Classrooms," Lenski, Ehlers-Zavala, Daniel, and Sun-Irminger provide valuable suggestions for amending our assessment routines to accommodate ELLs. Extra time to partake in an assessment, clarification of assessment instructions and requests, repeating directions—all of these may help us get the best possible information about students' reading without impacting the validity and reliability of the measure. Students with learning disabilities, and other students, may also benefit from accommodations that include extra time and repetition of directions. A key point here is that if we are to invest our time and resources in reading assessment, we must consider how assessment accommodations optimize our efforts to gather useful information.

Assessment in Relation to Our Evolving Understanding of Reading

Finally, the readings focus on how our understanding of reading changes. In our lifetimes, we have seen traditional, print-based texts joined by electronic Internet and hypertexts. Reading may now involve text, pictures, embedded video, and audio. As our understandings, definitions, and descriptions of reading change, we must determine whether our assessments are keeping pace with this dynamic. Callow's "Show Me: Principles for Assessing Students' Visual Literacy" challenges us to ask, "What is the construct and definition of reading?" and "What are the implications for reading assessment?" Such a forward-looking perspective on reading and reading assessment is necessary, as is one that is retrospective. One of my hopes is that this volume prompts new thinking about reading and reading assessment and that it reminds us that much good work is already complete and ready for our perusal. The state of the art is a creation of new information—tried and true information.

Complex acts of reading demand accordingly complex assessments. If reading is conceptualized as a single act—a single session in which a reader constructs meaning and is then done reading—then we can assess for the strategies and skills that we hope are operating to construct meaning, and we can assess the meaning that students construct. However, if we envision reading as a series of acts of reading—in which the student reader must (1) reconcile disparate information from across different texts, (2) incorporate information that is presented as text, graphics, illustrations, and videos, and (3) synthesize meaning—we then can ask what types of assessment are suitable for describing such performance. As assessment evolves a capability to describe such complex acts of reading, we should expect that these assessments will sometimes demand considerable amounts and diversities of information. In "Using Electronic Portfolios to Make Learning Public," Fahey, Lawrence, and Paratore describe a program that takes advantage of technology to both streamline and bolster portfolio assessment. Here, evolution in reading and evolution in assessment are accommodated through the use of evolving understanding of the role that technology can play in reading assessment.

In conclusion, *Essential Readings on Assessment* represents a broad spectrum of practice and theory related to the critical enterprise of gathering, interpreting, and using information related to our students' reading development. We know much about reading, assessment, and effective reading assessment. The collected readings in this volume describe important aspects of reading assessment and hint at the considerable resources contained in IRA's reading assessment archives. I consider the included writing but a sample of the work that can, and should, inform our assessment practices. It is my hope that these readings will continue to contribute to discussions about how reading assessment is most useful to teachers and students and to our using reading assessments in their most effective manner.

References

Afflerbach, P. (2005). National Reading Conference policy brief: High stakes testing and reading assessment. *Journal of Literacy Research, 37*(2), 151–162.

Afflerbach, P. (2007). *Teacher questioning. Understanding and using reading assessment, K–12*. Newark, DE: International Reading Association.

Common Core Standards Initiative. (2010). *Common Core state standards for English language arts & literacy in history/social studies, science, and technical subjects*. Washington, DC: Author. Retrieved July 7, 2010, from www.corestandards.org/assets/CCSSI_ELA%20 Standards.pdf

Frederiksen, N. (1984). The real test bias: Influences of testing on teaching and learning. *American Psychologist, 39*(3), 193–202.

Guthrie, J.T., & Wigfield, A. (2000). Engagement and motivation in reading. In M.L. Kamil, P.B. Mosenthal, P.D. Pearson, & R. Barr (Eds.), *Handbook of reading research* (Vol. 3, pp. 403–422). Mahwah, NJ: Erlbaum.

Hamilton, K. (2005, June 2). Big business: Educational testing is a multimillion-dollar industry, with revenues only expected to increase with NCLB mandated tests. *Black Issues in Higher Education*. Retrieved May 10, 2010, from findarticles.com/p/articles/mi_m0DXK/is_8_28/ai_n15399787/?lstpn = article_results&lstpc = search&lstpr = external&lstprs = other&lstwid = 1&lstwn = search_results&lstwp = body_middle

Johnston, P.H. (1987). Teachers as evaluation experts. *The Reading Teacher, 40*(8), 744–748.

Johnston, P.H. (1989). Constructive evaluation and the improvement of teaching and learning. *Teachers College Record, 90*(4), 509–528.

Johnston, P.H. (2004). *Choice words: How our language affects children's learning*. Portland, ME: Stenhouse.

Kaestle, C.F. (1991). Studying the history of literacy. In Kaestle, C.F. (Ed.), *Literacy in the United States: Readers and reading since 1880* (pp. 3–32). New Haven: Yale University Press.

Leipzig, D.H., & Afflerbach, P. (2000). Determining the suitability of assessments: Using the CURRV framework. In L. Baker, M.J. Dreher, & J.T. Guthrie (Eds.), *Engaging young readers: Promoting achievement and motivation* (pp. 159–187). New York: Guilford.

Lemann, N. (1999). *The big test: The secret history of the American meritocracy*. New York: Farrar, Straus and Giroux.

McDonnell, L.M. (2008). The politics of educational accountability: Can the clock be turned back? In K.E. Ryan & L.A. Shepard (Eds.), *The future of test-based educational accountability* (pp. 47–68). New York: Routledge.

National Assessment Governing Board. (2008). *Reading framework for the 2009 National Assessment of Educational Progress*. Washington, DC: Author. Retrieved July 8, 2010, from www.nagb.org/publications/frameworks/reading09.pdf

National Institute of Child Health and Human Development. (2000). *Report of the National Reading Panel. Teaching children to read: An evidence-based assessment of the scientific research literature on reading and its implications for reading instruction* (NIH Publication No. 00-4769). Washington, DC: U.S. Government Printing Office.

Pellegrino, J.W., Chudowsky, N., & Glaser, R. (2001). *Knowing what students know: The science and design of educational assessment*. Washington, DC: National Academy Press.

Rasinski, T. (2006). Reading fluency instruction: Moving beyond accuracy, automaticity, and prosody. *The Reading Teacher, 59*(7), 704–706. doi:10.1598/RT.59.7.10

Schön, D.A. (1987). *Educating the reflective practitioner: Toward a new design for teaching and learning in the professions.* San Francisco: Jossey-Bass.

Stanovich, K. (1986). Matthew effects in reading: Some consequences of individual differences in the acquisition of literacy. *Reading Research Quarterly*, *21*(4), 360–407. doi:10.1598/RRQ.21.4.1

Vygotsky, L.S. (1978). *Mind in society: The development of higher psychological processes* (M. Cole, V. John-Steiner, S. Scribner, & E. Souberman, Eds. & Trans.). Cambridge, MA: Harvard University Press.

Teachers as Evaluation Experts

Peter Johnston

The process through which we examine and keep track of children's literacy development is currently dominated by multiple choice, product oriented, group administered, norm referenced reading tests. These tests have been developed in the names of science and efficiency by "experts" so that the teacher need only be a technician who administers a test and later receives scores.

The goal is to collect efficiently objective data which can be used for a variety of purposes such as classification, accountability, and progress monitoring. However, these so called goals are properly subgoals. The most fundamental goal of all educational evaluation is optimal instruction for all children and evaluation practices are only legitimate to the extent that they serve this goal.

In this context, current evaluation practices are extraordinarily inefficient and we have been valuing the wrong sort of evaluation expertise. Rather than refining tests and testing, we should be dealing with the fact that the bulk of instructional decision making takes place in the classroom on a moment to moment basis. Teachers must evaluate individual students' needs and respond to them. Informal observations and hunches about how and why children behave in particular ways form the basis of instruction decisions far more that do test scores (Shavelson and Stern, 1981).

Thus we must ensure that teachers' hunches and informal observations are as accurate, insightful, and valid as possible. In other words we must help teachers become experts at evaluating the process of literacy development.

Detecting Patterns

What makes an expert in classroom literacy evaluation? A very important characteristic of experts in general is their ability to recognize patterns.

A good analogy for classroom evaluation expertise is provided by chess masters who recognize around 50,000 board patterns (Chase and Simon, 1973). If we think of students engaging in recognizable patterns of behavior which are motivated, organized, and goal directed, the analogy to the chess master is accurate. Indeed, Peterson and Comeaux (1985) found that expert teachers could recall many more incidents from videotapes of teaching than could novice teachers.

The analogy is most appropriate in exhibition matches in which a master chess player plays 20 or 30 club players simultaneously. The analogy is not perfect, however. The chess player faces a less complex problem, because the context beyond the board is of little concern. Teachers, on the other hand, must not only know what patterns to look for but also the conditions under which the patterns are likely to occur. In a sense, unless teachers understand the patterns *and* how and where to look for them, they simply will not see them.

A novice at classroom evaluation will pick up the sample of beginning writing in this article and see scribble. The expert will look at the same piece and see signs of the child's development of hypotheses about the nature of written language, an understanding of the format of a letter, the development of some concepts about print, skill at phonemic segmentation, and a strong "literacy set." In addition, the expert will have spent some time watching the writing being

Reprinted from Johnston, P. (1987). Teachers as evaluation experts. *The Reading Teacher, 40*(8), 744–748.

Sample of Beginning Writing

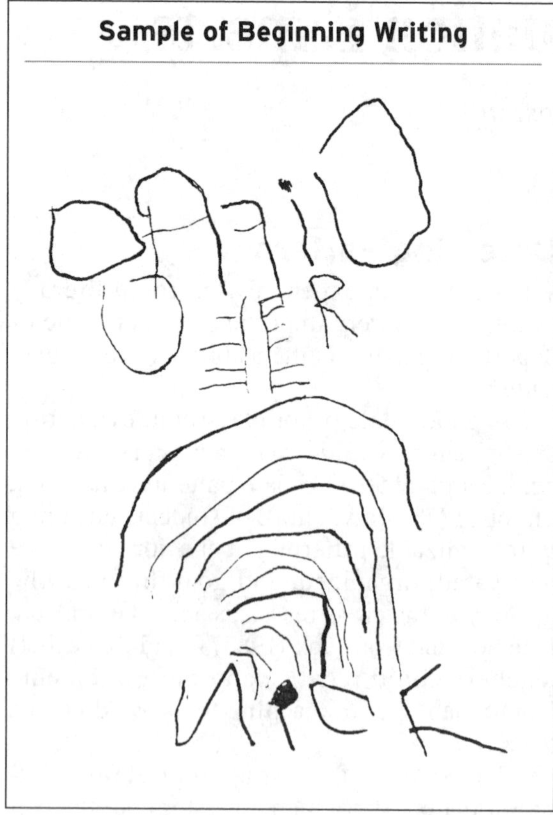

done, and possibly discussing it with the author, enabling an even more insightful analysis.

Similarly, the novice listens to oral reading, including disfluency and self correction, and simply hears many errors. The expert hears in the same rendition the development of voice-print matching, prediction, self monitoring, self correction, and independent learning. The expert has knowledge of reading and writing processes and of the process of development.

Knowing Classroom Procedures

Aside from the ability to see and hear patterns in the development of reading and writing processes, experts have procedural knowledge. In the case of the classroom evaluation expert, this involves, for example, how to set a context so that certain behaviors are most likely to occur, how to record those behaviors, file and update the records, and prevent some children from being missed.

The expert would know, for example, how to take (and interpret) regular running records (Clay, 1985) of children's oral reading behaviors and use them to describe reading growth. An expert will also know how to keep writing files, schedule interviews with individual children, and plan and carry out daily observations of the children's independent literacy behaviors.

Even simple classroom management skills are part of evaluation expertise. Without a well managed classroom in which the children have learned to work independently, a teacher cannot step back from instruction and watch the class as a whole, or work uninterrupted with particular individuals.

Listening

Teachers who are evaluation experts have even more complex skills. They know how important it is to listen and they know how to listen with appropriate attention, patience and thoughtful questioning.

Listening is at the heart of the writing conference portrayed by Graves (1983) and others and the interview described by Nicholson (1984). Listening, the expert evaluator strives to understand the child's understanding of the reading or writing process and helps the child come to grips with what she is doing and how to extend it.

Conferences, which last about 5 minutes, are focused and concern manageably sized pieces of information. Both teacher and student are likely to respond to such exchanges actively and accurately.

Evaluation That Serves Instruction

To suggest that individualized evaluation is efficient may seem counterintuitive. But consider this. Efficiency is the ability to produce the desired effect with a minimum of effort, expense, or waste. Current evaluation procedures have been designed to produce efficiently the sort of objective data which can be compared across individuals and groups, but they are singularly inefficient at helping attain the goal of optimal instruction for all children. Indeed, in many ways they afford obstructions to this end as well as being expensive and wasteful (see Frederiksen, 1984; Johnston, in press).

Current test centered evaluation procedures cast teacher and learner in fundamentally adversarial roles which preclude effective teaching, but classroom evaluation is process oriented and requires the teacher to adopt the role of an advocate (Graves, 1983). An advocate sits beside the child at a comparable height, engaging in eye contact, and waits to be offered the child's work. This role conveys respect, recognizable control by both parties, and a recognition that the learner's concerns deserve serious consideration.

Holdaway (1979) refers to this as a professional–client relationship. It is a relationship based on trust which involves the alignment of the goals and task definitions of teacher and student and the development of collaboration. The concept is clearly reflected in the early reading evaluation work of Clay (1985). Her informal "running records" and more formal Concepts About Print test both involve the teacher and student sitting side by side sharing the same text and working toward the same end.

This view of evaluation implies the need to liberate teachers and students from the disempowering and isolating burden of centralized, accountability testing. The cost of that liberty is increased responsibility on the part of the classroom teacher, some of which is passed on to the student. A learning process or teaching process (or any other process for that matter) cannot be controlled without feedback.

Empowering the Learner

Thus process oriented evaluation strongly emphasizes the development of continual *self* evaluation so that learners may be responsible for and direct their own learning. Not only are self assessed difficulties caught at the most teachable point, but the development of self evaluation is critical if learners are to become independent.

Indeed, probably the clearest indicator of reading difficulties is failure to self correct. Similarly, self evaluation is at the center of the revision and editing processes in writing.

Process oriented evaluation is thus continually directed toward causing "intelligent unrest." Teachers ask reflective questions, questions that teach (Graves, 1983). These questions provide the teacher with information, but also give responsibility back to the student and simultaneously model the self evaluation process.

Teachers are often encouraged to model reading processes, but rarely to model self evaluation. Similarly, they do not seem to be encouraged to model listening. The type of questioning to which I have referred is part of listening. Indeed, Easley and Zwoyer (1975) refer to this general notion as "teaching by listening."

By making process evaluation an integral part of teaching and learning, we get multiple returns on our time investment, and at the same time, in good management style, we delegate responsibility for evaluation to those closest to the teaching–learning process, making that process more efficient.

Timely Assessment

Individualized, process oriented evaluation by the teacher can boast efficiency even beyond this. The roles of teacher and evaluator allow teaching and evaluation to occur at the same time, while encouraging and modeling independence. The information gathered is instructionally more relevant and timely, and teachers are more likely to use it.

When teachers observe a child actually performing a task, the knowledge gained will influence their instructional interactions. The teacher "owns" it. If the information is secondhand, no matter how detailed, it is much less likely to influence the automatic instructional interactions.

Some may respond "Of course we need such evaluation but we need *real* evaluation too." I want it clearly understood that this *is* the real evaluation. There is a place for the more intrusive norm referenced, product oriented approach but it is a small one, certainly much smaller than the pretentious position it currently occupies.

Showing Our Skill

One cannot be an expert teacher without being an expert evaluator. I hope that it is apparent that this expertise is complex and does not simply come with years of classroom experience. Indeed, as Marie Clay points out, such experience can easily produce a "naive theory that prevents accurate observation." Teachers should not expect this expertise to be gained without effort. There is much to know.

If teachers are ever to gain public trust and win professional status we must show that we are responsible. While children are our primary clients, parents, among others, have rights too.

When parents wish to know about their child's development, there should be no hesitation. A teacher should be able to say "Let me show you how Jane has developed since last month. This is what she was doing at the beginning of the year. Last month she had developed to this point. Now she has begun to...." As The Scottish Council for Educational Research put it:

> We stopped short of asking the parents bluntly: "Do you trust the teachers?" If they do not, then it is time we took steps to remedy our public relations. If we are not to be trusted, then the whole edifice of the school falls down, whatever the external supports. We have to show that we can be trusted.... *Perhaps if we prove that we know our pupils, this will challenge the community to value our work more highly.* (Broadfoot, 1979, p. 23, italics added.)

I have a simple test of teacher evaluation expertise which can be used as a self test. Look at the extent and quality of an impromptu description of a particular child's literacy development. Two features which will be most evident in an expert's description will be an emphasis on processes and an emphasis on what the child *can* do.

Unless we know our children it is not possible to tailor our instruction to their needs, particularly in the language arts, which require a supportive, communicative context. We must observe and listen, and if they will not talk, we cannot listen.

This principle holds at levels of evaluation outside of the classroom. Indeed, without the foundation of trusting relationships at all levels, development of the educational enterprise will be beyond our grasp.

References

Broadfoot, Patricia. *Assessment, Schools and Society.* New York, N.Y.: Methuen, 1979.

Chase, William, and Herbert Simon. "Perception in Chess." *Cognitive Psychology*, vol. 4 (January 1973), pp. 55–81.

Clay, Marie. *The Early Detection of Reading Difficulties*, 3rd ed. Portsmouth, N.H.: Heinemann, 1985.

Easley, Jack, and Russel Zwoyer. "Teaching by Listening—Toward a New Day in Math Classes." *Contemporary Education*, vol. 47 (Fall 1975), pp. 19–25.

Frederiksen, Norman. "The Real Test Bias: Influences of Testing on Teaching and Learning." *American Psychologist*, vol. 39 (March 1984), pp. 193–202.

Graves, Donald. *Writing: Teachers and Children at Work.* Exeter, N.H.: Heinemann, 1983.

Holdaway, Don. *The Foundations of Literacy.* Gosford, Australia: Ashton-Scholastic, 1979.

Johnston, Peter. "Assessing the Process and the Process of Assessment in the Language Arts." In *The Dynamics of Language Learning: Research in the Language Arts*, edited by James Squire. Urbana, Ill.: National Council of Teachers of English, in press.

Nicholson, Tom. "You Get Lost When You Gotta Blimmin Watch the Damn Words: The Low Progress Reader in the Junior High School." *Topics in Learning and Learning Disabilities*, vol. 3 (January 1984), pp. 16–23.

Peterson, Penelope, and Michelle Comeaux. "Teachers' Schemata for Learners and Classrooms: The Mental Scaffolding of Teachers' Thoughts During Classroom Instruction." Paper presented at the American Educational Research Association annual meeting, Chicago, Ill., April 1985.

Shavelson, Richard, and Paula Stern. "Research on Teachers' Pedagogical Thoughts, Judgments, Decisions, and Behavior." *Review of Educational Research*, vol. 41 (Winter 1981), pp. 455–98.

Questions for Reflection

- According to the author, at the time this article was written assessment was "dominated by multiple choice, product oriented, group administered, norm referenced reading tests. These tests have been developed in the names of science and efficiency by 'experts' so that the teacher need only be a technician who administers a test and later receives scores." Do you think this has improved in today's schools? How have assessment processes changed since this article was written?
- The author posits that an expert in literacy evaluation should be skilled at detecting patterns, knowing classroom procedures, listening, using individualized evaluation, empowering the learner, and providing timely assessment. What can teachers do to expand their assessment expertise? What can schools do to help teachers develop their expertise?

Reading Assessment: Time for a Change

Sheila W. Valencia and P. David Pearson

Reading assessment has not kept pace with advances in reading theory, research, or practice. On the one hand we argue vehemently for richer and more liberating instructional materials and practices—practices that help students become sophisticated readers, readers who have a sense of ownership and awareness of their reading habits and strategies.

On the other hand, we stand idly by and observe yet another round of standardized or end-of-unit basal tests. Even those of us who argue that the current tests do not measure what we mean by reading take secret pride that our pet instructional technique produces greater gains than another technique on one of those very tests.

In this article, we explain the nature, contributing factors, and consequences of this frightening dilemma in order to set the stage for some possible solutions.

The accountability movement of the 1970s, the wave of recent national reports (Education Commission of the States, 1983) and the focus of the effective schools research (Fisher et al., 1978) have set the stage for major educational reforms in the U.S. In most instances, these reports have had reading achievement as one major focus, and in many cases they have relied on students' standardized test scores as measures of educational effectiveness. Such reliance has led to an increased focus on minimal competency, norm referenced, and criterion referenced testing.

As evidence of the increasing use of tests, one need only note that there are at least 40 statewide competency testing programs in place. Add to this the thousands of locally regulated programs, the criterion referenced tests accompanying every basal reading program, and the countless school and teacher made tests, and the picture of a nation of schools, teachers, and students engulfed by tests is complete. No matter the perspective one takes, the conclusion is inescapable: The influence of testing is greater now than at any time in our history.

The time has come to change the way we assess reading. The advances of the last 15–20 years in our knowledge of basic reading processes have begun to impact instructional research (Pearson, 1985) and are beginning to find a home in instructional materials and classroom practice (Pearson, 1986). Yet the tests used to monitor the abilities of individual students and to make policy decisions have remained remarkably impervious to advances in reading research (Farr and Carey, 1986; Johnston, in press; Pearson and Dunning, 1985).

New Views of the Process

A major contribution of recent research has been to articulate a strategic view of the process of reading (e.g., Collins, Brown, and Larkin, 1980; Pearson and Spiro, 1980). This view emphasizes the active role of readers as they use print clues to "construct" a model of the text's meaning. It deemphasizes the notion that progress toward expert reading is the aggregation of component skills. Instead, it suggests that at all levels of sophistication, from kindergartner to research scientist, readers use available resources (e.g., text, prior knowledge, environmental clues, and potential helpers) to make sense of the text.

Progress toward expert reading is guided by the increasing sensitivity of readers to issues of *how*, *when*, and *why* those resources can best be used. This strategic view also suggests

Reprinted from Valencia, S.W., & Pearson, P.D. (1987). Reading assessment: Time for a change. *The Reading Teacher, 40*(8), 726–732.

that skilled, but not unskilled, readers can use knowledge flexibly—they can apply what they have learned from reading to new situations (e.g., Campione and Brown, 1985; Spiro and Meyers, 1984); in fact, the ability to use knowledge flexibly predicts how well students will acquire future knowledge.

Assessment has not been touched by this strategic view of reading. The Figure describes the litany of conflicts we see between what is known about reading and what is done to assess it.

The point is simple but insidious: As long as reading research and instructional innovations are based upon one view of the reading process while reading assessment instruments are based upon a contradictory point of view, we will nurture tension and confusion among those charged with the duel responsibility of

A Set of Contrasts Between New Views of Reading and Current Practices in Assessing Reading

New views of the reading process tell us that...	Yet when we assess reading comprehension, we...
Prior knowledge is an important determinant of reading comprehension.	Mask any relationship between prior knowledge and reading comprehension by using lots of short passages on lots of topics.
A complete story or text has structural and topical integrity.	Use short texts that seldom approximate the structural and topical integrity of an authentic text.
Inference is an essential part of the process of comprehending units as small as sentences.	Rely on literal comprehension test items.
The diversity in prior knowledge across individuals as well as the varied causal relations in human experiences invite many possible inferences to fit a text or question.	Use multiple choice items with only one correct answer, even when many of the responses might, under certain conditions, be plausible.
The ability to vary reading strategies to fit the text and the situation is one hallmark of an expert reader.	Seldom assess how and when students vary the strategies they use during normal reading, studying, or when the going gets tough.
The ability to synthesize information from various parts of the text and different texts is hallmark of an expert reader.	Rarely go beyond finding the main idea of a paragraph or passage.
The ability to ask good questions of text, as well as to answer them, is hallmark of an expert reader.	Seldom ask students to create or select questions about a selection they may have just read.
All aspects of a reader's experience, including habits that arise from school and home, influence reading comprehension.	Rarely view information on reading habits and attitudes as being as important information about performance.
Reading involves the orchestration of many skills that complement one another in a variety of ways.	Use tests that fragment reading into isolated skills and report performance on each.
Skilled readers are fluent; their word identification is sufficiently automatic to allow most cognitive resources to be used for comprehension.	Rarely consider fluency as an index of skilled reading.
Learning from text involves the restructuring, application, and flexible use of knowledge in new situations.	Often ask readers to respond to the text's declarative knowledge rather than to apply it to near and far transfer tasks.

instructional improvement and monitoring student achievement.

Instruction and Assessment

During the last 20 years, the relationship between assessment and instruction in reading curriculum has been framed by the logic of master learning, introduced in the early 1960s and developed fully by the end of the decade. The goal in mastery learning is to assure a given achievement across students by varying input such as the amount and kind of instruction and practice, or the attention paid to presumably prerequisite skills or to aptitudes of individual learners (matching the method to the child).

What has happened, of course, is that with reading conceptualized as the mastery of small, separate enabling skills, there has been a great temptation to operationalize "skilled reading" as an aggregation—not even an integration—of all these skills; "instruction" becomes operationalized as opportunities for students to practice these discrete skills on worksheets, workbook pages, and Ditto sheets.

The essence of the relationship is this: Mastery learning encourages us to think of instruction in reading as a matter of making certain that students master a "scope and sequence" of enabling skills. The "reader" moves along an assembly line, picking up a new part (new skill) at each station. Then all the parts are in place, we have a reader ready to tackle real reading. Or do we?

Hidden Dangers

There are serious consequences of using one model to define skilled reading and the assessment–instruction link and another to define reading assessment. One danger lies in a false sense of security if we equate skilled reading with high scores on our current reading tests. A close inspection of the tasks involved in these tests would cast doubt upon any such conclusion.

A second danger stems from the potential insensitivity of current tests to changes in instruction motivated by strategic views of reading. Educators bold enough to establish new programs might abandon it as ineffective on the basis of no (or only a small) measurable advantage over a conventional program; they might never consider the alternative interpretation that the tests they are using are insensitive to effective instruction.

A third danger is that given the strong influence of assessment on curriculum, we are likely to see little change in instruction without an overhaul in tests. Conscientious teachers want their students to succeed on reading tests; not surprisingly, they look to tests as guides for instruction. In the best tradition of schooling, they teach to the test, directly or indirectly. Tests that model an inappropriate concept of skilled reading will foster inappropriate instruction.

A fourth danger stems from the aura of objectivity associated with published tests and the corollary taint of subjectivity associated with informal assessment. For whatever reasons, teachers are taught that the data from either standardized or basal tests are somehow more trustworthy than the data that they collect each day as a part of teaching. The price we pay for such a lesson is high; it reduces the likelihood that teachers will use their own data for decision making.

An Alternative Relationship

Consider a completely different relationship between instruction and assessment, based upon a strategic view of the reading process: Every act of reading requires the orchestration of many resources, including the text, the reader's prior knowledge, other learners, and the constraints of the situation. The goal of every act of reading, and therefore every act of assessment, is identical regardless of who is performing it. What varies across readers, situations, and levels of sophistication is exactly how readers orchestrate available resources.

Given such a view, the best possible assessment of reading would seem to occur when teachers observe and interact with students as they read authentic texts for genuine purposes. As teachers interact with students, they evaluate the way in which the students construct meaning, intervening to provide support or suggestions when the students appear to have difficulty. This model, referred to as dynamic assessment (Campione and Brown, 1985), emanates from Vygotsky's notion of the "zone of proximal development," that region of just far enough—but not too far—beyond the students' current level of competence such that sensitive teachers, using scaffolding tools such as modeling, hints, leading questions and cooperative task completion, can assist learners in moving to their next level of learning. In such a model, instruction consists of guiding learning through the interplay of assessment and meaningful application of skills; the "measure" of students' ability is not a score but an index of the type and amount of support required to advance learning.

A scenario in which there is no difference between reading, instruction and assessment is the ideal. While this model may never be fully integrated into large scale testing, it holds enormous promise for classroom and individual student assessment.

The Near Future

What we must do, then, is to help educators and policymakers at all levels begin to think about assessment strategies that are consistent with strategic reading and that redefine the instruction/assessment link. What we need are not just new and better tests. We need a new framework for thinking about assessment, one in which educators begin by considering types of decisions needed and the level of impact of those decisions.

We propose a framework for developing a complete assessment system based on known attributes of strategic reading and reading programs, and the decision making levels of our educational system. Imagine a matrix in which the attributes of skilled reading and effective reading programs are listed down the first column—those outcomes which students and teachers agree are desirable. Across the top of this matrix, heading columns 2, 3 and 4, are the levels of decision—state/provincial or district, school or classroom, classroom or individual. The underlying assumption is that different sorts of decisions must be made at each level and that each type of decision may require or lend itself to different types of assessment.

Note 3 critical features of such a matrix:

(1) The attributes listed must reflect a sound model of the reading process.

(2) These attributes are interdependent and cannot be measured discretely, but they may be loosely clustered—prior knowledge, comprehension, metacognition habits and attitudes—and described in terms of their interrelations.

(3) Whatever is worthy of assessment ought to be assessable in different contexts for different purposes using different strategies.

For example, because of the large number of students involved, units as large as national and state education agencies and even most large school districts need some measures that can be administered to large groups to determine trends. However, since these tools sample such a limited range of the achievements of any individual, they are likely to prove invalid and unreliable for making decisions about individuals.

Some decisions made about individuals may simply require interview techniques. In trying to validate our paper and pencil measures of reading (some examples appear later in this article), we have conducted hundreds of interviews with individual children who have answered novel machine scorable items. We found that there are some things you can learn only by talking to a student one on one. And student constructed responses of the type generated on daily assignments may even be useful in making decisions about groups or whole classes.

It should not be inferred that we are advocating machine scorable formats for large scale testing and constructed response formats for individual assessment. There are possibilities for both formats at different levels of impact.

For example, while the constraints of large scale assessment have led to multiple choice, machine scorable tests, there is some indication that this is changing. In fact, the writing assessment done by the National Assessment of Educational Progress, along with those administered by most states, requires students to write compositions that are evaluated by human judges. This change in writing assessment reflects the advances in our understanding of the writing process. Those of us in reading can take at least one lesson from the writing field: Those professionals stood firm in demanding large scale assessments that exhibited face, curricular, and instructional validity until they got them.

Conversely we can see the usefulness of some machine scorable formats at the individual level if items can be constructed to provide opportunities that are usually reserved for student constructed responses.

We suspect there will be machine scorable formats useful at the individual assessment level and open ended formats useful and necessary at the district, state, or national levels. Nonetheless, if something like our proposed "imaginary" matrix ever does come to pass, we predict that, on average, as one moves from large scale to school to classroom to individual levels, assessment will become more informal, open ended, and frequent. Dynamic, interactive, daily assessment could become a norm at the reading group level.

A Call for Action

Because standardized, norm referenced tests are still the most prevalent in U.S. schools, one important focus for immediate research should be to develop and evaluate new assessment techniques that are both consistent with our understanding of reading and its instruction *and* amenable to large scale testing. Unless we can influence large scale assessment, we may not be able to refocus assessment at all.

To this end, a group of us in Illinois has begun to reshape statewide assessment of reading. Within the constraints of large scale formats, we are using concepts that encourage strategic reading and redefine the assessment/instruction link. In our pilot work with 15,000 students in grades 3, 6, 8, and 10, we are evaluating many novel formats:

- **Summary writing.** Students read 3 or 4 summaries written by other students in response to the selection they read and pick the one they think best. In one version, they get a list of features of summaries and check off the reasons for their choice.
- **Metacognitive judgments.** Students encounter a scenario about a task they might have to perform in response to the selection they just read, such as retelling it to different audiences (peer, younger child, teacher). They rate the helpfulness of several different retellings for each audience.
- **Question selection.** From 20 questions, students pick the 10 they think will help a peer best understand the important ideas about a selection.
- **Multiple acceptable responses.** In a discussion, a group can consider many alternative acceptable responses to good questions, especially inferential or evaluative questions. In one format, students select all responses they find plausible. In another, students grade responses as "really complete" or "on the right track" or "totally off base" (much as a teacher grades short answer or essay responses).
- **Prior knowledge.** We have two machine scorable formats for assessing prior knowledge. In one, students predict (yes/no/maybe) whether certain ideas are likely to be included in a selection on a specified topic. In another, they rate the relatedness of vocabulary terms to a central concept of the selection, for example blood circulation. However, while we begin to explore new large scale formats and techniques, we are committed to developing valid, reliable and usable strategies to be included in all three columns of our "imaginary" matrix—to provide educators and policymakers with a portfolio approach to assessment that can be used to fit the types of decisions they need to make.

While we have argued that there is an urgency about these issues in 1987 not felt in previous eras, we would not want to leave readers with the impression that the battle is new. In fact, we have located a similar concern nearly a century old. In 1892 H.G. Wells bemoaned the influence of the external examiners in determining curricula in England:

> The examiner pipes and the teacher must dance—and the examiner sticks to the old tune. If the educational reformers really wish the dance altered they must turn their attention from the dancers to the musicians. (p. 382)

While some amongst us will argue that musical instruments ought to be outlawed, others will strive to change the tune, perhaps in a way that reflects less concern for melody but greater concern for harmony.

References

Campione, Joseph C., and Ann L. Brown. *Dynamic Assessment: One Approach and Some Initial Data.* (Technical Report No. 361). Urbana, Ill: Center for the Study of Reading, 1985.

Collins, Allan, John Seely Brown, and Kathy M. Larkin. "Inference in Text Understanding." In *Theoretical Issues in Reading Comprehension*, edited by Rand J. Spiro, Bertram C. Bruce, and William F. Brewer. Hillsdale, N.J.: Erlbaum, 1980.

Education Commission of the States. *Calls for Educational Reform: A Summary of Major Reports.* Denver, Colo.: ECS, 1983.

Farr, Roger, and Robert F. Carey. *Reading: What Can Be Measured?* Newark, Del.: International Reading Association, 1986.

Fisher, Charles, W., David Berliner, Nikola Filby, Richard Marliave, Leonard Cahen, Marilyn Dishaw, and Jeffrey Moore. *Teaching and Learning in Elementary Schools: A Summary of the Beginning Teacher Evaluation Study.* San Francisco, Calif.: Far West Regional Laboratory for Educational Research and Development, 1978.

Johnston, Peter. "Steps Toward a More Naturalistic Approach to the Assessment of the Reading Process." In *Content-Based Educational Assessment*, edited by James Algina. Norwood, N.J.: Ablex, in press.

Palinscar, Annemarie S., and Ann L. Brown. "Reciprocal Teaching of Comprehension-Fostering and Comprehension-Monitoring Activities." *Cognition and Instruction*, vol. 2 (Spring 1984), pp. 117–75.

Palinscar, Annemarie S., and Ann L. Brown. "Interactive Teaching to Promote Independent Learning from Text." *The Reading Teacher*, vol. 39 (April 1986), pp. 771–77.

Pearson, P. David, and Rand J. Spiro. "Toward a Theory of Reading Comprehension." *Topics in Language Disorders*, vol. 1 (December 1980), pp. 71–88.

Pearson, P. David. Changing the Face of Reading Comprehension Instruction. *The Reading Teacher*, vol. 38 (April 1985), pp. 724–38.

Pearson, P. David, and David B. Dunning. The Impact of Assessment on Reading Instruction. *Illinois Reading Council Journal*, vol. 3 (Fall 1985), pp. 18–19.

Pearson, P. David. "Twenty Years of Research in Reading Comprehension." In *The Context of School-Based Literacy*, edited by Taffy E. Raphael. New York, N.Y.: Random House, 1986.

Spiro, Rand J., and Ann Meyers. "Individual Differences and Underlying Cognitive Processes." In *Handbook of Reading Research*, edited by P. David Pearson (pp. 471–504). New York, N.Y.: Longman, 1984.

Wells, Herbert G. "On the True Lever of Education." *Educational Review*, vol. 4 (June–December 1892), pp. 380–85.

Questions for Reflection

- The authors argue that at the time the article was written, tests used to measure reading achievement did not reflect current understandings of the reading process. Do you think this is still true today? How can teachers resolve the discrepancy between what we know and what we must measure?
- What are some examples of "things you can learn only by talking to a student one on one"? Why is it impossible for standardized assessments to measure these skills or ways of thinking?

Meeting AYP in a High-Need School: A Formative Experiment

Douglas Fisher, Nancy Frey, and Diane Lapp

Having just presented the components of our schoolwide literacy plan, as well as the outcomes of our work, at an after-school staff meeting, a science teacher asked, "Is it possible?" Her school had been identified by the state as chronically underperforming and in program improvement. She continued, "Can we really impact the reading skills of our students? It's my dream, but I'm losing faith." Her statements echo the hopes of many secondary teachers who want to support students' learning but are not exactly sure how to accomplish this.

Faculties in secondary schools across the country are working hard to address the current literacy skills of their students, engage teenagers in new literacies, prepare young adults for the world of work and college, and meet state and federal accountability demands. Despite teachers who work really hard and try to develop their students' reading, writing, and thinking, these schools are not places in which students achieve. To address this, researchers often recommend the use of content literacy strategies (e.g., Vacca & Vacca, 2008), which should provide students with the skills necessary to read and write across the curriculum. However, as O'Brien, Stewart, and Moje (1995) pointed out, many secondary school teachers are resistive to content literacy strategies and simply do not use them. There are probably a number of reasons for this, but the fact remains that students in many schools have difficulty accessing the texts required of them. As a result, students do not learn, and schools fall into program improvement.

On the other hand, there are a number of secondary schools that have beat the odds and made impressive progress in integrating reading and writing into their daily operation such that students do achieve (e.g., Langer, 2001; Schoenbach, Braunger, Greenleaf, & Litman, 2003). There are any number of examples that demonstrate the power of content literacy instruction in helping students learn but very few systematic analyses of the ways in which failing schools change over time to meet the needs of their students. This study focuses on one such school as the faculty and administration attempted to meet state accountability targets and ensure that their students were successful.

Western High School

Western High School (pseudonym) educates over 2,000 students, 60% of whom qualify for free lunch. Western is somewhat unique in that it is geographically isolated from any major city, yet it educates a diverse student population with over 40% of the students homeless and living in cars, tents, or on the street; 23% of them identified as having a disability; and 93% of them identified as Latino, African American, Asian/Pacific Islander, or Native Peoples. In the nearby town, people talk negatively about the school's population because it is known for its violence, illicit drug use, gang activity, pregnancy rates, and other indicators of urban stress. In 2002, only 12% of the Western students scored proficient or advanced on the state assessment in reading. As a result, the school was in program

Reprinted from Fisher, D., Frey, N., & Lapp, D. (2009). Meeting AYP in a high-need school: A formative experiment. *Journal of Adolescent & Adult Literacy, 52*(5), 386–396.

during their preparation periods. Historically, these sessions focused on small learning communities, test preparation, guidance and counseling, and the like. The LLT requested that at least three of the four meetings per month be dedicated to the literacy plan.

Given our commute to the school, we could not be the primary providers of weekly professional development. Instead, the literacy peer coach would have to coordinate the sessions, and members of the LLT would engage their colleagues. We developed a schedule of topics for the remainder of the school year, and members of the LLT signed up to lead the sessions. As part of the plan, teachers would be compensated for observing one another teach during their prep periods. These peer observations were voluntary, and teachers could be paid once per month for peer observations. The literacy coach would also conduct feedback sessions aligned with the literacy plan, and we established a classroom observation and coaching schedule for times that one of us would be on campus. The LLT understood that job-embedded training, teacher-led professional development, and collegial conversations about teaching and learning, as well as coaching and feedback, were required if these schoolwide instructional routines were going to become permanent features of the school (Joyce & Showers, 2002).

Process 3: Collect Data

Our data collection system included results on annual state achievement tests as well as a num- ber of common formative assessments given by he school to gauge success and theoretically sed to plan instruction. On each visit, we inter- iewed the literacy peer coach and principal. hese interviews were conducted separately and ere used to inform our staff development ses- ns as well as our interactions with faculty. e interviews always focused on a few ques- s, including the following:

- What's working better this month?
- Who do we need to recognize for their contributions?
- What are you seeing that needs to be addressed to ensure that the literacy plan is implemented?

These interviews ranged from the shortest being 12 minutes to the longest lasting 93 minutes, with an average of 38 minutes. Information from the interviews was integrated immediately into our work with the school, often resulting in changes to our professional development plan or focus of classroom observations. Interviews were recorded and summarized on the commute home.

In addition, we conducted classroom observations and feedback sessions monthly for the two and a half years of this study. For each trip to Western, at least two of us were on campus. The total number of person days of data collection was 86. These were in addition to the days we were on campus for administrator meetings, staff development sessions, or the annual faculty retreat. On each of these days, each of us conducted at least 12 classroom observations (3 per 90-minute block period); the total number of classroom observations was 1,161. Using a constant comparative method (Glaser & Strauss, 1967), we reviewed and discussed our classroom field notes during the commute home from the school. We also summarized our notes and e-mailed them to the principal and peer coach, inviting them to comment. We did not discuss any specific teacher but noted trends in instructional routines and made recommendations for the use of professional development time.

Process 4: Use Data

The first two days of our engagement with Western left us and the LLT excited about the possibilities and eager to get to work. Our plan included weekly professional development on specific components of a schoolwide literacy intervention as well as regular coaching and feedback for teachers. The week following our visit, at their first professional development session, members of the LLT presented their plan to the faculty. They repeated the content four times so that every teacher had an opportunity to participate. This structure was familiar to the

improvement level 5, the highest level, when we began our work. The graduation rate for Western during that year was 67%.

For the two years before our visit, Western focused on creating small learning communities (SLCs) in specific career pathways (business, tourism, health, etc). This initiative was brought to the school by the district as a result of federal grant support. The principal reported spending nearly every professional development minute on this initiative "debating about who goes where." Yet, as a history teacher told us after the meeting, "We've spent the last two years rearranging the Titanic deck chairs." Western had career academies in place, but this effort in and of itself had not resulted in improved student achievement. Prior to our visit, teachers were told that the school faced state sanctions, including an imposed curriculum and regular classroom monitoring.

Unlike our previous work with neighborhood schools, visiting Western required a six-to-seven hour commute. This posed a unique opportunity to test our ideas about the establishment of a schoolwide literacy plan based on the local capacity building necessary for long-term change.

Our Formative Experiment

Given that we would be involved in ongoing professional development, coaching, and technical assistance designed to improve student achievement and that we would naturally make midcourse corrections in our recommendations with this school, the most appropriate methodology for this study was a formative experiment (Reinking & Bradley, 2007).

Formative experiments have been used to study engagement in reading of beginning English language learners (Ivey & Broaddus, 2007), the use of computers to affect reading and writing (Reinking & Pickle, 1993), vocabulary learning (Baumann, Ware, & Edwards, 2007), and the effectiveness of cognitive strategy instruction for Latina/o readers (Jiménez, 1997). Western High School provided a unique opportunity to document and study a whole school change as teachers attempted to increase student achievement.

Formative experiments allow for inquiry and investigation using both qualitative and quantitative traditions. Formative experiments focus on what it takes to achieve a pedagogical goal as well as the factors that inhibit or enhance the effectiveness of the intervention. Our study borrows from the procedures as outlined by Reinking and Watkins (1998) in our attempt to develop, refine, and confirm an intervention designed to increase student achievement in an underperforming school. These six procedures are as follows:

1. Identify and justify a valued pedagogical goal.
2. Specify an instructional intervention and provide a rationale for why it might potentially be effective.
3. Collect data to determine which factors in the educational environment enhance or inhibit the specified intervention's effectiveness.
4. Use data to modify the intervention to achieve the pedagogical goal more efficiently and effectively.
5. Consider what positive or negative effects the intervention is producing beyond those associated with the pedagogical goal.
6. Consider the extent to which the educational environment has changed as a result of the intervention.

We will discuss each of these processes in turn.

Process 1: Identify and Justify Goals

As a condition of our longer term involvement in the school, the school elected a building-level literacy leadership team (LLT). Given that the school had over 130 teachers and 41 support staff, we needed a group that could function as a communication route. We recommended that the school elect this group of people to ensure that there was a balance of perspectives and ideas about the work ahead. Consistent with Taylor and Collins's (2003) and Cobb's (2005) recommendations, we understood that literacy leadership had to come from the school and that members of this elected body could serve as change agents and ambassadors for literacy instruction.

During our first session with the LLT, we explained the components of the formative experiment and the plan for our collective work. In response, one of the members said, "We've had a lot of consultants with a lot of answers, but they didn't work." Acknowledging this, we discussed the development of their schoolwide literacy plan and reminded them that we did not have a plan to impose upon the school.

The conversation then moved to the first component of the formative experiment: a pedagogical goal. The members of the LLT were clear: They had one goal, which was to meet Adequate Yearly Progress (AYP). As an English teacher said, "It's not lofty, but when you hit that mark, you get a lot of freedom. And that's what we need, a little freedom." We argued that meeting AYP was not a pedagogical goal and urged them to consider the idea that making AYP was a byproduct of meeting their own goals. This conversation lasted nearly two hours, and we were regularly reminded of the reality faced by teachers working in failing schools: They begin to define success not in terms of student progress but rather in terms of performance on state tests.

Through a process of give and take in which we discussed and debated pedagogical goals, we realized that we all agreed that student achievement was important, and we acknowledged that students at Western did not yet have habits that they could deploy automatically while reading and writing. As such, most students were unable to complete many classroom assignments and performed poorly on the state achievement tests. By the end of our first meeting, we had agreed on a pedagogical goal, namely that students would develop literacy habits that they could take with them from class to class, and eventually to college.

That afternoon, the LLT presented the goal to the rest of the faculty at their regular staff meeting while we observed. They answered questions skillfully and guided their colleagues in a conversation similar to the one we had during the day. They acknowledged the importance of "gaining freedom" as well as the value of thinking beyond state tests. They also noted that their work on small learning communities was not in vain but that they now needed to turn their attention "from structure to instruction." The chairperson of the LLT, a peer coach staff developer, then made a motion that the school approve the proposed pedagogical goal. In an anonymous paper vote, 82% of the teachers approved the goal. In announcing the decision, the principal commented, "We've really come together on this. I can't remember a vote with more agreement. We're on our way to freedom."

Process 2: Specify an Intervention and Provide a Rationale

The day following the staff meeting, we met with the LLT. The agenda for the day was the development of an instructional intervention that could be taken schoolwide. Armed with every content literacy or "strategy" book the group could find, we set out to determine the ways in which teachers would engage students in reading, writing, speaking, and listening across content areas. In introducing this session, we acknowledged "there might be 50 ways to leave a lover, but there are at least 100 ways to engage in literacy learning." We discussed the fractured nature of most high schools and the fact that students experienced different instructional routines in every class.

During the first hour of the meeting, we collectively established the criteria we would use to select components of the schoolwide instructional intervention, namely that each

- Had a solid evidence base
- Could be used across content areas
- Had high utility in college or adult life

While many instructional routines and instructional interventions would meet our criteria, the LLT selected four that would be the focus of ongoing professional development for the first year of work. These are detailed in the following sections.

Cornell Note-Taking. The first instructional routine suggested by the LLT centered on note-taking. As one of the committee members noted, "You struck a cord with me. I see all of the different systems we require students to use at this school. I'd be so confused if I had to change methods every hour or so." In reviewing the evidence on note-taking, LLT members were impressed with Cornell style notes (Pauk, 1974). Using Cornell notes, students take notes and complete the tasks on the right side of the page. The left side provides them with a guide and the key points. These key points will help students quickly find information, locate references, and study for exams. Students can also use this column to add their own notes, drawings, and ideas. As Faber, Morris, and Lieberman (2000) found, the Cornell note-taking system increases comprehension and achievement. The committee recommendation was that Cornell notes be used for all note-taking activities.

Think-Alouds. Following the conversation on "external storage functions" during which note-taking was agreed upon, members of the LLT noted that comprehension was an issue for most students at Western and that previous efforts to address comprehension (such as test practice and homework packets) had not significantly impacted student achievement. The literacy peer coach reported that very few students performed poorly on assessments of phonics or phonemic awareness and that most were reasonable fluent readers. We explored the evidence based on think-alouds, read-alouds, and shared readings (e.g., Wilhelm, 2001) and discussed the ways in which content teachers could use this instructional intervention with students. We noted that thinking aloud while reading might serve a number of purposes, including the development of general comprehension skills as well as discipline specific thinking (Shanahan & Shanahan, 2008). We shared a piece of text and considered how scientists, historians, art critics, and literary critics might view this same piece of text. The committee recommended that every teacher conduct a think-aloud with a piece of text, broadly defined, every day in every class.

Writing to Learn. Researchers have argued that writing is thinking (Dean, 2006), yet members of the LLT reported that students at Western did very little writing. For much of the conversation about writing, the LLT focused on the role of the English teachers. The two English teachers on the committee pushed back, saying that writing had to be a requirement in all classes. The debate about writing continued among members of the LLT without a decision. Following the lunch break, we asked members of the team to sum- marize in writing the arguments presented th far for and against writing as a schoolwide init tive. We asked them to talk with a partner fro different content area about what they had v ten. During the debriefing session, we clar that writing to learn was not process writin that teachers were not expected to grade pers for spelling, grammar, or mec Instead, they could use their students' w a way to check for understanding and t struction. The LLT did eventually reac sus about writing to learn and recomm students write to learn every day in e

Dedicated Reading Time. The nent of the plan was dedicated rea current school schedule at the ti provided an optional time for re alternatively be used as a stud work center. Members of the L the majority of teachers allowe do their homework, or talk time. In acknowledging the ing volume (Cunningham the committee members should "just read" for 20 n day (Ivey & Broaddus, 2

These four instructi tified by the literacy lea of possible ways for en in content literacy wo ule at Western, teach a 60-minute profes

faculty as this is how they regularly engaged in professional development.

In an e-mail to us following this session, the peer coach stated, "All I can say is amazing. Nobody, not even the electives teachers, complained. They are with us and feel like we're finally doing something real." For the next several weeks, the preparation period sessions were implemented as we had planned during our two-day team meeting. The following month, we visited Western again to participate in professional development sessions and to observe classrooms. There was clear evidence of the professional development plan as teachers experimented with think-alouds, Cornell notes, and writing-to-learn prompts.

This continued, with teachers attending weekly sessions and our visiting monthly for several months. Teachers were generally positive about the feedback we provided and often asked questions about our recommendations. By the fourth month, however, we noticed that the classroom implementation wasn't progressing. Teachers were going through the motions of the literacy intervention, but we often felt like we were watching a literacy commercial and not like the instructional routine was embedded into the lesson. For example, during an observation of a science teacher, the field notes say, "Students *are* taking notes in Cornell form, but they're copying information from an overhead projector that is in Cornell format." In another observation that day, we noted, "The teacher is thinking aloud, but it's just a collection of personal stories. He's not labeling the cognitive strategies he's using nor is he doing much other than making personal connections with the text."

Modification #1: Supporting the LLT. In sharing this information with the LLT, a history teacher confessed that he had run out of information that he could share during the professional development sessions. In his words, "I don't understand much more than the teachers, but I'm supposed to provide them training. I feel like the blind leading the blind." Most of the members of the LLT agreed that they had reached the end of their comfort zone. We promised to collect video footage from our local schools that they could use during the sessions. We also wrote discussion guides to facilitate discussions about the videos. This modification worked for several months because it allowed teachers to directly observe examples of the instructional routines their school had selected. The discussion guides provided an opportunity for teachers to consider the ways in which the lesson worked for students as well as the ways in which the lesson could be improved. For example, in a video clip of a science teacher modeling her thinking, she revealed the following discussion prompts:

- What supports does the teacher provide for students during the modeling?
- What are the student's responsibilities during modeling?

While we wanted to provide a teacher-to-teacher approach to professional development, we realized that the level of understanding was limited and that we needed to expand the knowledge base of the members of the LLT. We hypothesized that team members would ask to be replaced if they felt uncomfortable in their role. As such, we requested additional release days for the LLT to meet and work with us. The structure of these quarterly sessions focused on preparing for each of the weekly sessions that the team would lead. We regularly read articles together, talked about implications, and discussed the best way to deepen understanding with the faculty. We also previewed videos and provided members of the team with the backstory for each video such that they could share this information during the sessions.

During one of the sessions with the LLT, we realized we needed some video footage of a teacher modeling connections that were not personal but that were related to the world around us. We didn't have any such video footage with us, and the team really wanted to address this the following day during professional development. Amazingly, within an hour we had a student ready to film and a teacher ready to model his thinking. We stayed after school to edit the video footage with a group of students. The next day, when we showed the video, a teacher in first period cried. Concerned, we asked her about her reaction following the session. Tearing up again, she said, "He's one of us and he can do it. It's not just the people from San Diego. It's a local. I'm so proud of us."

While we needed to provide the LLT with materials they could use during their professional development sessions, filming a local teacher engaged in the work of the literacy plan proved to be a major breakthrough. Over the next several months, the literacy coach visited classrooms with student camera people and sent the footage to us. We edited the footage and sent them short videos that they could use in the professional development sessions. Our edits focused on the behaviors we hoped would become schoolwide, and it worked. The principal reported a culture shift as someone told her, "If Ms. Ramirez can do it, you better believe I can." Perhaps teachers needed to see their students and their colleagues engaged in content literacy work to believe it's possible.

Modification #2: New Teacher Support. Upon our return to Western after the summer break, we learned that the school had 36 new, first-year teachers, many of whom were out of the field and teaching on provisional permits. We were depressed when we considered the amount of training and support that had been provided to a group of teachers who would not start the school year with us. The principal, however, was excited. This was the smallest group of new teachers in years, and she attributed the decline in transfers to a sense of possibility that had been created by the work of the LLT. We asked her why she didn't tell us about the number of new teachers, and she was genuinely surprised. She said that there were large numbers of new teachers every year and that it never occurred to her to talk about it; it just was.

As a result of the significant number of new teachers, despite the fact that there were fewer than in the past, we recommended a number of revisions to the professional development plan. The district induction plan was known to be paperwork heavy, and new teachers regularly complained about the demands of teaching, participating in professional development, attending new teacher meetings, and keeping up with the paperwork. Our revision created a site-based induction program in which the new teachers at Western would use their weekly preparation periods to observe other teachers, complete the required paperwork, talk with mentors, and be introduced to the schoolwide literacy intervention.

One of the authors took the primary role in the revision of the induction effort and spent time while on campus with the new teachers. Acknowledging the tension between their early career support needs and the priority for a schoolwide literacy intervention, the principal said, "We can't have them playing catch-up to the school, but we also want them to stay another year." New teachers received a modified version of the literacy intervention while being mentored into their careers. While this is not ideal and likely impacted student achievement overall, the long-term investment in reducing turnover seemed to outweigh the cost. Having said that, we recognize that most schools do not have the resources to create a site-based induction program and are forced to have new teachers participate in the district support program as well as the site-based initiatives. This demand seems to be exacerbated in urban schools that educate large numbers of students who live in poverty and might explain part of the achievement gap.

The following year, the number of new teachers was reduced almost by half (to 19), and for the first time in recent history, veteran teachers from other schools requested transfers to Western. The site-based induction program continued with support from the administration as part of a grant-funded effort to reduce turnover.

Modification #3: Student Behavior Concerns. We were also forced to revise the literacy intervention almost from the start as a result of student behavior concerns. During our first classroom observations, we observed significant numbers of students who were sleeping, talking with one another, leaving the class when they wanted to roam the halls, being disrespectful to teachers, sending text messages, answering their phones in class, and displaying a host of other problematic behaviors. When asked about this, one of the teachers told us, "That's the way it is here. You just gotta put up with it to get by."

When we asked the principal about this, she acknowledged the problem and said that the small learning communities were designed to address this. They had placed vice principals and counselors in each academy who were supposed to address behavioral issues. However, the principal said, "We've gone from bad to worse" over the past couple of years. We urged the principal to address this issue, and the following month she hired a full-time behavior specialist who provided professional development (once per month) to the teachers and coached the vice principals and counselors daily. In addition, the principal dedicated time at each after-school staff meeting to behavioral issues.

For example, a few months into our work with Western, we attended a staff meeting. The focus was on the student ID policy. The faculty decided, with leadership from the behavior specialist, that no one (faculty, student, administrator, or visitor) would be allowed on campus without a lanyard and ID. The faculty voted on this at the meeting and acknowledged that the change would cause a temporary absence problem and enforcement issue. A few months later, the faculty discussed a tardy policy in which they decided to lock the classroom doors when the bell rang and require students who were late to miss class, resulting in a truancy and the possible failure of the class. The overall success of this effort outweighed the cost of transferring focus from the literacy plan once a month.

Process 5: Consider Effects

As teachers engaged in the implementation of the instructional routines selected for schoolwide implementation, new questions were raised. For example, after nearly nine months of work on Cornell note-taking, the teachers began talking about students' lack of ability to summarize. In response, during a professional development session, the literacy coach said, "Our students didn't just forget how to summarize, we just didn't notice before. The Cornell notes have forced us to notice a need our students have." The following month's session with the LLT focused on teaching summarizing, which led to a discussion about main ideas and details. The team designed a number of professional development sessions on summarizing as a result of this revelation.

We are not sure that most teachers in secondary schools would accept the responsibility of teaching students to summarize. However, this need came from teachers who were looking at student work and realized that there was a gap. As a result, just a few months later, we observed a number of lessons in which content area teachers were focused on teaching, summarizing, and engaging students in conversations about how, why, and when to summarize.

The think-aloud component was the most difficult to institutionalize at Western. We hypothesized that this may be because modeling requires a change in teacher behavior whereas writing to learn, Cornell note-taking, and wide reading focus more on the use of time. Most teachers we observed did not really model, per se. Instead, they often explained how something worked or what the author was doing or what students might do to understand. Our regular feedback about this, over several months, caused tension in the teaching staff and some resentment among teachers. They wanted to do well and appreciated the feedback on the other components of the plan. However, during the first 15 months of this study when we talked about think-alouds, we would regularly be challenged or debated. As an example, in frustration, one of the teachers said, "Then you come into my class and do it." We took this as an invitation and later the next day did model thinking while reading to her students.

Thankfully, we had support from the principal and LLT to maintain the focus on think-alouds. Over time, teachers began to incorporate this new behavior into their habits. One of the early naysayers was later interviewed and she said, "My [think-aloud] time has the most student engagement. They can't wait to hear what I think about what we're reading." Hopefully, there were no long-term negative feelings about the feedback we or the peer coach provided.

The one major, negative effect this intervention produced came from the vice principals. Given that their day was mainly devoted to student discipline, they felt left out and neglected as the school turned its attention to literacy. Before this effort, they were the "keepers of information" and "had a lot of power" because teachers went to them for support and guidance. According to the peer coach, the work of the LLT shifted the balance of power away from the vice principals, and teachers spent less time with them and more time with literacy resource staff. As a result, the principal was forced to address back-stabbing comments from her vice principals, including questions about her ability to run the school and periodic reports to the superintendent's office about how she spent her time.

Process 6: Consider the Result of the Intervention

The most obvious change in the school came just a few months into our work together—students regularly read during the reading period. In observation after observation of this time of day, we noticed students reading. We had a hard time finding a student who did not have a book and didn't seem to be reading. Indicators of this change were all around us. Library use by students had increased. The number of students carrying books across campus increased. Referrals to the vice principals during this time of day decreased significantly. In conversations we had with teachers and administrators, we regularly heard about their "success with wide reading." We believe that this early success in the climate of the school for this portion of the day encouraged teachers to try other parts of the literacy intervention.

Over the course of the two years, our observation and interview data had shown a significant trend in the use of content literacy interventions. With extensive professional development and coaching, teachers were able to incorporate these four instructional routines into their habits. Students were able to predict some aspects of each of their classes and to develop habits that they could use across the school day. While these are positive trends, the school really wanted to earn their freedom from the accountability system.

As we noted, only 12% of the students at Western were proficient in reading on the state assessment. That number was virtually unchanged for the previous five years until the results of the first assessment following the development of the schoolwide literacy instruction intervention. Following just over six months of work, achievement increased to 21% proficient. This is nearly double the achievement of 2002 but still not enough to meet AYP.

Two years later, 47% of the students were proficient in reading, and the school met state and federal accountability targets. Following our two and a half years of work, Western students continued to progress, and 54% of them scored proficient on the state assessment. In addition, the graduation rate increased from 67% to 73%. While still depressing, more students at Western earned a diploma than had done so in the past. When asked about this during a classroom observation, one of the teachers said, "They're more engaged now and they feel like they can succeed. They know what's expected and how to pass a class."

Schoolwide Approach Raises Achievement

This study adds to the evidence that a schoolwide approach to content literacy instruction is an effective way for raising achievement. The four schoolwide approaches selected by the school-based LLT are not new, but they are effective. As Shanahan and Shanahan (2008) noted, discipline-specific literacy is built on basic and intermediate (generic) literacy skills. Given the profile of the students at Western, it seemed reasonable to focus on intermediate and generic skills that could be integrated into all classes.

For many secondary schools, the problem is not the development of such a plan but rather the implementation of the plan. This formative experiment provides a glimpse into the workings of one high school over a two-and-a-half year period as the teachers worked to build students' literacy habits. In reality, the plan had to be changed a number of times to address the needs of the school. For example, evidence-based recommendations for professional development center on teacher-to-teacher implementation. While this was certainly the goal at Western, we quickly realized that the leadership team needed resources to effectively engage their peers in adult learning situations. We also had to modify the plan to account for student behavioral concerns and the number of new teachers starting at the school each year.

This study also points to the number of ways that schoolwide plans for improving student achievement can be sidetracked and sabotaged. Lack of support from the administrative team was a problem at Western; other schools will be forced to address similar or related challenges. Having said that, it is important to note the significant changes in achievement realized at Western as a result of purposeful integration of content literacy instruction. Interestingly, the changes extended beyond what can be measured by state tests. Students at Western read more and better than ever before. They engaged with their teachers at levels not previously witnessed. At the outset, the teachers at Western wanted freedom from state mandates, which they understood could only be attained by meeting AYP. Through hard work and personal change, this freedom was realized.

References

Baumann, J.F., Ware, D., & Edwards, E.C. (2007). "Bumping into spicy, tasty words that catch your tongue": A formative experiment on vocabulary instruction. *The Reading Teacher, 61*(2), 108–122. doi:10.1598/RT.61.2.1

Cobb, C. (2005). Literacy teams: Sharing leadership to improve student learning. *The Reading Teacher, 58*(5), 472–474. doi:10.1598/RT.58.5.7

Cunningham, A., & Stanovich, K. (2003). Reading can make you smarter! *Principal, 83*(2), 34–39.

Dean, D. (2006). *Strategic writing: The writing process and beyond in the secondary English classroom.* Urbana, IL: National Council of Teachers of English.

Faber, J.E., Morris, J.D., & Lieberman, M.G. (2000). The effect of note taking on ninth grade students' comprehension. *Reading Psychology, 21*(3), 257–270. doi:10.1080/02702710050144377

Glaser, B.G., & Strauss, A.L. (1967). *The discovery of grounded theory: Strategies for qualitative research.* New York: Aldine.

Ivey, G., & Broaddus, K. (2001). "Just plain reading": A survey of what makes students want to read in middle school classrooms. *Reading Research Quarterly, 36*(4), 350–377. doi:10.1598/RRQ.36.4.2

Ivey, G., & Broaddus, K. (2007). A formative experiment investigating literacy engagement among adolescent Latina/o students just beginning to read, write, and speak English. *Reading Research Quarterly, 42*(4), 512–545. doi:10.1598/RRQ.42.4.4

Jiménez, R.T. (1997). The strategic reading abilities and potential of five low-literacy Latina/o readers in middle school. *Reading Research Quarterly, 32*(3), 224–243. doi:10.1598/RRQ.32.3.1

Joyce, B.R., & Showers, B. (2002). *Student achievement through staff development* (3rd ed.). Alexandria, VA: Association for Supervision and Curriculum Development.

Langer, J.A. (2001). Beating the odds: Teaching middle and high school students to read and write well. *American Educational Research Journal, 38*(4), 837–880. doi:10.3102/00028312038004837

O'Brien, D.G., Stewart, R.A., & Moje, E.B. (1995). Why content literacy is difficult to infuse into the secondary school: Complexities of curriculum, pedagogy, and school culture. *Reading Research Quarterly, 30*(3), 442–463. doi:10.2307/747625

Pauk, W. (1974). *How to study in college.* Boston: Houghton Mifflin.

Reinking, D., & Bradley, B.A. (2007). *On formative and design experiments: Approaches to language and literacy research.* New York: Teachers College Press.

Reinking, D., & Pickle, J.M. (1993). Using a formative experiment to study how computers affect reading and writing in classrooms. In D.J. Leu & C.K. Kinzer (Eds.), *Examining central issues in literacy research, theory, and practice* (42nd yearbook of the National Reading Conference, pp. 263–270). Chicago: National Reading Conference.

Reinking, D., & Watkins, J. (1998). Balancing change and understanding in literacy research through formative experiments. In T. Shanahan & F.V. Rodriguez-Brown (Eds.), *47th yearbook of the National Reading Conference* (pp. 461–471). Chicago: National Reading Conference.

Schoenbach, R., Braunger, J., Greenleaf, C., & Litman, C. (2003). Apprenticing adolescents to reading in subject-area classrooms. *Phi Delta Kappan, 85*(2), 133–138.

Shanahan, T., & Shanahan, C. (2008). Teaching disciplinary literacy to adolescents: Rethinking content-area literacy. *Harvard Educational Review, 78*(1), 40–59.

Taylor, R., & Collins, V.D. (2003). *Literacy leadership for grades 5–12*. Alexandria, VA: Association for Supervision and Curriculum Development.

Vacca, R.T., & Vacca, J.A. (2008). *Content area reading: Literacy and learning across the curriculum* (9th ed.). Boston: Allyn & Bacon.

Wilhelm, J.D. (2001). *Improving comprehension with think-aloud strategies: Modeling what good readers do.* New York: Scholastic.

Questions for Reflection

- The literacy leadership team that was the focus of this article chose four specific instructional routines for their intervention: Cornell note-taking, think-alouds, writing to learn, and dedicated reading time. Which of these instructional routines has your school implemented? Which of these routines has been met with the most success? How do you go about truly embedding the routine in the lessons?
- The authors found that filming a local teacher engaged in the work of the literacy plan proved to be a major breakthrough—seeing their students and their colleagues in action helped teachers build their confidence in content literacy work. Do you think this strategy could be met with similar success in your school? What other strategies might help you during situations when you must leave the safe boundaries of your teaching "comfort zone"?
- A growing body of research suggests that a schoolwide approach to content literacy instruction is an effective way for raising achievement. Based on the profile of the students at the school in this study, the authors and LLT focused on intermediate and generic skills that could be integrated into all classes. What do you think needs to be the focus of your school's approach for raising achievement?

Developing the IRIS: Toward Situated and Valid Assessment Measures in Collaborative Professional Development and School Reform in Literacy

Theresa Rogers, Kari Lynn Winters, Gregory Bryan, John Price, Frank McCormick, Liisa House, Dianna Mezzarobba, and Carollyne Sinclaire

In the context of a collaborative literacy reform effort, we explored the use of a situated assessment tool to support and evaluate our project, providing an alternative or complement to standardized or published tests. By situated assessment, we mean an assessment tool that is collaboratively developed and used in the context of a particular reform effort and is meant to benefit teachers who use it by informing their instruction. We contrast this to standardized measures that are used solely for accountability rather than for professional development (cf. Dillon, 2003).

The role of the first three authors (university researchers Rogers, Winters, and Bryan) was to help conceptualize, support, and evaluate the project along with five teachers from the local school board who serve as consultants and mentor teachers (authors Price, McCormick, House, Mezzarobba, and Sinclaire). This project required us to build relationships among administrators, teachers, and researchers to assess progress and pitfalls and respond to the gaps and tensions in the project through collaborative "on-the-ground" theorizing—particularly about the uses of assessment in school reform.

The Context

Many educational reform initiatives in North America include external assessments from state or provincial governments, or from publishing companies, to make decisions about the nature and outcome of the reform efforts. However, in contrast to the current climate of reform in the United States, where accountability is tied to high-stakes standardized testing, provincial governments in Canada have asked individual districts to create their own accountability contracts with a range of possible indicators of success. The school board (district) with which we worked has named literacy as the key area for improvement in the current accountability contract, and both provincial tests and school or classroom-based measures are included as indicators of progress.

Within the context of this literacy reform effort in western Canada, we worked together to develop a project to improve reading comprehension among students in grades 4 through 8. The call for increased comprehension instruction is hardly new (cf. Durkin, 1978/1979); however, there is evidence to suggest that comprehension strategy instruction is still not getting the attention it deserves as a critically important

Reprinted from Rogers, T., Winters, K.L., Bryan, G., Price, J., McCormick, F., House, L., Mezzarobba, D., & Sinclaire, C. (2006). Developing the IRIS: Toward situated and valid assessment measures in collaborative professional development and school reform in literacy. *The Reading Teacher, 59*(6), 544-553.

component of effective and successful reading programs (Taylor, Pearson, Clark, & Walpole, 2002). Indeed, Cassidy and Cassidy (2004/2005) have cited comprehension as a "hot topic." This should not be surprising given that reading text strategically is particularly important in a time when the ability to garner, negotiate, synthesize, and critique information across a range of print and nonprint genres is acknowledged as a key component of participating in an information or knowledge economy (cf. Luke & Elkins, 1998).

On the basis of our evaluation of the first year of the project, we decided that collaboratively developing a situated and valid reading strategies measure would be key to supporting effective professional development in the larger school reform project. A major goal of this literacy project was to improve reading comprehension by supporting students from grades 4 to 8 in the development and use of comprehension strategies (Pearson & Dole, 1987) in flexible ways across a range of texts, with a focus on informational texts. We developed the project around six reading comprehension strategies: Making Connections, Engaging With the Text, Active Meaning Construction, Monitoring Understanding, Analysis and Synthesis, and Critical Reading (see Table 1).

These comprehension strategies are adapted from the work of Pearson and colleagues (Duke & Pearson, 2002; Fielding & Pearson, 1994; Pearson, Roehler, Dole, & Duffy, 1992) and are compatible, for instance, with the best practice comprehension methods recommended by the National Reading Panel (National Institute of Child Health and Human Development, 2000).

Table 1
A Description of the Strategies on the IRIS

- **Making Connections:** drawing on background knowledge and experiences, using your knowledge of genre and the author's craft, developing purposes for reading (e.g., what you would like to learn).
- **Engaging With the Text:** visualizing, entering the world of the text, taking perspectives, responding to the author's craft.
- **Active Meaning Construction:** questioning, connecting ideas, hypothesizing and drawing inferences, predicting, and using text-structure cues.
- **Monitoring Understanding:** awareness of lack of understanding, cross-checking ideas, revising hypotheses and predictions, using repair/fix-up strategies.
- **Analysis and Synthesis:** distinguishing more important ideas from less important ones, drawing conclusions from the ideas in the text, constructing themes, connecting information across texts (and other media).
- **Critical Reading:** questioning the author, the relationship of the text to yourself and to the world, evaluating ideas, developing alternative interpretations.

Background

Results from a provincial-wide fundamental skills assessments in reading were one impetus for the school board to develop the comprehension focus of the literacy project: In 2001, only 77% of grade 4 students in the district met expectations in reading comprehension; at grade 7, it was only 73%; and at grade 10, it was only 74%. At the same time, a grade 8 (the first year of high school in this province) formal assessment of incoming students indicated that, at some schools, a considerable proportion of the student population was reading below grade level. In addition, anecdotal accounts by teachers repeatedly indicated that significant numbers of their students struggled to comprehend texts across the curriculum. These were among the reasons the board initiated the 4 to 8 Literacy Project as a major professional development and reform effort and included it in the 2003/2004 District Accountability Contract, which cites the improvement of literacy as a main goal.

While naming literacy as a priority, we recognized that successful school reform is closely related to effective teacher professional development (Fullan, 1992). Indeed, professional development is often recognized as one of the key ingredients to which the successful implementation of school reform might be attributed (e.g., Taylor et al., 2002). While many teachers develop effective techniques in one aspect or another of the literacy curriculum, they also need time to share and build on that acquired knowledge and experience and to connect it to the growing body of literature in this area. To effect real improvement in schools, teachers need an opportunity to engage in sophisticated and long-term professional support that allows for inquiry, reflection, and dialogue and that provides instructional interventions to meet specific goals. These interventions also need to be relatively easy to implement and adapt to particular classroom settings (cf. Anders, Hoffman, & Duffy, 2000).

The 4 to 8 Literacy Project drew on models of school improvement that include focused professional development work by classroom teachers who share beliefs and understandings about their goals (Hill, 1998); an emphasis on a range of teaching approaches and integration of assessment and instruction (Langer, 1999); and an opportunity for teachers to exchange ideas and gain new knowledge, reflect on their current and new practices, and provide feedback on the goals and methods of the project. As we (the project team) reflected on the professional development of the first year, however, we realized that a missing aspect of the project was a reading comprehension strategies assessment tool that might connect teachers' understanding of the comprehension strategies with their professional development goals.

Our evaluation of the first year of the project included an analysis of school board documents, teacher surveys from the beginning and end of the year, and examinations of field notes from teacher-leader meetings for the project and from meetings at one case study school. We found that the implementation of an informal process writing assessment in the first year was key to the teachers' engagement in and understanding of their students' strengths and weaknesses in writing. At that point, the reading component of the project was being assessed with a standardized test (Canadian Achievement Test, or CAT). This test, however, was not yielding similar engagement by the teachers in understanding students' reading abilities and the role of teaching reading strategies in the curriculum. We recognized the need for a reading comprehension strategies measure that was less formal and addressed the needs of the teachers and students in the project. We then undertook the collaborative development of the Informal Reading Inventory of Strategies (IRIS) to support and enhance the project goals.

Grappling With Issues of Validity

As we began to think about developing this tool, we recognized the need to think not only about issues of content validity (measuring use of the comprehension strategies that were at the core of the project), but also to think about the potential uses of the measure at all levels of the project (see Table 2).

The concept of validity in testing is still being established (Hubley & Zumbo, 1996) and has expanded beyond notions of content validity tied to issues of procedure to a more dynamic notion tied to social processes and interpretations (Murphy, 1998). For instance, the International Reading Association and the National Council of Teachers of English (1994) Joint Task Force on Assessment called for measures that, among other standards, have as their purpose the improvement of teaching and learning, recognize and reflect the intellectually and socially complex

Table 2
Validity in Assessment

Content validity: Assumes the knowledge and skills assessed represent the larger domain of knowledge and skills that are being taught (in this case, reading comprehension strategies).

Consequential validity: Takes into account how and why the assessment is used and who is being assessed.

Transactional validity: Involves all stakeholders in the negotiation and development of the assessment measures, including teachers, students, and administrators.

nature of reading and writing in various contexts, take into account the interests of the students, are fair and equitable, consider the consequences of assessment, and allow for critical inquiry into curriculum and instruction.

Definitions such as these include more expansive views of validity that incorporate not only questions of what is being testing but also who is being tested, why and how they are being tested, as well as the consequences of testing (Johnston, 1998; Moss, 1998); that is, validity in measurement and literacy "is a complex interplay between evidence and values" (Murphy, 1998, p. 27).

In collaboratively developing the IRIS, we took into account these notions of consequential validity (Johnston, 1998), including the idea that development of assessment measures should take into account the instructional effects in the educational context (cf. Frederiksen & Collins, 1989). Finally, we were also influenced by the argument that validity should be responsive and transactional (Tierney, Crumpler, Bertelsen, & Bond, 2003) by including stakeholders in the negotiation and development of the assessment measures.

The Structure of the Project

The university involvement in the project was part of a larger school board and university partnership with literacy as one major focus along with technology, social development, Indigenous education, and research and development. The school board serves approximately 70,000 students and has a diverse population in terms of ethnicity and language. This three-year literacy project began in the 2002–2003 school year, with approximately 100 teachers and 2,500 students participating. The focus of the project was both reading comprehension and writing, but the main focus of the university partnership was on supporting and evaluating the reading comprehension component.

This framework for teaching reading comprehension was adopted by the 12 schools (7 elementary and 5 secondary) encompassing teachers in grades 4 through 8 who volunteered to participate in the project. Support was provided to over 100 participating teachers and approximately 25 teacher leaders through mentorship, professional development, and material resources.

The project team members included three university researchers, two school board curriculum consultants (intermediate and secondary) with over 20 years' experience in elementary and secondary classrooms, two literacy mentors who are part-time teachers, and one Aboriginal support consultant. Each school also has one to three project leaders and up to eight teachers of grades 4 through 8 involved in the project.

The professional development and support is extensive and varied in the project. There were team meetings to conceptualize the project and plan professional development. Teacher-leader meetings were held several times a year, and schools were given resources to participate in various sorts of professional development workshops, all-day project conferences, and school-team professional development time along with time to visit other classrooms. The two mentor teachers and the two school board consultants provided professional development workshops on reading strategies as requested. Each school is also provided with a "resource tub" of professional books and teaching materials.

The role as university consultants and collaborators was complex because we have helped to conceptualize the project, support its implementation, participate in professional development as speakers and workshop leaders, and plan evaluation. However, these multiple levels of involvement contributed to our approach to developing a more valid and situated reading comprehension strategies measure.

Developing and Implementing the IRIS

In response to the need for an assessment tool for this project, initially we attempted to develop rubrics for the teachers to use with any text or lesson they chose. We developed several rubric prototypes with the project team and shared them at school meetings. The feedback from teachers made it clear that they preferred an assessment tool that would be complete with a passage, questions, and scoring rubric to measure comprehension strategy use among their students. It was also evident from conversations with teachers that they wanted the scoring rubric to correspond to their provincial literacy rubrics outlined in a document on reading performance standards from the Ministry of Education that used a four-level scale (1 = not yet meeting expectations, 2 = minimally meeting expectations, 3 = fully meeting expectations, and 4 = exceeding expectations). The corresponding scale developed for the IRIS is 1 = no use of strategies, 2 = minimal use of strategies, 3 = appropriate use of strategies, and 4 = rich use of strategies.

In our visits to project school sites, teachers also shared with us other reading assessment tools they had seen, including one from a local district that included an oral reading measure that they thought would be useful for grouping students early in the year. We decided to include an oral reading excerpt and to provide the scoring guide for miscue analysis (adapted from Rhodes & Shanklin, 1990). The most important aspect of this assessment was its potential to be used by teachers to guide their instructional decision making and practice; that is, that it carried validity in terms of use as well as content.

The IRIS Written Form

We wanted the assessment tool to be as transparent as possible to students and teachers, so we listed the reading strategies that are central to the project on the first page of the written or student form (see Table 1). Below that, we listed two prereading questions focusing on connecting ideas (see questions 1 and 2 in Table 3). After

Table 3
Pre-, During-, and Postreading Questions on the IRIS

1. After taking a quick look at the reading selection, do you think this passage is fiction (e.g., a story) or nonfiction (true)? What clues helped you decide? (Making Connections)
2. What do you already know about this topic? (Making Connections)
3. Now that you have read the first part, what do you think you will find out in the rest of the passage? (Active Meaning Construction)
4. If you drew a picture of something in this passage, what would it look like? (Engaging With the Text)
5. What do you find most interesting so far? (Engaging With the Text)
6. What do you think were the two or three most important ideas in the passage? (Analysis and Synthesis)
7. If the author were sitting here, what questions would you ask him or her? (Critical Reading)
8. If someone were having problems understanding this passage, what suggestions would you have for him or her? (Monitoring Understanding)
9. What was the most confusing aspect of the passage? What did you do when you were confused?
10. Do you think that this reading selection was too difficult, too easy, or just right for your reading ability? Why do you think that?

reading the first part of the nonfiction selection, students answer several more questions focusing on constructing meaning and engaging with text (see questions 3–5 in Table 3). Then, after students read the second half of the passage, there are more questions related to analysis and synthesis, critical reading, and monitoring of understanding (questions 6–8). Finally, there are two self-assessment questions (questions 9 and 10).

The IRIS Follow-Up Interview Form

Because a written test is not necessarily an accurate measure of each student's strategy use (e.g., some students struggle with writing or writing in English as their second language), we developed a follow-up oral interview to ask about students' answers to the pre-, during-, and postreading questions. Using the teacher record-keeping form of the IRIS, teachers copy answers given by students as they are probed about their written answers. Students may refer to their written tests that are in front of them. Ultimately, teachers can choose how many students with whom they would like to do follow-up interviews. Teachers might choose to interview only struggling students or students about whom they need more information.

In our first administration of the IRIS, we interviewed four proficient students, four average students, and four struggling students in each grade. We have found that students typically increase their comprehension strategy score by 1 or 2 points (out of 24 total points) on the oral interview form of the assessment. Because the scores of the written version are highly correlated with the oral version (.98), it is not necessary to do this with all students—just a subset of students about whom teachers would like to learn more or who, for various reasons, find writing answers more challenging than providing verbal responses.

Students are also asked to read aloud a short excerpt from the same reading passage. This is scored for accuracy and for sense (Rhodes & Shanklin, 1990). They are also asked to retell what they remember from their oral reading of the short excerpt. The back page of the IRIS provides a rubric for scoring the written (student) and oral (teacher record keeping) forms of the strategies assessment (see Table 4).

Administering and Scoring the IRIS

Teachers can give this written version of the IRIS to all of their students in approximately 30 minutes, and they can score it with the rubric provided on the back of the teacher record-keeping form. All participating schools gave this assessment to their students in grades 4 to 8 in autumn of 2003 and spring 2004 (there are two versions of the assessment, A and B). The project team then conducted follow-up, one-on-one interviews with 12 students per grade per school, because at that point not all teachers had been to the training sessions and did not feel they would have time to interview the students. (In the third year of the project, teachers conducted the follow-up interviews, which take about 15 minutes per student.) Interrater reliability on 5% of the IRIS written and follow-up interviews ranges between 80 and 100% across the six strategies assessed.

We have found that the IRIS is highly correlated with the CAT subtests in reading (e.g., 0.79 correlation for grade 4 IRIS scores and grade 4 CAT Total Reading scores, $N = 42$). This assures us that we are measuring similar constructs (reading comprehension ability), although we argue that the IRIS is more directly related to the particular goals of this project, which focus on reading strategy use and instructional decision making.

Emerging Profiles of Intermediate Readers Based on the IRIS

From our experience conducting over 400 written and follow-up interviews, we have developed emerging profiles (cf. Wade, 1990) of intermediate readers that have been useful to teachers in understanding the strengths and instructional needs of their students in terms of the six reading comprehension strategies (and the oral reading and retelling measure). We include the caveat that while these profiles are useful for identifying general types of student readers, each student is unique in the combinations of strengths and weaknesses

Table 4
Scoring Rubric for Written and Oral Responses

	1	2	3	4
Making Connections Questions 1 & 2	No connections between background knowledge or experiences and the text in terms of purposes for reading or text ideas, genre, or writer's craft.	Makes some minimally related connections between background knowledge or experiences and the text in terms of purposes for reading, text ideas, genre, or writer's craft to support comprehension.	Makes appropriate connections between background knowledge or experiences and the text in terms of purposes for reading, text ideas, genre, or writer's craft that seem to support comprehension.	Makes rich connections between background knowledge or experiences and the text in terms of purposes for reading, ideas, genre, or writer's craft, including some that extend beyond the scope of the text.
Active Meaning Construction Question 3	No questioning, hypothesizing, or predicting; no connecting of ideas, inferencing, or use of text structure cues to support comprehension.	Does some minimally related questioning, hypothesizing, or predicting; or minimal connecting of ideas, inferencing, or use of text structure cues to support comprehension.	Appropriate use of questioning, hypothesizing, or predicting; or appropriate connecting of ideas, inferencing, or use of text structure cues to support comprehension.	Rich use of questioning, hypothesizing, or predicting; or appropriate connecting of ideas, inferencing, or use of text structure cues, including some that extend beyond the scope of the text.
Engaging With the Text Questions 4 & 5	No visualizing, engaging in world of text, perspective taking, or responding to author's craft.	Does some minimally related visualizing, engaging in world of text, perspective taking, or responding to author's craft to support comprehension.	Appropriate use of visualizing, engaging in world of text, perspective taking, or responding to author's craft to support comprehension.	Rich use of visualizing, engaging in world of text, perspective taking, or responding to author's craft to support and extend comprehension.
Analysis and Synthesis Question 6	No distinguishing more important ideas or events, drawing conclusions, identifying main ideas, themes, or connecting ideas to other texts.	Some minimal distinguishing of more important ideas or events, drawing of conclusions, main ideas, theme identification, or connecting of ideas to other texts to support comprehension.	Distinguishes more important ideas or events, draws conclusions, identifies main ideas, themes, or connects ideas to other texts to support comprehension.	Distinguishes important ideas or events, draws conclusions, identifies main ideas, themes, or connects ideas to other texts in rich ways that support and extend comprehension.
Critical Reading Question 7	No questioning of author, relating of text to self or world, evaluating ideas, or developing alternate interpretations.	Some minimally related questioning of author, relating of text to self or world, evaluating ideas, or developing alternate interpretations to support comprehension.	Appropriate use of questioning of author, relating of text to self or world, evaluating ideas, or developing alternate interpretations to support comprehension.	Rich use of questioning of author, relating of text to self or world, evaluating ideas, or developing alternate interpretations to support and extend comprehension.

(continued)

Table 4 *(continued)*
Scoring Rubric for Written and Oral Responses

	1	2	3	4
Monitoring Understanding Questions 8, 9, & 10	No awareness of lack of understanding, revising hypotheses predictions, cross-checking of ideas, or using fix-up strategies.	Some awareness of lack of understanding but little or no revising of hypotheses, predictions, cross-checking of ideas, or use of fix-up strategies.	Awareness of lack of understanding and appropriate revising of hypotheses or predictions, cross-checking of ideas, or use of fix-up strategies to support comprehension.	Awareness of lack of understanding and rich use of revising of hypotheses or predictions, cross-checking of ideas, or use of fix-up strategies to support and extend comprehension.

	Score for written responses		Score for responses to oral interview	
Questions 1 & 2	Making Connections	___/ 4	Making Connections	___/ 4
Question 3	Active Meaning Construction:	___/ 4	Active Meaning Construction:	___/ 4
Questions 4 & 5	Engaging With the Text:	___/ 4	Engaging With the Text:	___/ 4
Question 6	Analysis and Synthesis:	___/ 4	Analysis and Synthesis:	___/ 4
Question 7	Critical Reading:	___/ 4	Critical Reading:	___/ 4
Questions 8, 9, & 10	Monitoring Understanding:	___/ 4	Monitoring Understanding:	___/ 4
	Overall written response score:	___/24	Overall oral response score:	___/24

he or she brings to the reading process and may fit in more than one category. Also, this is just one assessment based on one nonfiction passage, and each student is interviewed in an unfamiliar situation. We recognize that a student may have a somewhat different profile in a different context. The following are the profiles we found.

Word-Level, Processing Problems. Students with this profile are constructing little to no meaning from the passage. When we perform the oral reading measure, we find that they have decoding, word-identification, or fluency problems. These students need support for these skills in the context of meaningful text and discussions that support comprehension.

"Reading" but Not Making Meaning. Students with this profile read fluently with perfect or near-perfect decoding and word identification but have little to no comprehension of the passage. They sometimes answer questions by "borrowing" phrases from boxed information, bolded information, or titles, but they do not provide evidence of constructing their own meaning from the text. These students need to begin using strategies that help them make meaningful connections to the text.

Local Meaning Makers. These students decode adequately, usually at the instructional level, and they retell fairly well but focus on meaning at the local or sentence-by-sentence level instead of constructing overall passage meaning or extending meaning beyond the passage. These students would benefit from strategies that help them construct meaning across the text, analyze and synthesize the ideas in the text, and read critically.

Global Meaning Makers. These students have rich connecting and engaging strategies and construct global meaning, but they only minimally attend to the structure and particulars of the passage. They may have some word-identification weakness, and they compensate by using a rich background knowledge and "guessing" at some of the content and structure. These students need to focus more on the structure and ideas in the text as evidence for their conclusions.

The Strategic Majority. Students who indicate no use or minimal use of some reading comprehension strategies and appropriate use of others (e.g., an overall average score of 14 to 16 out of 24). They often are able to connect ideas, engage with the text, and construct meaning (with attention to text as opposed to top-down readers), yet they may not read critically, make text-to-world connections, or monitor themselves when they are experiencing comprehension problems.

The Critics. We hope all students become this type of reader. These students are very competent readers and exhibit strengths in most or all areas of comprehension and critical reading and thinking strategy use. They sometimes point out weaknesses in a reading passage or in a teacher's questions.

Making Instructional Decisions

When the project team shared the profiles with the teacher leaders from each school at a meeting in late autumn of 2003 (year 2), we noted that they recognized the types of students described and saw the potential usefulness of these profiles for making instructional decisions. For instance, at one school, teachers who scored their IRISs said it helped them to see the specific differences between their stronger and weaker readers in terms of the strategies the students were using. They decided to focus on constructing meaning and critical reading strategies because of the students' lack of questioning of the text and the author. They decided to use a QAR (Question–Answer Relationship) Strategy (Raphael, 1982), noting that "when the question and answer are farther away from each other in the text it is more difficult for [students]."

Other teachers have chosen to use a mix of print and nonprint strategies to encourage the use of particular strategies, such as engaging (visualizing) and constructing meaning (predicting) for both literary and informational texts. In response, the mentors adapted a technique they called Read–Sketch–Predict to encourage students to read one stanza of a poem, sketch what they see, and then predict what will come next. After doing this for each stanza, the students wrote what they noticed about their thinking, which reinforces the Monitoring Understanding strategy. Many other examples have either been provided to the teachers in the resource tub or workshops or have been developed by the teachers at each school, including lessons that encourage the use of all six comprehension strategies with one informational book. For instance, along with the book *Should There Be Zoos?* (Stead, 2002), teachers created the following strategy lessons: K-W-L sheets (Ogle, 1986) for drawing on background knowledge, using illustrations to predict, collaboratively filling out sheets that provide a column for key opinions and evidence in the text, developing arguments for and against zoos, writing down arguments, and revising papers with a buddy using guidelines for persuasive writing.

It is important to note that the IRIS was developed to complement and inform the kinds of strategy work teachers were already doing, but it also gives them an opportunity to see if students are developing their use of particular strategies after instructional implementation. Some schools have chosen to use this measure as one indicator of literacy growth in their yearly school accountability contracts. Such a use illustrates our notion of a "situated" assessment that integrates assessment and practice, informing teachers rather than simply holding them accountable with measures unrelated to their practices.

Support and Encourage Accountability and Literacy Improvement

When we began collaborating on this project in the spring of 2002, we did not envision creating a specific assessment tool of reading comprehension strategies to support or evaluate the project. As the project developed, and we began to see the need for another kind of measure, we looked at a range of commercial informal reading inventories and realized none of them fully matched the goals of our project or the needs of the teachers. Over time we have simultaneously developed the instrument and conceptualized the role of assessment in this large professional development and reform project. Our on-the-ground, collaborative theorizing has led us to believe that not only do measures of projects such as this need to be valid in their content but also in terms of consequences and uses of the assessment. Teachers, school board consultants, and researchers were all actively engaged in developing the IRIS as it went through many draft stages, constantly being refined in consultation with stakeholders and as a result of their feedback. The transactional validity is reflected in this collaborative development and piloting of the assessment, as well as in the careful consideration of its uses. The uses (and consequences) of the instrument are consistent with the layers of systemic goals among the group using it. Teachers wanted a tool that they could use and score themselves—one that would inform their instruction and their students' understanding of what kinds of strategies were important in the reading process. In this way, the instructional changes "engendered by the use of the test" have the potential to "contribute to the development of knowledge and/or skills that the test purportedly measures" (Frederiksen & Collins, 1989, p. 27).

We know that the assessment is limited to one passage (per grade level) that any individual student may or may not find interesting. It is therefore a measure that should be used in relation to other classroom assessments to gauge a student's use of reading comprehension strategies. Over time, we will have even more information about how teachers use the assessment as part of their instructional decision making in relation to teaching reading comprehension strategies in their classrooms and to what extent reading strategy use increases among their students. We also will have more information about how they might use such an assessment for accountability. For instance, one inner-city secondary school analyzed its autumn and spring scores and calculated how many students were at each of the 4 levels and set goals for the next year: 100% of students scoring at least at the minimal range in using the six comprehension strategies (with overall scores of 12 and above out of 24) and 75% of students using appropriate comprehension strategies (scores of 18 and above out of 24).

In this way, we hope to respond to the growing demand for assessment approaches that are sensitive to the contexts in which they are used, build on notions of consequential and transactive validity, and allow for critical inquiry into the relationship between curriculum and instruction. This approach also supports and encourages teachers and school administrators who set their own goals for accountability and improvement in literacy.

References

Anders, P.L., Hoffman, J.V., & Duffy, G.G. (2000). Teaching teachers to teach reading. In M.L. Kamil, P.B. Mosenthal, P.D. Pearson, & R. Barr (Eds.), *Handbook of reading research* (Vol. 3, pp. 719–742). Mahwah, NJ: Erlbaum.

Cassidy, J., & Cassidy, D. (2004/2005, December/January). What's hot, what's not for 2005. *Reading Today, 22*(3), pp. 1, 8–9.

Dillon, D. (2003). In leaving no child behind have we forsaken individual learners, teachers, schools and communities? Presidential address. In C.M. Fairbanks, J. Worthy, B. Maloch, J.V. Hoffman, & D.L. Schallert (Eds.), *52nd Yearbook of the National Reading Conference* (pp. 1–31). Oak Creek, WI: National Reading Conference.

Duke, N.K., & Pearson, P.D. (2002). Effective practices for developing reading comprehension. In A.E. Farstrup & S.J. Samuels (Eds.), *What research has to say about reading instruction* (3rd ed., pp. 205–242). Newark, DE: International Reading Association.

Durkin, D. (1978/1979). What classroom observations reveal about reading comprehension instruction. *Reading Research Quarterly, 14*, 481–533.

Fielding, L.G., & Pearson, P.D. (1994). Synthesis of research/reading comprehension: What works. *Educational Leadership, 51*(5), 62–68.

Fullan, M. (1992). *Successful school improvement.* Buckingham, England: Open University Press.

Frederiksen, J.R., & Collins, A. (1989). A systems approach to educational testing. *Educational Researcher, 18*(9), 27–32.

Hill, P. (1998). Shaking the foundations: Research-driven school reform. *School Effectiveness and School Improvement, 9*, 419–436.

Hubley, A.M., & Zumbo, B.D. (1996). A dialectic on validity: Where we have been and where we are going. *The Journal of General Psychology, 123*, 207–215.

International Reading Association & National Council of Teachers of English. (1994). *Standards for the assessment of reading and writing.* Newark, DE; Urbana, IL: Authors.

Johnston, P. (1998). The consequences of the use of standardized tests. In S. Murphy (Ed.), *Fragile evidence: A critique of reading assessment* (pp. 89–101). Mahwah, NJ: Erlbaum.

Langer, J. (1999). *Excellence in English in middle and high school: How teachers' professional lives support student achievement.* Albany: Center on English Learning and Achievement, State University of New York.

Luke, A., & Elkins, J. (1998). Editorial: Reinventing literacy in "New Times." *Journal of Adolescent & Adult Literacy, 42*, 4–7.

Moss, P. (1998). Enlarging the dialogue in educational measurement. Voices from interpretive traditions. *Educational Researcher, 25*(1), 20–28.

Murphy, S. (1998). *Fragile evidence: A critique of reading assessment.* Mahwah, NJ: Erlbaum.

National Institute of Child Health and Human Development. (2000). *Report of the National Reading Panel. Teaching children to read: An evidence-based assessment of the scientific research literature on reading and its implications for reading instruction* (NIH Publication No. 00-4769). Washington, DC: U.S. Government Printing Office.

Ogle, D. (1986). K-W-L: A teaching model that develops active reading of expository text. *The Reading Teacher, 39*, 564–570.

Pearson, P.D., & Dole, J.A. (1987). Explicit comprehension instruction: A review of research and a new conceptualization of instruction. *The Elementary School Journal, 88*, 151–165.

Pearson, P.D., Roehler, L.R., Dole, J.A., & Duffy, G.G. (1992). Developing expertise in reading comprehension. In S.J. Samuels & A.E. Farstrup (Eds.), *What research has to say about reading instruction* (2nd ed., pp. 145–199). Newark, DE: International Reading Association.

Raphael, T.E. (1982). Question-answering strategies for children. *The Reading Teacher, 36*, 186–191.

Rhodes, L.K., & Shanklin, N.L. (1990). Miscue analysis in the classroom. *The Reading Teacher, 44*, 252–254.

Stead, T. (2002). *Should there be zoos? A persuasive text.* New York: Mondo.

Taylor, B.M., Pearson, P.D., Clark, K., & Walpole, S. (2002). Effective schools and accomplished teachers: Lessons about primary-grade reading instruction in low-income schools. In B.M. Taylor & P.D. Pearson (Eds.), *Teaching reading: Effective schools, accomplished teachers* (pp. 3–72). Mahwah, NJ: Erlbaum.

Tierney, R.J., Crumpler, T.P., Bertelsen, C.D., & Bond, E.L. (2003). *Interactive assessment: Teachers, parents and students as partners.* Norwood, MA: Christopher-Gordon.

Wade, S.E. (1990). Using think-alouds to assess comprehension. *The Reading Teacher, 43*, 442–451.

Questions for Reflection

- Consider the profiles of intermediate readers that emerged from the authors' study of IRIS—can you think of students who match these profiles or combinations of these profiles? How can you use these profiles to inform your instructional decisions? How can you adjust your strategy instruction to account for the strengths and weaknesses identified in these profiles?
- The IRIS is an assessment tool that is meant to help teachers determine the literacy needs of their students. However, it is also created to support effective professional development in the larger school reform project. How can assessments help you set your own goals for accountability and contribute to your own professional development?

A Framework for Authentic Literacy Assessment

Scott G. Paris, Robert C. Calfee, Nikola Filby, Elfrieda H. Hiebert, P. David Pearson, Sheila W. Valencia, and Kenneth P. Wolf

Assessment is fundamental to the improvement of education; it provides measures of success for students' learning, for educator's leadership, and for continuous evaluations of instructional programs. Many researchers and educators have argued that traditional psychoeducational tests are no longer adequate for these diverse assessment purposes (e.g., Resnick & Resnick, 1990; Valencia & Pearson, 1987). The proposals offered to improve literacy assessment include a wide variety of suggestions from new national tests based on performance measures to classroom assessments of individuals based on portfolios of work samples. It is unlikely that a single test or alternative assessment will meet the needs of all stakeholders, but it seems clear to us that the efforts are stimulating many new and useful approaches to assessment.

The purpose of this article is to describe a framework for literacy assessment that can be adapted to suit the assessment needs of particular schools and districts. The framework involves five phases of decision making that policymakers should consider as they revise assessment practices. Because the decisions about what outcomes are valued, how to assess literacy achievements, and how to use the data directly affect teachers, parents, and students, we believe that the decision making should be shared among the various stakeholders. In this manner, all the participants are informed about the goals and criteria of assessment, and they are motivated to participate fully in assessment. Although this article describes a process of decision making about authentic literacy assessments that was created by the authors for an external program evaluation, we encourage educators to emulate this process in schools and districts because it can establish an informed consensus among local stakeholders about the literacy outcomes and processes that will be assessed and valued in each community.

Our team was assembled as a group of consultants to the Far West Laboratory for Educational Research and Development charged with designing a framework for the evaluation of literacy achievement in the Kamehameha Elementary Education Program (KEEP). The overall evaluation conducted by the Southwest Regional Educational Laboratory, is part of a U.S. federally funded project designed to assess the effectiveness of the K–3 KEEP literacy curriculum and to compare the achievement of KEEP students at the end of third grade to similar students in other classrooms in Hawaii. What began as a program evaluation of a "whole literacy" curriculum grew into the creation of alternative literacy assessments because of the limitations of standardized tests to capture critical aspects of the curriculum objective of both KEEP and the Hawaii Department of Education (DOE) curricula (Giuli, 1991). The situation provided a unique opportunity for our team to work together on a specific practical problem. We believe that both the process and the outcome can serve as models for others to design authentic literacy assessments.

Reprinted from Paris, S.G., Calfee, R.C., Filby, N., Hiebert, E.H., Pearson, P.D., Valencia, S.W., & Wolf, K.P. (1992). A framework for authentic literacy assessment. *The Reading Teacher, 46*(2), 88–98.

The Hawaiian Context of KEEP

KEEP began in 1972 as an experimental project at the Kamehameha School to foster literacy among native Hawaiian students (Tharp & Gallimore, 1988) It is now disseminated in eight schools throughout the islands of Hawaii and serves annually approximately 3,000 students in K–3 classes. The curriculum has recently been extended to some grade 4, 5, and 6 classrooms also. The KEEP curriculum has been revised several times and may be described most appropriately as a dynamic rather than static set of guidelines for curriculum, instruction, and assessment. For example, the KEEP *Literacy Curriculum Guide* (Au, Blake, Herman, Oshiro, & Scheu, 1990) describes instruction that includes language experience and whole literacy activities relevant for native Hawaiian children.

The *Guide* also describes a portfolio assessment system of observations and checklists that teachers can use to assess students' progress against developmental benchmarks. The checklists summarize children's literacy in four broad areas: ownership and voluntary reading, reading comprehension, writing processes, and emergent literacy (Au, Scheu, Kawakami, & Herman, 1990). Although the *Guide* provided us with valuable information about the goals of the KEEP curriculum and assessment, our suggestions for authentic assessments were not constrained by extant practices. The portfolio system described by Au et al. is used primarily by paraprofessional aides for diagnostic purposes although teachers are gradually learning about the system so that they can record similar observations. In contrast, the assessment system that we were charged to create will be used by external evaluators to make quantitative comparisons between the achievements of KEEP and nonKEEP students.

The *Language Arts Program Guide* (Hawaii Department of Education, 1988) describes an integrated language arts curriculum that is similar to the KEEP framework but less oriented to whole language instruction and the sociocultural backgrounds of native Hawaiian children. Learner outcomes for each grade level and domain of language arts are specified in more detail than the KEEP benchmarks, but the objectives of both curricula are generally congruent. It is important to note that we used the curricular goals and activities of both KEEP and the Department of Education (DOE) to determine which aspects of literacy are emphasized in daily instruction and which outcomes are valued.

The assessment problems in Hawaii are similar to those faced by most school districts, that is, how to create assessments that (a) measure critical features of the curriculum, (b) are consistent with instructional practices, (c) motivate students, and (d) provide measures of accountability (Winograd, Paris, & Bridge, 1991). The traditional practice in Hawaii has been to test all students above second grade every spring with the Stanford Achievement Test which does not measure many of the goals in the KEEP and Hawaii DOE curricula. Many teachers spend months preparing their students for the Stanford with materials and activities that are inconsistent with their regular curriculum. Likewise, many students regard the Stanford as the goal of literacy learning and the pinnacle of the academic year. Administrators report a "canyon effect" of low motivation for the last month of school following the Stanford. The Stanford results have been used historically to evaluate the KEEP program without regard for the variable time that teachers and students have participated in actual KEEP classrooms or for the misalignment between the Stanford and the curricula.

Given these problems, it is not surprising that evaluations of KEEP using scores from the Stanford and the Metropolitan Achievement Test (Yap, Estes, & Nickel, 1988) revealed poor performance of KEEP students and frustrated KEEP staff. There was a clear and compelling need to design alternative assessments to measure literacy development in KEEP classrooms. The assessments needed to measure reading and writing proficiency as well as students' literacy ownership, habits, attitudes, and strategies in a manner that reflected the interactive, collaborative, and constructive nature of learning in Hawaiian classrooms. This is the problem we tackled.

Negotiating a Framework for Alternative Assessment

We began meeting in January 1991 as a group, met periodically during the year, collected pilot data, and corresponded regularly about the framework. As with many new projects, we realized the shape of the task and the solutions only after being immersed in them for many months. In the end, we can identify five discrete phases to our decision making that may be a heuristic for others.

Phase 1: Identifying Dimensions of Literacy

Our discussions about alternative assessments always hinged on issues of curriculum and instruction because we all agreed that "authentic assessment" must reflect daily classroom practices and goals. Thus, the initial task was to decide which aspects of students' literacy development are important to measure in Hawaiian schools and, correspondingly, which aspects are not assessed by current procedures. We began by considering various taxonomies that included elements such as knowledge, skills, and attitudes or reading, writing, listening, and speaking. None of these were satisfactory because they failed to capture the interconnectedness and the psychological characteristics of motivated literacy that were central to the curricula. From discussions with educators from KEEP and the DOE, as well as our observations and knowledge of KEEP, we gleaned a list of 5–10 dimensions that were the basis for continuing discussions. We subsequently identified seven critical dimensions of literacy, described in Table 1, that we considered to be at the core of both curricula. These dimensions embody a view of literacy that is interactive, social, constructive, metacognitive, motivated, and integrated with functional language uses. The assessment of these dimensions transcend the Stanford scores and traditional emphases on basic reading skills.

The results of this phase of decision making included both a product and a process. The process of examining the curricula, observing classroom instruction, and operationalizing the objectives of "whole literacy" took several months and involved brainstorming, clarifying values, and building consensus among our team. We also discussed our assessment proposals with Kathy Au and Chuck Giuli at KEEP and with Betsy Brandt at the DOE. It was remarkably illuminating to negotiate the alignment of curriculum and assessment, and we were all struck by the value this process can have for teachers and administrators. Indeed, students who understand the connections between daily activities for learning and assessment might also become more informed about the purposes of assessment and the criteria for success. Knowing what counts in literacy performance in the classroom can help create a shared vision for teaching and learning.

Phase 2: Identifying Attributes of Literacy Dimensions

As we identified potential dimensions we also discussed the kinds of literate performance that distinguish skilled from less skilled students on each dimension. These attributes could be described at general or specific levels. For example, in the dimension of Engagement With Text Through Reading, we discussed how good readers are constructive, strategic, reflective, and evaluative. For each of these general attributes, we generated three specific literacy indicators that could be verified empirically from students' performance, such as using appropriate strategies for monitoring comprehension or making inferences. Each of these indicators is describe in Table 2 and provides a tangible referent point for evaluating students' literacy. These indicators lie on continua, but anchored descriptions are provided only for the high and low ends. More detailed standards and scoring rubrics can be generated for each indicator.

One virtue of this activity for educators in general is that the participants share their theories of literacy with each other so that ideas about literacy development are reconsidered within this collaborative context. We believe that this exercise is extremely valuable for groups of teachers,

Table 1
Critical Dimensions and Attributes of Literacy

1. Engagement with text through reading
A critical aspect of literacy is the extent to which readers and writers interact with the ideas conveyed in text. They need to relate their background knowledge and experiences to new textual information and integrate the ideas. Thoughtful engagement with text implies that readers construct meaning sensibly, that they employ strategies as they read, and that they reflect on the meaning and style of the text. Comprehension is a key element of engagement, but the dimension also includes the demonstration of thinking strategies and personal responses to text that extend the basic interpretation of text.

2. Engagement with text through writing
Writing is a constructive expression of ideas that are communicated coherently and accurately. Students' involvement with writing and reading should provide mutual support for effective literacy strategies, habits, and motivation. Writing should be embedded in everyday activities and based on genuine communicative purposes. It should allow students to compose their ideas on a variety of topics with different genres and styles. Students' writing should include their personal opinions, reflections, and elaborations to texts they have read. The message and voice should be clear. The technical aspects of writing such as spelling, word choice, punctuation, grammar, and organization should be appropriate for the students' grade level.

3. Knowledge about literacy
Students should understand that language can be expressed through reading and writing according to literacy conventions and that adherence to these conventions helps people to understand each other through written communication. For example, effective readers and writers understand the different purposes and structures of various literary genres and know how strategies can be used while reading and writing. Their knowledge about literacy also includes their metalinguistic understanding of the nuances of language, such as ambiguity and figurative language, as well as their understanding about the connections among reading, writing, listening, and speaking.

4. Orientation to literacy
Reading and writing require more than engagement with text and the construction of meaning. They also require motivation so that children can read, write, and learn independently. Learners must set appropriate goals for literacy and persevere in the face of difficulty. Motivated readers see challenges in what they read just as motivated writers extend themselves to compose more text, to write in various genres, or to write creatively. A positive orientation to literacy also includes feelings of confidence, optimism, enjoyment, and control so that children regard their achievements with pride and satisfaction.

5. Ownership of literacy
Good readers develop independent reading habits, identify their favorite topics and books, and monitor their own progress and achievements. In this sense, they develop "ownership" of their reading that reflects pride in their accomplishments and their enjoyment in recreational reading. Likewise, good writers engage in writing independently, read their own compositions, and develop preferences for writing about some topics or writing with particular genres. This sense of ownership fosters lifelong literacy habits and is evident in children's preferences for reading and writing, their independence, and their initiative for literacy.

6. Collaboration
Reading and writing are not always private activities; they often involve discussion and cooperation so that meaning can be negotiated among individuals. The social construction of meaning is especially important in school where instruction activities may involve shared reading and writing, cooperative learning, and peer tutoring arrangements. Effective readers and writers can work with others in "communities of learners" to create meaning, revise compositions, present and share their ideas, and solve problems while they read and write. Frequent participation with other students in school is one mark of collaboration; social respect for others and mutual benefits for learning are also desirable consequences of collaboration.

7. Connectedness of the curriculum
Reading and writing are pervasive activities in school and are fundamental for learning across the entire school curriculum. It is important, therefore, that children read and write in order to learn in subjects such as social studies, science, and mathematics and that the skills, motivation, and collaboration evident in literacy instruction are reinforced in content areas. It is also important for children to understand the connections among reading, writing, listening, and speaking so that they regard language arts as integrated, purposeful, and pragmatic. Literacy also needs to be connected between school and home so that families can support school-based literacy skills and habits and so that teachers can be sensitive to the unique backgrounds and talents of each child.

Table 2
Performance Indicators for Each Attribute and Dimension of Literacy

Low engagement	High engagement
ENGAGEMENT WITH TEXT THROUGH READING	
Reading is constructive	
a. Fails to build on prior knowledge	a. Integrates new ideas with previous knowledge and experiences
b. Few inferences or elaborations; literal retelling of text	b. Exhibits within text and beyond text inferences
c. Focus is on isolated facts; does not connect text elements	c. Identifies and elaborates plots, themes, or concepts
Reading is evaluative	
a. Fails to use personal knowledge and experience as a framework for interpreting text	a. Uses prior knowledge and experience to construct meaning
b. Is insensitive to the author's style, assumptions, perspective, and claims	b. Is sensitive to, and may even question, the author's style, assumptions, perspective, and claims
c. Fails to examine or go beyond a literal account of the ideas in the text	c. Expresses opinions, judgments, or insights about the content of the text
ENGAGEMENT WITH TEXT THROUGH WRITING	
Low engagement	**High engagement**
Writing is constructive	
a. Writes disconnected words or phrases with few identifiable features of any genre	a. Writes well-constructed, thematic, cohesive text that is appropriate to the genre
b. Fails to use personal knowledge as a base for composing text	b. Draws on personal knowledge and experiences in composing text
c. Little evidence of voice, personal style, or originality	c. Creative writing reveals a strong sense of voice, personal style, and originality
Writing is technically appropriate	
a. Writing includes numerous violations of the conventions of spelling, punctuation, and usage	a. Displays developmentally appropriate use of the conventions of spelling, punctuation, and usage
b. Inappropriate or inflexible use of grammatical structures	b. Writing exhibits grammatical structures appropriate to the purpose and genre
c. Limited and contextually inappropriate vocabulary	c. Rich, varied, and appropriate vocabulary
KNOWLEDGE ABOUT LITERACY	
Low knowledge	**High knowledge**
Knowledge about literacy conventions and structures	
a. Unaware of the functions of print conventions and punctuation in written communication	a. Understands the functions that print conventions and punctuation play in written communication
b. Unaware of text structures and genres	b. Can identify and use several specific text structures and genres
c. Unaware of the subtleties of language use; does not understand or use connotative meaning, ambiguity, or figurative language	c. Understands that words have multiple meanings; can use and understand ambiguity and figurative language

(continued)

Table 2 *(continued)*
Performance Indicators for Each Attribute and Dimension of Literacy

Low knowledge	High knowledge
KNOWLEDGE ABOUT LITERACY *(continued)*	
Knowledge about strategies	
a. Unaware of the strategies that can be applied while reading and writing	a. Knows strategies that can be applied before, during, and after reading and writing
b. Limited understanding of how strategies can be applied while reading or writing	b. Can explain how strategies are applied or might be used
c. Naive about the value of strategies; does not use strategies selectively	c. Understands how and when strategies can be used and why they are helpful
ORIENTATION TO LITERACY	
Low orientation	**High orientation**
Motivation for reading and writing	
a. Goals for literacy are task completion and extrinsic rewards	a. Goals are intrinsic and mastery oriented
b. Gives up easily in the face of difficulty	b. Persists when confronted with obstacles or difficulties
c. Chooses tasks where success or failure are certain	c. Chooses challenging tasks on the edge of current abilities
Attitudes about reading and writing	
a. Negative attitudes about reading and writing	a. Exhibits enthusiasm for reading and writing
b. Exhibits embarrassment, passivity, and insecurity about self as reader or writer	b. Exhibits pride and confidence about self as a reader or writer
c. Views literacy events as under the control of others	c. Views self as in charge of own literacy and feels that others respect contributions
OWNERSHIP OF LITERACY	
Low ownership	**High ownership**
Interests and habits	
a. Expresses little or no preference for different topics, genres, and authors	a. Exhibits clear preferences for topics, genres, and authors
b. Avoids reading and writing as free choice activities	b. Voluntarily selects reading and writing as free choice activities
c. Does not choose texts to read or topics to write about appropriately	c. Chooses appropriate texts to read and topics for writing
Self-assessment of reading and writing	
a. Rarely evaluates own work, learning, or progress	a. Frequently assesses own work, learning, and progress
b. Shows little initiative in evaluating own work	b. Takes initiative to review and monitor own performance
c. Uses single, vague, or unclear criteria in assessing own work	c. Employs appropriate criteria to evaluate what has been read or written

(continued)

Table 2 *(continued)*
Performance Indicators for Each Attribute and Dimension of Literacy

Low collaboration	High collaboration
COLLABORATION	
Cooperation among peers	
a. Little participation with others; engages in isolated activities	a. Frequently engages in collaborative literacy activities
b. Unwilling to engage in the collaborative construction of meaning	b. Initiates discussion, dialogue, or debate about text meaning
c. Reluctant to give or seek help; does not encourage the literacy development of peers	c. Provides positive support, affect, and instructional scaffolding for peers
Community of learners	
a. Does not share goals, values, and practices with others	a. Shares goals, values, and practices with others
b. Does not participate, or plays only a limited array of roles, in the learning community	b. Plays a variety of roles (performer, audience member, leader, supporter) within the learning community
c. Is unaware of the contribution others can make to one's own literacy development	c. Values the contributions of others; respects others' opinions and help
CONNECTEDNESS OF THE CURRICULUM	
Low connectedness	**High connectedness**
Within school	
a. Views reading and writing as decontextualized activities	a. Understands that reading and writing are tools for learning and personal insight
b. Views reading, writing, speaking, and listening as independent of each other	b. Views reading, writing, speaking, and listening as mutually supportive activities
c. Sees little relation between reading and writing and other content areas	c. Understands that what one learns in reading and writing is useful in other content areas
Beyond school	
a. Rarely engages in reading and writing outside of school	a. Reading and writing are part of daily routine activities
b. Views the school literacy curriculum as unrelated to one's own life	b. Connects school literacy activities with reading and writing in daily life
c. Feels discouraged and unsupported for reading and writing outside of school	c. Feels encouraged and supported to read and write outside of school

administrators, and parents who design assessment. A second virtue of identifying specific attributes of literacy is that it forces us to consider jointly the questions "What is important?" and "How can we measure it?" Although the ease and economy of measurement are important, we need to ensure that new forms of assessment are aimed at critical aspects of students' learning and development and not just those skills that are readily tested. Of course, the dimensions, attributes, and indicators are interrelated, so they all must be negotiated together. We often expanded and reduced the lists we produced because there appeared to be an imbalance in the level of detail or emphasis. We cannot emphasize too strongly the importance of the *process* of negotiating what is important to assess because it allows local stakeholders to create a shared set of values and concepts about literacy development.

Evaluating Literacy Performance

The next three phases in the design of alternative assessments translate the values and specific attributes identified in phases 1 and 2 into assessment procedures. There are several options available to decision makers at this point for gathering evidence about students' learning, including conventional tests, checklists, structured lessons, observations, etc. We chose to analyze students' ordinary literacy artifacts and activities rather than their responses to specific instruction or uniform content for three reasons. First, we wanted the literacy assessment to reflect authentic activities in classrooms, including the variety and quality of students' literacy experiences. Second, we wanted to design a prototypical assessment model based on students' work samples that could be used flexibly and adapted by other educators. Third, the overall KEEP evaluation plan includes several other assessments of children's literacy development that are not based on students' daily performance.

Phase 3: Methods for Collecting Evidence About Literacy Proficiency

Work that students produce in class every day reveals their usual learning and motivation. Such work samples are authentic performance measures that reflect instructional opportunities afforded in classrooms as well as achievements of students. Ordinary work samples, therefore, are not pure ability measures, but they can provide illuminating evidence about students' typical and best work in class. Conversely, a paucity of outstanding work samples may indicate a lack of opportunities in the classroom, an "instructional deficit," rather than some kind of deficit in the student. Additional information about the students' achievements, including their perceptions, understanding, and self-assessment, can be gained when students are given opportunities to reflect on their strengths, weaknesses, and progress. The method of reflective interviews about work samples is consistent with portfolio approaches, but it is an equally fair assessment in classrooms where portfolio systems are not used.

The method we devised was to collect all literacy work samples produced in one week by children who represented a range of achievement levels in each classroom. The artifacts included reading logs, journal entries, letters, essays, spelling lists, worksheets, and book reports. In the pilot project, teachers collected work samples from four students in each class who were then interviewed about their work as well as their literacy habits and attitudes. In our pilot project with four teachers and 16 third graders, there was an abundance of diverse materials that reflected the curricular units and literate activities occurring in each classroom.

At the end of the week, an interviewer discussed the materials with students individually for 20–30 minutes. Approximately 20 questions were assembled in a structured yet conversational interview, described fully in Wolf et al. (1991), that was designed to yield information about the attributes and indicators of each dimension so that a score could be assigned. For example, students were asked questions such as:

- Here is a sample of your writing that you did this week. Are you finished with it? What do you like about this piece? What would you change to make it better? Did other students in the class help you to write or revise it?
- What book have you read this week? Tell me about it. How did it make you feel? Was there anything surprising in the book?
- Do you think you are a good reader and writer? What makes someone a really good reader? When you think of yourself as a

reader, what would you like to do differently or better?

The interview was tape recorded and transcribed later so that we could discuss the students' answers as we created the scoring system. In the future, we anticipate that trained interviewers can score the students' reflections and work samples during the interview so that the process is speedy and efficient.

Phase 4: Scoring Students' Work Samples

The next phase in our project was to score the pilot data from 16 students to determine if the system could yield reliable and informative measures of differences among students. We gathered the data in May and discussed whether the data should be scored at the level of indicators (the 42 "a, b, c" items in Table 2) or at the level of attributes (the 14 subcategories in Table 2, e.g., "Reading is constructive") or at the general level of dimensions (the 7 major entries in Table 2, e.g., "Engagement With Text Through Reading"). We settled on an intermediate level of attributes as most appropriate for the holistic, quantitative judgments that we wanted to make. However, teachers who use a similar system may elect a more holistic evaluation or choose to record narrative comments rather than quantitative scores.

The scoring procedure involved reading the transcript of the student's interview, examining the work samples, and assigning a score of 1–4 for each attribute. The four-point scale was anchored at both ends with descriptions of the attributes (e.g., "Integrates new ideas with previous knowledge and experiences"; see Table 2) which aided the judgments considerably because they were tangible examples of students' knowledge, attitudes, or behavior for each attribute. The scores can be aggregated across the two attributes per dimension (values range from 2–8) and across the seven dimensions (values range from 14–56) to give summary scores about the literacy performance of individual students. As we evaluated different students' work samples, we achieved greater consensus in scoring. Although the evaluations were conducted by our team, we are optimistic that trained and knowledgeable teachers can use this holistic scoring procedure to obtain trustworthy assessments of students' literacy development.

An example might help to illustrate the scoring procedures. Alice's collection of work included nearly 20 pages of her own writing, including poems, a response journal, and a long story entitled "Ghost Dad." During her interview, Alice told how she liked to choose her own journal topics and how she chose her best poems to include in a portfolio. She also identified her favorite books and described how she enjoyed reading frequently. These remarks, coupled with the tangible evidence, earned her a score of three out of four points for the attribute of "Interests and Habits" with the dimension of "Ownership" (see Table 2). The other attribute in that dimension, "Self-Assessment," only received two points because Alice said that her writing goal was to write faster, a negative piece of evidence that was offset modestly by her discussion of choosing her best poem. In a similar fashion, Alice's comments and reflections, coupled with a review of her work samples, were used to determine scores for each of the 14 attributes.

Because this was a pilot project and the scoring system was generated and refined as we examined students' work, we do not have numerical indices of the validity and reliability of the performance assessments. However, we believe that this model yields data that are authentic and trustworthy because the work samples are derived from daily curricular activities and interpreted by students (cf., Valencia, 1990). Traditional notions of reliability, based on the similarity of scores from tests to retest, may no longer apply to performance assessments that provide opportunities for reflection and learning. Indeed, low test–retest reliability may be desirable if students benefit from the process of assessing their own literacy.

Assessments grounded in performance may provide dynamic descriptions of students' rates of learning and degrees of change. Furthermore, Linn, Baker, and Dunbar (1991) have suggested that performance-based assessments be judged by expanded notions of validity that include concepts such as the consequences of assessment, the fairness of tasks and scoring, the generalizability of results, and the quality and complexity of the content of the assessments. We think that evaluations of students' work samples like we've done will encourage teachers and students to produce complex, high quality, diverse, and fair collections of literacy artifacts. The consequences of such assessment will stimulate motivated learning by students as well as effective instruction by teachers that is aligned with curricular objectives.

These brief comments about reliability and validity illustrate the need to expand traditional psychometric definitions. We believe that various assessment models, such as the one we designed for KEEP, should be examined against standards of validity and reliability, but we also recognize that those psychometric constructs are being redefined as new kinds of assessment are created. Revisions of assessment and criteria for evaluating assessment are intertwined, so we encourage researcher to substantiate the usefulness of new assessment procedures against a wide variety of criteria.

Phase 5: Interpreting and Using the Data

We have not yet had an opportunity to implement the system and use the data derived from the interviews and work samples. However, the framework we created was guided by certain intended uses of the data, and we strongly believe that stakeholders must consider the uses and consequences of assessment *before* creating alternative measures. The data derived from the interviews and artifacts can be reported in several ways. One option is to report the scores for each attribute or dimension. These can be compared directly across students, classrooms, or programs. Another option is to report the percentage of students meeting some criterion (e.g., a "High orientation"; see Table 2), on each dimension. A third option is to aggregate the data across dimensions and report single scores for each student, although this mixes evaluations from quite different dimensions of literacy. A fourth option is to record students' achievements with narrative comments rather than numerical scores, noting areas of particular talent or weakness.

Regardless of the format of the data, the results of authentic assessments can serve a variety of purposes, all of which can improve opportunities for students to learn. First, alternative assessments can provide richer diagnostic information about students' development because the assessments are tied directly to the curriculum objectives and to instructional procedures and goals in the classroom (Calfee & Hiebert, 1990). In this model, assessment and instruction become overlapping and symbiotic activities. A second use of the data is to inform parents about their children's progress as well as the curriculum objectives and instructional practices. We believe that parents can become more involved in their children's literacy when they understand how they can support and extend instructional efforts at school. Third, authentic assessments help students to engage in monitoring and evaluating their own work, to reflect on their efforts and accomplishments, and to gain insights into the processes of learning that will help them in future tasks (Tierney, Carter, & Desai, 1991). Fourth, we think that authentic assessments can yield summative data for administrators who must provide quantitative indicators of accountability. These multiple functions can be served by authentic assessments when they are designed with these purposes in mind.

Modifying and Applying the Framework

The strength of the five-phase framework is that it can serve as a dynamic, flexible system for any district or state revising or creating alternative assessments of educational progress. Our project illustrates the feasibility of the framework for large-scale literacy assessments. We see the coherence, flexibility, and local control as strengths of the process. For example, a district might identify different dimensions of literacy than we did, but the process of identifying what is valued in a curriculum and building consensus among stakeholders clarifies what needs to be assessed. The specification of characteristics and attributes of literacy can also be negotiated to reflect the level of specificity desired for different purposes. Teachers who want fine-grained assessments to use diagnostically may use the evidence in a different manner that administrators who may need only general descriptions; however, the same kinds of dimensions and evidence undergird both assessments. For example, a teacher who reviews a student's work in an interview may notice that the student is unaware of text structures, genre, and specific comprehension strategies suitable for expository text. The teacher might design specific projects involving documents and library research skills to improve the student's knowledge about literacy. An administrator who notices low scores on this dimension across many students may look for concomitant low reading scores in social studies and science and may suggest instructional strategies for content area reading.

There is also flexibility in the ways that evidence is collected and scored. We believe that a broad array of evidence is needed to augment traditional test scores, evidence that should include students' daily work samples collected periodically throughout the year. The collection of evidence need not be disruptive nor undermine the curriculum if assessment, instruction, and curricula are mutually supportive. Local decision makers can choose to score students' work quantitatively or qualitatively. In our project there was a need for quantitative data to make yearly comparisons among programs so the data could serve summative evaluation purposes. If the data are used primarily for formative purposes, then qualitative descriptions might suffice.

We consider the local control and implementation of assessment reform to be essential, but at the same time, we see a need for districts to generate coherent frameworks to guide their decision making. As districts move away from using "off-the-shelf, one-size-fits-all" commercial tests of literacy, they need to clarify what they value, what they measure, what standards will be used for evaluation, how they will collect the evidence, and how the data will be used. Our framework for creating alternative literacy assessment provides a starting point that can be expanded and revised to fit the needs of any district. We are enthusiastic about the opportunities that exist today for designing new kinds of educational assessment, not just new tests, but whole new systems of assessing teaching and learning in schools. Creative solutions to longstanding problems of assessment hold great promise for enhancing students' learning, motivation, and achievement.

References

Au, K.H., Blake, K., Herman, P., Oshiro, M., & Scheu, J. (1990). *Literacy curriculum guide.* Honolulu, HI: Center for the Development of Early Education, Kamehameha Schools.

Au, K.H., Scheu, J.A., Kawakami, A.J., & Herman, P.A. (1990). Assessment and accountability in a whole language curriculum. *The Reading Teacher, 43*, 574–578.

Calfee, R., & Hiebert, E. (1990). Classroom assessment of reading. In R. Barr, M. Kamil, P. Mosenthal, & P.D. Pearson (Eds.), *Handbook of reading research* (2nd ed.) (pp. 281–309). New York: Longman.

Giuli, C. (1991). Developing a summative measure of whole language instruction: A sonata in risk-taking. *The Kamehameha Journal of Education, 2*, 57–65.

Hawaii Department of Education. (1988). *Language arts program guide.* Honolulu, HI: Office of Instructional Services.

Linn, R.L., Baker, E.L., & Dunbar, S.B. (1991). Complex, performance-based assessment: Expectations and validation criteria. *Educational Researcher, 20*, 15–21.

Resnick, L. & Resnick, D. (1990). Tests as standards of achievement in school. *The uses of standardized tests in American education* (pp. 63–80). Princeton, NJ: Educational Testing Service.

Tharp, R.G., & Gallimore, R. (1988). *Rousing minds to life: Teaching, learning, and schooling in social context.* New York: Cambridge University Press.

Tierney, R.J., Carter, M.A., & Desai, L.E. (1991). *Portfolio assessment in the reading–writing classroom.* Norwood, MA: Christopher-Gordon.

Valencia, S.W. (1990). Alternative assessment: Separating the wheat from the chaff. *The Reading Teacher, 44*, 60–61.

Valencia, S.W., & Pearson, P.D. (1987). Reading Assessment: A time for change. *The Reading Teacher, 40*, 726–733.

Winograd, P., Paris, S., & Bridge, C. (1991). Improving the assessment of reading. *The Reading Teacher, 45*, 108–116.

Wolf, K., Filby, N., Paris, S., Valencia, S., Pearson, P.D., Heibert, E., & Calfee, R. (1991). *KEEP literacy assessment system.* Final report from the Far West Laboratory for Educational Research and Development.

Yap, K.O., Estes, G.D., & Nickel, P.R. (1988, September). *A summative evaluation of the Kamehameha elementary education program as disseminated in Hawaii public schools.* Northwest Regional Educational Laboratory, Evaluation and Assessment Program.

Questions for Reflection

- In the first phase of the study described in this article, the initial task was to decide which aspects of students' literacy development are important to Hawaii schools and which aspects are not assessed by current procedures. Consider how you could apply this task to your school—which aspects of literacy development are most important in your school at the grade level you teach? Which aspects are not covered in current assessments?
- At the end of the article, the authors suggest ways that schools can modify and apply the five-phase framework. How would you go about adapting the framework for your school? Would your district identify different dimensions of literacy than the dimensions offered here?

Reading Fluency Assessment and Instruction: What, Why, and How?

Roxanne F. Hudson, Holly B. Lane, and Paige C. Pullen

Reading fluency is gaining new recognition as an essential element of every reading program, especially for students who struggle in reading. Reading fluency is one of the defining characteristics of good readers, and a lack of fluency is a common characteristic of poor readers. Differences in reading fluency not only distinguish good readers from poor, but a lack of reading fluency is also a reliable predictor of reading comprehension problems (Stanovich, 1991). Once struggling readers learn sound–symbol relationships through intervention and become accurate decoders, their lack of fluency emerges as the next hurdle they face on their way to reading proficiency (Torgesen et al., 2001; Torgesen, Rashotte, Alexander, Alexander, & MacPhee, 2003). This lack of fluent reading is a problem for poor readers because they tend to read in a labored, disconnected fashion with a focus on decoding at the word level that makes comprehension of the text difficult, if not impossible.

The speed with which text is translated into spoken language has been identified as a major component of reading proficiency (Adams, 1990; Allington, 1983; Fuchs, Fuchs, Hosp, & Jenkins, 2001; Hasbrouk & Tindal, 1992; Samuels, Schermer, & Reinking, 1992). Many struggling readers may not gain reading fluency incidentally or automatically. In contrast to skilled readers, they often need direct instruction in how to read fluently and sufficient opportunities for intense, fluency-focused practice incorporated into their reading program (Allinder, Dunse, Brunken, & Obermiller-Krolikowski, 2001). The National Research Council (Snow, Burns, & Griffin, 1998) recommended that reading fluency be regularly assessed in the classroom and effective instruction be provided when dysfluent reading is detected. Despite the importance of reading fluency and the need for direct teaching (National Institute of Child Health and Human Development [NICHD], 2000), it is often neglected in reading instructional programs (Allington, 1983; Kame'enui & Simmons, 2001). Teachers who are concerned about meeting the needs of all students in their classrooms should consider whether they know who their dysfluent readers are and what types of instruction they plan to provide for those readers.

What Is Reading Fluency and Why Is It Important?

Fluent reading comprises three key elements: *accurate* reading of connected text at a conversational *rate* with appropriate *prosody* or expression (Hudson, Mercer, & Lane, 2000). A fluent reader can maintain this performance for long periods of time, can retain the skill after long periods of no practice, and can generalize across texts. A fluent reader is also not easily distracted and reads in an effortless, flowing manner.

The most compelling reason to focus instructional efforts on students becoming fluent readers is the strong correlation between reading fluency and reading comprehension (Allington, 1983; Johns, 1993; Samuels, 1988; Schreiber, 1980). Each aspect of fluency has a clear connection to text comprehension. Without accurate

Reprinted from Hudson, R.F., Lane, H.B., & Pullen, P.C. (2005). Reading fluency assessment and instruction: What, why, and how? *The Reading Teacher, 58*(8), 702–714.

word reading, the reader will have no access to the author's intended meaning, and inaccurate word reading can lead to misinterpretations of the text. Poor automaticity in word reading or slow, laborious movement through the text taxes the reader's capacity to construct an ongoing interpretation of the text. Poor prosody can lead to confusion through inappropriate or meaningless groupings of words or through inappropriate applications of expression.

Automaticity and Working Memory

Laberge and Samuels (1974) suggested that there is a limited capacity of attention and working memory in cognitive processing and that learning one aspect of reading (word identification) to a criterion of automaticity frees the processing space for higher order thinking (comprehension). Attentional capacity is limited, so more resources are available for comprehension if word identification processes occur relatively effortlessly. Because comprehension requires higher order processes that cannot become automatic, word identification must become the automatic process. The only other option (and the one most commonly attempted by beginning readers) is to switch attention rapidly back and forth from identifying words on the page to constructing meaning, thus limiting the ability to do either one well.

Quick and effortless word identification is important because when one can read words automatically, one's limited cognitive resources can be used for comprehension (e.g., NICHD, 2000), and many times the differences in comprehension between good and poor readers can be attributed to differences in the level of automatic decoding (Perfetti & Hogaboam, 1975; Torgesen, 1986). Fawcett and Nicholson (1994) hypothesized that the difficulties experienced by students with dyslexia are due to an underlying deficit in automaticity (i.e., processing speed deficits). Fluent readers are better at seeing a word in a single eye fixation and do not need as many refixations or regressions. The placement and overlap of the eye fixations of fluent readers are more efficient than those of less skilled readers. Faster readers also make shorter fixations, longer jumps between fixations, and fewer regressions than slow readers (NICHD, 2000).

Link Between Reading Accuracy and Reading Proficiency

Word-reading accuracy refers to the ability to recognize or decode words correctly. Strong understanding of the alphabetic principle, the ability to blend sounds together (Ehri & McCormick, 1998), and knowledge of a large bank of high-frequency words are required for word-reading accuracy. Poor word-reading accuracy has obvious negative influences on reading comprehension and fluency. A reader who reads words incorrectly is unlikely to understand the author's intended message, and inaccurate word reading can lead to misinterpretations of the text. In the 2002 Oral Reading Fluency Study, conducted as part of the National Assessment of Educational Progress (NAEP), researchers found that when children made errors that changed the meaning of the text, there was a more direct relationship to reading comprehension than the errors that did not result in a change of meaning (National Assessment Governing Board, 2002). They also noted that errors that do not affect meaning are rare.

When words cannot be read accurately from memory as sight words, they must be analyzed. Thus it is important to teach word-identification strategies, such as decoding and use of analogy (Ehri, 2002), to figure out unknown words. Decoding is a sequentially executed process where the reader blends sounds to form words from their parts. This can take place by blending individual phonemes (beginning decoding) or phonograms (a more advanced form of decoding; Ehri, 2002). In order to accurately decode words, readers need to be able to accurately (a) identify the sounds represented by the letters or letter combinations, (b) blend phonemes, (c) read phonograms (common patterns across words), and (d) use both letter–sound and meaning cues to determine exactly the pronunciation and meaning of the word that is in the text (e.g., knowing how to correctly pronounce *bow* in two different sentences: The dog had a *bow* tied around her neck. The *bow* of the ship was tall). Instruction in all of these subprocesses is necessary for the first part of reading fluency: accurate word identification.

> Because the ability to obtain meaning from print depends so strongly on the development of word recognition accuracy and reading fluency, both should be regularly assessed in the classroom, permitting timely and effective instructional response when difficulty or delay is apparent. (NICHD, 2000, p. 7)

Link Between Reading Rate and Reading Proficiency

Reading rate comprises both word-level automaticity and the speed and fluidity with which a reader moves through connected text. Automaticity is quick and effortless identification of words in or out of context (Ehri & McCormick, 1998; Kuhn & Stahl, 2000). The automaticity with which a reader can decode or recognize words is almost as important as word-reading accuracy. It is not enough to get the word right if a great deal of cognitive effort is required to do so; automaticity frees up cognitive resources that can be devoted to text comprehension (LaBerge & Samuels, 1974).

Most educators quantify rate in terms of reading speed—either the number of words read correctly per minute or the length of time it takes for a reader to complete a passage. Poor readers are often characterized by slow, laborious reading of connected text. Many fluency interventions focus on increasing reading rate, because slow reading can result in weakened comprehension (Mastropieri, Leinart, & Scruggs, 1999). Students who read slowly often fail to complete their work, lose interest in school, and seldom read for pleasure (Moats, 2001).

There is strong correlational evidence that increased reading rate is related to higher levels of comprehension in average and poor readers (Breznitz, 1987; Deno, Marston, Shinn, & Tindal, 1983; Dowhower, 1987; Perfetti & Hogaboam, 1975; Rasinski, 1989, 1990; Tenenbaum & Wolking, 1989), as well as in students with reading disabilities (Breznitz, 1991; Chard, Vaughn, & Tyler, 2002; Fuchs, Fuchs, & Maxwell, 1988). Fuchs et al. (2001) proposed that "oral reading fluency [i.e., rate and accuracy] represents a complicated, multifaceted performance" (p. 239) that captures a variety of processes related to reading: using sound–symbol relationships to translate text to sound, accessing word meanings, making connections between words and sentences, relating textual meaning to prior knowledge, and making inferences. Oral reading rate is also related to teacher judgments of proficiency; is correlated with criterion-referenced tests in basal curricula; and differentiates between students in special, compensatory, and general education programs (Deno et al., 1983). Thus, oral reading rate is considered an important measure of reading proficiency and a tool for progress monitoring, just as a thermometer can be used to measure the current temperature and ongoing changes (Deno, Mirkin, & Chiang, 1982; Fuchs & Fuchs, 1992; Fuchs et al., 1988; Hasbrouk & Tindal, 1992; Shinn, Good, Knutson, & Tilly, 1992).

Link Between Prosody and Reading Proficiency

Prosody is a linguistic term to describe the rhythmic and tonal aspects of speech: the "music" of oral language. Prosodic features are variations in pitch (intonation), stress patterns (syllable prominence), and duration (length of time) that contribute to expressive reading of a text (Allington, 1983; Dowhower, 1991; Schreiber, 1980, 1991). These elements signal question, surprise, exclamation, and other meanings beyond the semantics of the words being spoken. When these features are present and appropriate in oral reading, the reader is reading prosodically, or "with expression." A fundamental task of fluent reading is to supply the prosodic features in a text, although they are not graphically represented (Schreiber, 1980). Schreiber suggested that fluent readers use the other cues (i.e., morphemic, syntactic, semantic, and pragmatic) present in text to organize the text into meaningful phrases and read with correct prosody (i.e., reading that sounds like speaking). Struggling readers are often characterized as reading in a monotone without expression or with inappropriate phrasing. Because prosody and reading comprehension seem to have a reciprocal relationship, prosody is an important area of focus for fluency instruction.

Prosodic reading provides evidence that the reader understands what is being read (Kuhn & Stahl, 2000). Despite this connection, little research has been conducted exploring the relationship between prosody and reading comprehension, and what little research has been done has found an unclear relationship. While studying repeated readings, Dowhower (1987) found that as the students' reading rate, accuracy, and comprehension increased, so did their prosodic reading on practiced and unpracticed passages, but she could not determine which caused the other. Pinnell et al. (1995) rated a representative sample of fourth graders according to a prosody scale. They found that higher levels of prosody were associated with higher scores on the main NAEP reading proficiency scale and concluded that decisions about the causal relationships are unclear. It is unclear whether prosody is a cause or result of comprehension (Kuhn & Stahl, 2000) or if the relationship is reciprocal; however, it is clear that the amount of correct expression indicates to a trained ear how much the reader comprehended the text.

Assessing Reading Fluency

Teachers need to listen to students read aloud to make judgments about their progress in reading fluency (Zutell & Rasinski, 1991). Systematic observation helps assess student progress and determine instructional needs. Teachers observing students' oral reading fluency should consider each critical aspect of fluent reading: word-reading accuracy, rate, and prosody. Table 1 provides a summary of assessments for oral reading fluency, including standardized assessments and assessments for monitoring student progress.

Assessing Accuracy

Measurement of students' word-reading accuracy can take numerous forms. Simply listening to oral reading and counting the number of errors per 100 words can provide invaluable information for the selection of appropriate text for various instructional purposes for an individual or group of students. A running record and miscue analysis (Clay, 1984, 1993) provides more detailed information about the student's accuracy. Through careful examination of error patterns, a teacher can determine which strategies the student is using and which strategies the student is failing to use. For example, observation of a student's attempts to figure out an unknown word might yield evidence of phonemic blending, guessing based on context, or a combination of decoding and contextual analysis. These observations can provide information about areas in need of further instruction to improve word-reading accuracy.

Assessing Rate

Contextual reading rather than reading words in a list (Jenkins, Fuchs, van den Broek, Espin, & Deno, 2003) and oral reading rather than silent reading (Fuchs, Fuchs, Eaton, & Hamlet, 2000 cited in Fuchs et al., 2001) were both found to be the best measures of reading rate. Measuring reading rate should encompass consideration of both word-reading automaticity and reading speed in connected text. Assessment of automaticity can include tests of sight-word knowledge or tests of decoding rate. Tests of decoding rate often consist of rapid decoding of nonwords. Measurement of nonword reading rate ensures that the construct being assessed is the student's ability to automatically decode words using sound–symbol knowledge.

Measurement of reading speed is most typically accomplished through timed readings. Timings of a student's reading of connected text allows a teacher to observe the number of words read correctly and the number of errors made in a given time period. Data from timed readings are usually recorded on a timing chart (see Figure 1 for an example).

Table 1
Reading Fluency Assessments

Assessment	Publisher	Description
AIMSweb Standard Reading Assessment Passages (RAPs)	Edformation	AIMSweb RAPs provide teachers with passages for quick but accurate formative assessment of students' oral reading fluency. These assessments are a Curriculum Based Measurement (CBM) system that is intended to assist teachers in making instructional decisions and monitoring student progress. RAPs have been field-tested and validated. The AIMSweb system includes a Web-based software management system for data collection and reporting.
Dynamic Indicators of Basic Early Literacy Skills (DIBELS)	University of Oregon and Sopris West	DIBELS contains a subtest of Oral Reading Fluency and Retell Fluency for students in the first through third grades. The Oral Reading Fluency is standardized and individually administered. Students read a passage aloud for one minute. The number of correct words per minute is determined to provide the oral reading fluency rate. The Retell Fluency is a measure of comprehension that accompanies the Oral Reading Fluency assessment.
Gray Oral Reading Test, Fourth Edition (GORT-4)	PRO-ED	The GORT-4 is a norm-referenced measure of oral reading performance. Skills assessed include rate, accuracy, fluency (rate and accuracy combined), comprehension, and overall reading ability (rate, accuracy, and comprehension combined).
National Assessment of Educational Progress (NAEP) Fluency Scale	National Center for Education Statistics (NCES)	The NAEP Fluency Scale provides a descriptive guide for oral reading performance based on the student's "naturalness" of reading. The student's performance is rated on a four-point scale, with emphasis placed on phrasing of words, adherence to syntax, and expressiveness (Pinnell et al., 1995). Accuracy and rate are measured and determined by calculating the correct words read per minute.
Reading Fluency Monitor by Read Naturally	Read Naturally	The Reading Fluency Monitor is an assessment instrument that allows teachers to monitor student progress. Fall, winter, and spring administrations are recommended. Grade-level passages are available for grades 1–8, as well as a software program for reporting and record keeping.

Figure 1
Timing Chart

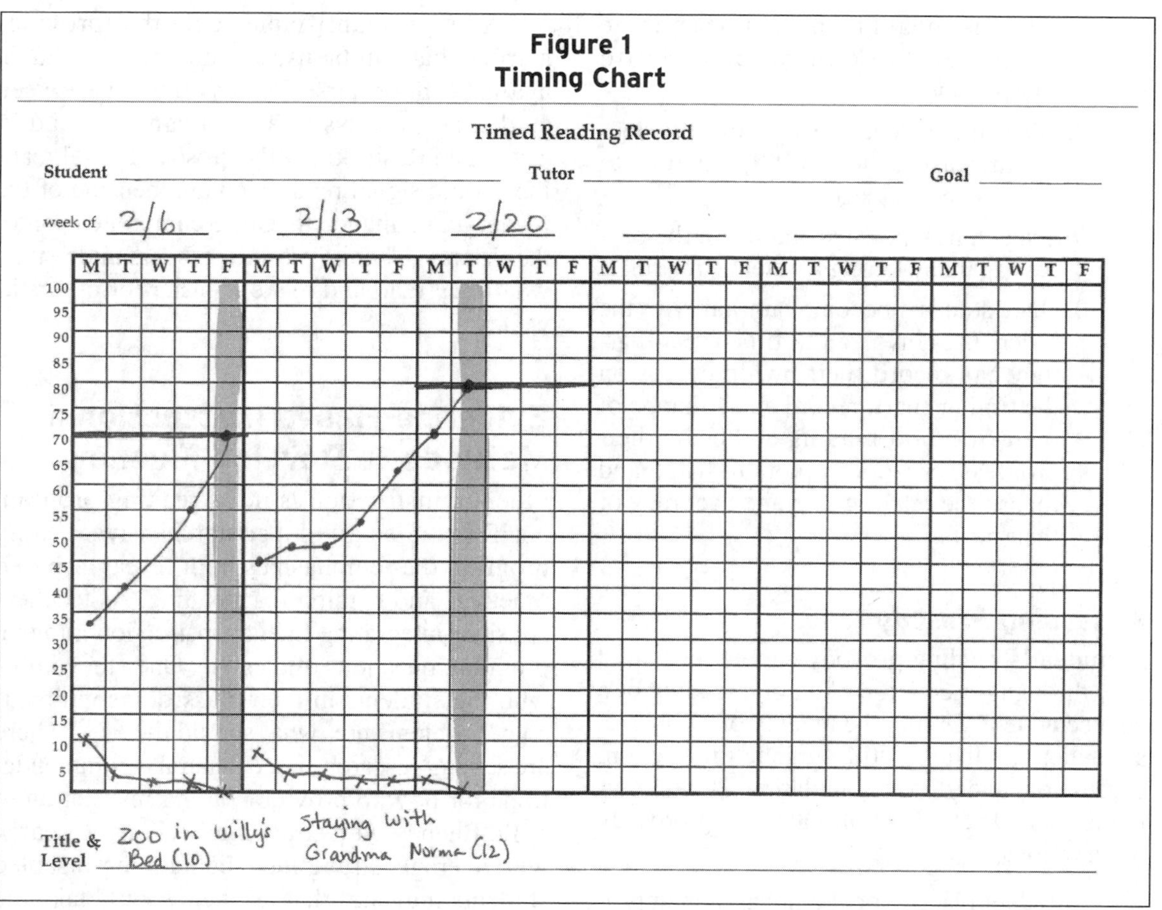

Timed readings (Samuels, 1979) can be used to measure and increase word-reading accuracy and passage-reading rate. Timed readings are conducted using books or passages the student has read before that are at an independent reading level (i.e., books the student can read with 95% accuracy or above). To conduct timed readings, follow these steps:

1. Record a baseline rate on a new passage by having the student read the passage without knowing that he or she is being timed. The number of words read correctly for that minute are recorded as the baseline.
2. Note the errors as the student reads. After the reading, discuss any errors and work on them by rereading the parts that were difficult or by doing word-study activities.
3. Set a goal for the next reading by asking the student to read five or six more words, or maybe another line. The goal should be a reasonable one that can be attained within the next few attempts. If the student made three or more errors in the first attempt, the goal may be to decrease the errors and keep the correct word per minute (CWPM) the same.
4. Record the goal on the graph with a highlighter.
5. Time the student again for one minute and record the CWPM and errors.
6. Discuss the errors; set another goal and repeat the process.

7. Timings should be done at least three times per week in order to build consistency.
8. When the student levels off and is no longer increasing the CWPM, it is time to select a new passage.
9. Select a new passage and begin the process again by taking a baseline reading.
10. Once students become familiar with the procedures involved in timed readings, they can record their own progress on the timing chart, record an audiotape of their own oral reading and chart their progress, or work in pairs to listen and record the reading rate and accuracy of their peers.

Assessing Prosody

A student's reading prosody can be measured only through observation of an oral reading of a connected text. During the reading of a passage, a teacher can listen to the student's inflection, expression, and phrase boundaries. The following is a simple checklist of oral reading prosody observation:

1. Student placed vocal emphasis on appropriate words.
2. Student's voice tone rose and fell at appropriate points in the text.
3. Student's inflection reflected the punctuation in the text (e.g., voice tone rose near the end of a question).
4. In narrative text with dialogue, student used appropriate vocal tone to represent characters' mental states, such as excitement, sadness, fear, or confidence.
5. Student used punctuation to pause appropriately at phrase boundaries.
6. Student used prepositional phrases to pause appropriately at phrase boundaries.
7. Student used subject–verb divisions to pause appropriately at phrase boundaries.
8. Student used conjunctions to pause appropriately at phrase boundaries.

A more quantifiable scale that provides a score that can be used to compare a student against him or herself across time or between students in a class or school can be found in Zutell and Rasinski (1991). Prosody in oral reading should signal reading comprehension of the reader and enhance listening comprehension of the listener. That is, prosodic readers understand what they read and make it easier for others as well.

Evidence-Based Instructional Methods to Develop Fluency

Fluency instruction is not a reading program itself, but it is part of a comprehensive reading program that emphasizes both research-based practices and reading for meaning. As teachers consider integrating fluency instruction into that program, questions often arise. Once they know who the students in their classrooms with fluency problems are, what should they do? There are several research-based general recommendations for how to provide reading instruction to build fluency with struggling readers. Research with average, struggling, and learning-disabled students indicates that teachers should take the following steps:

- Model fluent oral reading (Blevins, 2001; Rasinski, 2003) using teacher read-alouds and as part of repeated reading interventions (Chard et al., 2002).
- Provide direct instruction and feedback to teach decoding of unknown words, correct expression and phrasing, the return-sweep eye movement, and strategies that fluent readers use (NICHD, 2000; Snow et al., 1998).
- Provide oral support and modeling for readers (Rasinski, 2003) using assisted reading, choral reading, paired reading, audiotapes, and computer programs.
- Provide students with plenty of materials at their independent reading level to read on their own (Allington, 2000).

- Offer many opportunities for practice using repeated readings of progressively more difficult text (Chard et al., 2002; Meyer & Felton, 1999; Rasinski, 2003; Samuels, 1979).
- Encourage prosody development through cueing phrase boundaries (Rasinski, 2003; Schreiber, 1980).

Instructional Methods Primarily Focused on Rate and Accuracy

Repeated Readings

The repeated readings technique (Samuels, 1979) has many different approaches that vary in levels of support and emphasis on building speed. Repeated readings emphasizes practice as a way of working on all of the areas of reading fluency—accuracy, rate, and prosody—and is one of the most-studied methods for increasing reading fluency (Kuhn & Stahl, 2000; Meyer & Felton, 1999; NICHD, 2000).

Timed Repeated Readings. Samuels (1979) was the first to describe the repeated readings method that is used so often today. It consists of (a) selecting a short passage at the student's instructional level, (b) setting a rate criterion, and (c) having the student read and reread the passage over time until the rate criterion is reached. The oral reading rate is determined by timing the student for one minute and then counting how many correct words were read. Charting of the rate is recommended as a means of record keeping and of maintaining motivation with the student (Figure 1). Timed repeated readings are the basis for several methods available to develop reading fluency. These methods, which focus on increasing rate and accuracy, typically measure the number of words correctly read in one minute and involve the student in charting data. For example, Great Leaps Reading uses phonics timings to increase decoding automaticity, sight-phrase timings to increase recognition of high-frequency words, and story timings to increase the rate of reading connected text. (See Table 2 for more information.) In a study with middle school students, Great Leaps was found to have significant positive effects on reading achievement (Mercer, Campbell, Miller, Mercer, & Lane, 2000). Other timed reading programs include Jamestown Timed Readings Plus, which includes both narrative and related expository passages, and QuickReads, which focuses on nonfiction text (Table 2).

Repeated Readings With Recorded Models. Using audiotaped text to support repeated readings is an efficient method because it provides the student with a fluent model without requiring individual teacher assistance. In a comparison of assisted (audiotape) and unassisted repeated readings, Dowhower (1987) found that both resulted in significantly higher word reading accuracy, comprehension, fluency, and prosody. The assisted condition seemed to affect prosody more than the unassisted. There are several methods of repeated readings with recorded models.

Most recorded books found in classroom listening centers are designed for listening rather than for reading along. They are read too fast for struggling readers to keep up, and the addition of music or other sound effects can be distracting. Therefore, although a listening center may be useful for developing skills such as listening comprehension, vocabulary, or sense of story, it is unlikely to improve reading fluency, especially for struggling students. Marie Carbo developed a method of recording books that makes it possible for a developing reader to read along with the recording. Carbo Recorded Books are recorded at a much slower pace than listening center books, yet they maintain the expression and inflection necessary for understanding (see Table 2). Using this method, Carbo (1981, 1992) reported reading gains among struggling readers. Thus, adding a read-along center to a classroom reading program can promote reading fluency.

Read Naturally (Table 2) is a repeated reading method that includes both audiotaped and computer models. Read Naturally combines supported oral reading and independent repeated reading. The student begins with a one-minute "cold" reading to the teacher or computer. Then,

Table 2
Instructional Resources for Developing Reading Fluency

Program/resource	Publisher	Description
Carbo Recorded Books	National Reading Styles Institute	Carbo Recorded Books are audiotaped literature for children and adolescents. These materials provide a resource for audio-assisted repeated reading.
Great Leaps Reading	Diarmuid, Inc.	Great Leaps is a tutorial program for students with reading problems. Programs are available for students in Grades K–12 and adults. In the K–2 edition, fluency practice is provided for sound awareness, letter recognition, phonics, sight words and phrases, and stories. The editions for beyond grade 2 are divided into phonics, sight phrases, and reading fluency.
Jamestown Timed Readings Plus	Jamestown Education, Glencoe/McGraw-Hill	Jamestown Timed Readings Plus is a program designed to help secondary struggling readers increase their reading rate and fluency with 400-word nonfiction passages followed by related fiction passages and comprehension questions.
Phonics Phones	Crystal Springs Books	Whisper phones or Phonic Phones are pieces of PVC pipe elbows connected to form a telephone shape. This shape amplifies the sound of the student's voice, which focuses the student's attention on reading and allows the student to evaluate prosody and rate.
QuickReads	Modern Curriculum Press	QuickReads is a reading fluency program for students in grades 2–4. The lesson requires approximately 15 minutes and includes short nonfiction passages. The program has been field-tested and has shown positive effects on students' reading fluency and comprehension.
Read-Along Radio Dramas	Balance Publishing Company	This program includes a recording of a radio play with full cast and sound effects, a word-for-word read-along script and annotated script of the original story, and a variety of student activities.
Read Naturally	Read Naturally	Read Naturally is an individually paced program for improving students' reading fluency. A software version is available that guides students through lessons and tracks individual progress. An audio version is also available on CD or cassette tape with accompanying passage blackline masters.
Soliloquy Reading Assistant	Soliloquy Learning	Soliloquy Reading Assistant is a software program designed to increase students' opportunities for oral reading practice. The computer guides the reader by highlighting the words to be read and changing the color as they are read correctly. If a student hesitates on a word too long, Soliloquy supplies the challenging word. The computer also prompts the student to reread a sentence if it was read with poor fluency and includes a progress-monitoring feature that the student or teacher can use.

the student practices reading the same passage three or four times while listening to a recorded fluent model. The student then continues independent practice without the recording. Finally, the student reads to the teacher or computer again. In the computer version, the student can receive feedback during the independent reading by clicking on difficult words and noting where they stopped during each timed reading. Hasbrouk, Ihnot, and Rogers (1999) found encouraging improvements in reading fluency from Read Naturally with both beginning readers and struggling older readers.

Soliloquy Reading Assistant (Table 2) is a software program designed to increase students' opportunities for oral reading practice. Soliloquy employs speech recognition software to record what a student reads and to measure progress over time and offers a variety of text genres, including fiction, poetry, biographies, and folktales. Although Soliloquy was developed on a solid research base, as of this writing, no studies of its effectiveness have been published.

Common Instructional Questions Related to Developing Reading Rate

What Type of Text Should I Use? We recommend practicing with text at an independent level (95–100% accuracy). We also suggest using relatively short passages, texts from a variety of genres, and text that is motivating to the individual student. The accuracy, speed, and expressiveness of poor readers are more affected by text difficulty than average readers (Young & Bowers, 1995), and making proper text selection is much more critical when working with struggling readers. The number of shared words facilitates transfer from practiced text to unpracticed text (Dowhower, 1987; Rashotte & Torgesen, 1985). Rashotte and Torgesen found that passages that shared many of the same words led to transfer of training from repeated readings to another passage.

How Do I Know When to Move My Student to a New Passage? A question many teachers ask is "How fast should they have their students read?" Another is "How much progress should they expect?" These questions do not have definitive answers and depend on the student's age, the type of text the student is reading, and the purpose for which he or she is reading. However, Howell and Lorson-Howell (1990) suggested that fluency aims be determined by sampling the performances of successful students working in the target setting. Using similar reasoning, reading rates were established in "norming" studies designed to determine how varying fluency rates related to levels of reading achievement among large samples of students (Good, Simmons, & Kame'enui, 2001; Hasbrouk & Tindal, 1992; School Board of Alachua County, 1997). Recommendations from these studies should serve as a general guide for determining students' goals for oral reading rate (Table 3).

Fuchs, Fuchs, Hamlett, Walz, and Germann (1993) suggested that an essential step in assessing reading fluency was to establish how much

Table 3
Recommended Reading Fluency Rates in Connected Text

Grade		Correct words per minute
First grade	Winter	39
	Spring	40-60
Second grade	Fall	53
	Winter	72-78
	Spring	82-94
Third grade	Fall	79
	Winter	84-93
	Spring	100-114
Fourth grade	Fall	90-99
	Winter	98-112
	Spring	105-118
Fifth grade	Fall	105
	Winter	110-118
	Spring	118-128

Note. Adapted from Good, Simmons, & Kame'enui (2001); Hasbrouk & Tindal (1992); and the School Board of Alachua County (1997).

weekly growth a teacher should expect. A standard for weekly improvement helps teachers decide whether a student's rate of progress is sufficient or whether an adjustment in teaching strategies is needed. Using data from their norming study, Fuchs et al. (1993) suggested that on average, the following are reasonable expectations for improvement among average, poor, and disabled readers:

- First grade: 2–3 words per week increase in CWPM
- Second grade: 2.5–3.5 words per week increase in CWPM
- Third grade: 1–3 words per week increase in CWPM
- Fourth grade: .85–1.5 words per week increase in CWPM

Is Isolated Word Reading Practice a Good Idea? Single-word training, either in a list or on flashcards, appears to be valuable for helping struggling readers develop reading fluency. Several researchers (e.g., Levy, Abello, & Lysynchuk, 1997; Tan & Nicholson, 1997; van den Bosch, van Bon, & Schreuder, 1995) have found that with poor readers, practice reading words in isolation led to improved reading fluency in context; the practice of the words generalized to textual reading.

Instructional Methods Focused on Prosody

In addition to reading with recorded books, several methods have been designed with the specific goal of improving prosody. These methods emphasize how a student's reading sounds—its inflection, expression, and phrasing.

Repeated Reading Practice for Performance

Readers Theatre. Readers Theatre is a popular method of reading practice that can be a powerful way to increase prosody. For Readers Theatre, the teacher creates scripts from selections of children's literature that are rich in dialogue. The teacher begins by reading aloud the story on which the script is based and leads a discussion of the characters' emotions and how they might sound at different points in the story. Students then practice reading the entire script before the teacher assigns roles. Rehearsing and performing the play for peers provides an authentic purpose for rereading the text multiple times. Readers Theatre can help students develop accuracy, rate, and prosody.

Radio Reading. Radio reading is a variation of Readers Theatre for older students that adds sound effects to make the performance sound like an old-time radio show. Groups of students can create recorded versions of their "radio shows" that can become listening center readings for their classmates. Students can even generate questions to pose to listeners at the end of the recording. Radio reading reinforces the importance of prosody, because so much information from the story must be communicated through vocal variation. National Public Radio has an old-time radio show called Theatre of the Mind. From these radio shows, an instructional program called Read-Along Radio Dramas was developed. This program includes a recording of a radio play with full cast and sound effects, a word-for-word read-along script, an annotated script of the original story, and a variety of student activities (see Table 2).

Reader as Fluent Model

Self-Recordings. Hearing one's own voice on audiotape can be an eye-opening experience. For struggling readers, having the opportunity to record, listen, and rerecord can be a powerful method for increasing reading fluency. This approach promotes independent judgment and goal setting, along with ownership of the process.

Amplification. Whisper phones or phonic phones are a low-tech method of amplifying one's own voice. Whisper phones are pieces of PVC pipe elbows connected to form a telephone shape. This shape amplifies the sound of the student's voice, but only to the student. The whisper phone also masks other extraneous noises for the distractible reader. Whisper phones can be modified by twisting one end to form an S shape. With this modification, the whisper phone can be used for quiet partner reading. One student reads into the mouthpiece of the phone while the other student listens in the other end.

Calling the Reader's Attention to Phrase Boundaries

Appropriate placement of pauses around phrase boundaries can contribute substantially to meaning. For example, Rasinski (2003) used the following example of a sentence that can convey meaning or appear as a nonsensical string of words: The young man the jungle gym. Most readers pause after *man*, which results in nonsense. By pausing after *young*, the reader can construct meaning from those words.

The concept of phrase boundaries can be taught by cueing pauses in text with slashes. Single slashes represent shorter pauses, and double slashes indicate longer pauses. Table 4 illustrates a passage cued for phrase boundaries.

Table 4
Example of Phrase Boundaries

My favorite season / of the year / is summer.//
I am so glad / we don't have school / in the summer.//
I would rather / spend my time / swimming, / playing, / and reading.//

Assisted Reading Methods

There are several effective methods for improving prosody through assisted reading with fluent models. For example, echo reading is a technique in which the teacher reads a phrase or sentence and the student reads the same material just behind him or her. In unison reading, the teacher and student read together, and in assisted cloze reading, the teacher reads the text and stops occasionally for the student to read the next word in the text.

Explicit Teaching of Intonation

Blevins (2001) suggested a variety of ways to teach appropriate intonation. For example, students can be taught to recite the alphabet as a conversation, using punctuation to cue inflection (e.g., ABCD? EFG! HI? JKL. MN? OPQ. RST! UVWX. YZ!). By reciting the same sentence using different punctuation (e.g., Dogs bark? Dogs bark! Dogs bark.), students learn the importance of punctuation to meaning. A similar activity, in which the student places stress on different words in the same sentence (e.g., *I* am tired. I *am* tired. I am *tired*.), emphasizes the importance of inflection.

An Essential Skill

Research has clearly demonstrated the significance of fluency in the development of reading proficiency, and a variety of effective methods for assessment and instruction of reading fluency have been developed. Opportunities to develop all three areas of reading fluency are important for all readers, but teachers of struggling readers in particular must recognize the importance of incorporating explicit fluency-based instruction into their reading programs. Reading fluency has long been acknowledged as an essential skill that proficient readers need to have, and now is the time to focus attention on all areas to be developed—accuracy, rate, and prosody—for truly effective, comprehensive reading instruction for all children.

References

Adams, M.J. (1990). *Beginning to read: Thinking and learning about print*. Cambridge, MA: MIT Press.
Allinder, R.M., Dunse, L., Brunken, C.D., & Obermiller-Krolikowski, H.J. (2001). Improving fluency in at-risk readers and students with learning disabilities. *Remedial and Special Education, 22*(1), 48–54.
Allington, R.L. (1983). Fluency: The neglected reading goal. *The Reading Teacher, 36*, 556–561.

Allington, R.L. (2000). *What really matters for struggling readers: Designing research-based programs.* Boston: Longman.

Blevins, W. (2001). *Building fluency: Lessons and strategies for reading success.* Scranton, PA: Scholastic.

Breznitz, Z. (1987). Increasing first graders' reading accuracy and comprehension by accelerating their reading rates. *Journal of Educational Psychology, 79,* 236–242.

Breznitz, Z. (1991). The beneficial effect of accelerating reading rate on dyslexic readers' reading comprehension. In M. Snowling & M. Thomson (Eds.), *Dyslexia: Integrating theory and practice* (pp. 235–243). London: Whurr.

Carbo, M. (1981). Making books talk to children. *The Reading Teacher, 35,* 186–189.

Carbo, M. (1992). Eliminating the need for dumbed-down textbooks. *Educational Horizons, 70,* 189–193.

Chard, D.J., Vaughn, S., & Tyler, B.J. (2002). A synthesis of research on effective interventions for building reading fluency with elementary students with learning disabilities. *Journal of Learning Disabilities, 35,* 386–406.

Clay, M.M. (1984). *Observing the young reader.* Auckland, New Zealand: Heinemann.

Clay, M.M. (1993). *Reading Recovery: A guidebook for teachers in training.* Portsmouth, NH: Heinemann.

Deno, S.L., Marston, D., Shinn, M.R., & Tindal, G. (1983). Oral reading fluency: A simple datum for scaling reading disability. *Topics in Learning and Learning Disabilities, 2*(4), 53–59.

Deno, S.L., Mirkin, P.K., & Chiang, B. (1982). Identifying valid measures of reading. *Exceptional Children, 49,* 36–45.

Dowhower, S.L. (1987). Effects of repeated reading on second-grade transitional readers' fluency and comprehension. *Reading Research Quarterly, 22,* 389–406.

Dowhower, S.L. (1991). Speaking of prosody: Fluency's unattended bedfellow. *Theory Into Practice, 30,* 165–175.

Ehri, L.C. (2002). Phases of acquisition in learning to read words and implications for teaching. In R. Stainthorp & P. Tomlinson (Eds.), *Learning and teaching reading* (pp. 7–28). London: British Journal of Educational Psychology Monograph Series II.

Ehri, L.C., & McCormick, S. (1998). Phases of word learning: Implications for instruction with delayed and disabled readers. *Reading and Writing Quarterly: Overcoming Learning Difficulties, 14*(2), 135–164.

Fawcett, A.J., & Nicolson, R.I. (1994). Naming speed in children with dyslexia. *Journal of Learning Disabilities, 27,* 641–646.

Fuchs, L.S., & Fuchs, D. (1992). Identifying a measure for monitoring student reading progress. *School Psychology Review, 21*(1), 45–58.

Fuchs, L.S., Fuchs, D., Eaton, S., & Hamlet, C.L. (2000). [Relations between reading fluency and reading comprehension as a function of silent versus oral reading mode]. Unpublished raw data.

Fuchs, L.S., Fuchs, D., Hamlett, C.L., Walz, L., & Germann, G. (1993). Formative evaluation of academic progress: How much growth can we expect? *School Psychology Review, 22*(1), 27–48.

Fuchs, L.S., Fuchs, D., Hosp, M.D., & Jenkins, J. (2001). Oral reading fluency as an indicator of reading competence: A theoretical, empirical, and historical analysis. *Scientific Studies of Reading, 5,* 239–259.

Fuchs, L.S., Fuchs, D., & Maxwell, L. (1988). The validity of informal reading comprehension measures. *Remedial and Special Education, 9*(2), 20–28.

Good, R.H., Simmons, D.C., Kame'enui, E.J. (2001). The importance and decision-making utility of a continuum of fluency-based indicators of foundational reading skills for third-grade high-stakes outcomes. *Scientific Studies of Reading, 5,* 257–288.

Hasbrouk, J.E., Ihnot, C., & Rogers, G.H. (1999). "Read Naturally": A strategy to increase oral reading fluency. *Reading Research and Instruction, 39*(1), 27–38.

Hasbrouk, J.E., & Tindal, G. (1992). Curriculum-based oral reading fluency norms for students in grades 2 through 5. *TEACHING Exceptional Children, 24*(3), 41–44.

Howell, K.W., & Lorson-Howell, K.A. (1990). What's the hurry? Fluency in the classroom. *TEACHING Exceptional Children, 22*(3), 20–23.

Hudson, R.F., Mercer, C.D., & Lane, H.B. (2000). *Exploring reading fluency: A paradigmatic overview.* Unpublished manuscript, University of Florida, Gainesville.

Jenkins, J.R., Fuchs, L.S., van den Broek, P., Espin, C., & Deno, S.L. (2003). Accuracy and fluency in list and context reading of skilled and RD groups: Absolute and relative performance levels. *Learning Disabilities: Research & Practice, 18,* 237–245.

Johns, J.L. (1993). *Informal reading inventories.* DeKalb, IL: Communitech.

Kame'enui, E.J., & Simmons, D.C. (2001). Introduction to this special issue: The DNA of reading fluency. *Scientific Studies of Reading, 5,* 203–210.

Kuhn, M.R., & Stahl, S.A. (2000). *Fluency: A review of developmental and remedial practices.* Ann Arbor, MI: Center for the Improvement of Early Reading Achievement.

LaBerge, D., & Samuels, S.J. (1974). Toward a theory of automatic information processing in reading. *Cognitive Psychologist, 6,* 293–323.

Levy, B.A., Abello, B., & Lysynchuk, L. (1997). Transfer from word training to reading in context: Gains in reading fluency and comprehension. *Learning Disabilities Quarterly, 20,* 173–188.

Mastropieri, M.A., Leinart, A., & Scruggs, T.E. (1999). Strategies to increase reading fluency. *Intervention in School and Clinic, 34,* 278–283, 292.

Mercer, C.D., Campbell, K.U., Miller, M.D., Mercer, K.D., & Lane, H.B. (2000). Effects of a reading fluency intervention for middle schoolers with specific learning disabilities. *Learning Disabilities Research & Practice, 15*, 179–189.

Meyer, M.A., & Felton, R.H. (1999). Repeated reading to enhance fluency: Old approaches and new directions. *Annals of Dyslexia, 49*, 283–306.

Moats, L.C. (2001). When older students can't read. *Educational Leadership, 58*(6), 36–40.

National Assessment Governing Board. (2002). *Reading Framework for the 2003 National Assessment of Educational Progress*. Retrieved July 9, 2004, from http://www.nagb.org/pubs/reading_framework/toc.html.

National Institute of Child Health and Human Development. (2000). *Report of the National Reading Panel. Teaching children to read: An evidence-based assessment of the scientific research literature on reading and its implications for reading instruction* (NIH Publication No. 00-4769). Washington, DC: U.S. Government Printing Office.

Perfetti, C.A., & Hogaboam, T. (1975). Relationship between single word decoding and reading comprehension skill. *Journal of Educational Psychology, 67*, 461–469.

Pinnell, G.S., Pikulski, J.J., Wixson, K.K., Campbell, J.R., Gough, P.B., & Beatty, A.S. (1995). *Listening to children read aloud*. Washington, DC: U.S. Department of Education, National Center for Educational Statistics.

Rashotte, C.A., & Torgesen, J.K. (1985). Repeated reading and reading fluency in learning disabled children. *Reading Research Quarterly, 20*, 180–188. doi:10.1598/RRQ.20.2.4

Rasinski, T.V. (1989). Fluency for everyone: Incorporating fluency instruction in the classroom. *The Reading Teacher, 42*, 690–693.

Rasinski, T.V. (1990). Investigating measures of reading fluency. *Educational Research Quarterly, 14*(3), 37–44.

Rasinski, T.V. (2003). *The fluent reader: Oral reading strategies for building word recognition, fluency, and comprehension*. New York: Scholastic.

Samuels, S.J. (1979). The method of repeated readings. *The Reading Teacher, 32*, 403–408.

Samuels, S.J. (1988). Decoding and automaticity: Helping poor readers become automatic at word recognition. *The Reading Teacher, 41*, 756–760.

Samuels, S.J., Schermer, N., & Reinking, D. (1992). Reading fluency: Techniques for making decoding automatic. In S.J. Samuels & A.E. Farstrup (Eds.), *What research has to say about reading instruction* (2nd ed., pp. 124–144). Newark, DE: International Reading Association.

School Board of Alachua County. (1997). *Curriculum-based assessment in Alachua County, Florida: Vital signs of student progress*. Gainesville, FL: Author.

Schreiber, P.A. (1980). On the acquisition of reading fluency. *Journal of Reading Behavior, 7*, 177–186.

Schreiber, P.A. (1991). Understanding prosody's role in reading acquisition. *Theory Into Practice, 30*, 158–164.

Shinn, M.R., Good, R.H., Knutson, N., & Tilly, W.D. (1992). Curriculum-based measurement of oral reading fluency: A confirmatory analysis of its relation to reading. *School Psychology Review, 21*, 459–479.

Snow, C., Burns, S., & Griffin, P. (1998). *Preventing reading difficulties in young children*. Washington, DC: National Academy Press.

Stanovich, K.E. (1991). Word recognition: Changing perspectives. In R. Barr, M.L. Kamil, P. Mosenthal, & P.D. Pearson (Eds.), *Handbook of reading research* (Vol. 2, pp. 418–452). New York: Longman.

Tan, A., & Nicholson, T. (1997). Flashcards revisited: Training poor readers to read words faster improves their comprehension of text. *Journal of Educational Psychology, 89*, 276–288.

Tenenbaum, H.A., & Wolking, W.D. (1989). Effects of oral reading rate on intraverbal responding. *The Analysis of Verbal Behavior, 7*, 83–89.

Torgesen, J.K. (1986). Computers and cognition in reading: A focus on decoding fluency. *Exceptional Children, 53*, 157–162.

Torgesen, J.K., Alexander, A.W., Wagner, R.K., Rashotte, C.A., Voeller, K., Conway, T., & Rose, E. (2001). Intensive remedial instruction for children with severe reading disabilities: Immediate and long-term outcomes from two instructional approaches. *Journal of Learning Disabilities, 34*, 33–58.

Torgesen, J.K., Rashotte, C., Alexander, A., Alexander, J., & MacPhee, K. (2003). Progress towards understanding the instructional conditions necessary for remediating reading difficulties in older children. In B. Foorman (Ed.), *Preventing and remediating reading difficulties: Bringing science to scale* (pp. 275–298). Baltimore: York Press.

van den Bosch, K., van Bon, W., & Schreuder, P.R. (1995). Poor readers' decoding skills: Effects of training with limited exposure duration. *Reading Research Quarterly, 30*, 110–125.

Young, A., & Bowers, P.G. (1995). Individual difference and text difficulty determinants of reading fluency and expressiveness. *Journal of Experimental Child Psychology, 60*, 428–454.

Zutell, J., & Rasinski, T.V. (1991). Training teachers to attend to their students' reading fluency. *Theory Into Practice, 30*, 211–217.

Questions for Reflection

- Consider the recommended evidence-based instructional methods for developing fluency that are described in this article. Which of these methods have you used in your classroom? Which methods have you found to be most effective and why? Are there additional methods that you would recommend?
- Table 3 lists recommended reading fluency rates in connected text. How do these goals for oral reading rate align with your own goals for your students and with your students' current fluency skills? How do you go about deciding whether a student's rate of progress is sufficient or whether an adjustment in teaching strategies is needed?

QAR: Enhancing Comprehension and Test Taking Across Grades and Content Areas

Taffy E. Raphael and Kathryn H. Au

Promoting high levels of literacy for all children is a core responsibility for today's teachers. In this article, we describe the potential of Question Answer Relationships (QAR) for helping teachers guide all students to higher levels of literacy. We set this description within the current instructional and assessment context, with a particular focus on what it means to teach to high levels of literacy and why it is especially important to ensure that such instructional activities reach all students.

Educators agree that students must meet high standards for literacy achievement. In a democratic society, success depends on an informed citizenry who can participate effectively in the democratic process—reading a wide range of materials, interpreting and evaluating what they read, drawing conclusions based on evidence, and so forth. Furthermore, with increasing accountability at the district, state, and national levels, U.S. teachers know that they are often judged on the basis of how well their students perform on mandated, high-stakes tests. And certainly high levels of achievement in literacy are important for learning across the curriculum, for independence in engaging with print for personal satisfaction, and for success in an increasingly information-based economy.

But what does it mean to achieve high levels of literacy? Recent national panels and current reviews detailing what it means to comprehend text help inform us about current policies and future trends (e.g., Pressley, 2002; Snow, 2002; Sweet & Snow, 2003). For example, the RAND report (Snow), commissioned by the U.S. Department of Education, identifies literacy proficiency as reached when a

> reader can read a variety of materials with ease and interest, can read for varying purposes, and can read with comprehension even when the material is neither easy to understand nor intrinsically interesting.... [P]roficient readers...are capable of acquiring new knowledge and understanding new concepts, are capable of applying textual information appropriately, and are capable of being engaged in the reading process and reflecting on what is being read. (p. xiii)

This same view is reflected in the current National Assessment of Educational Progress (NAEP; Donahue, Daane, & Grigg, 2003), the only federally funded large-scale testing program in the United States, and the framework for the NAEP 2009 reading assessment (National Assessment Governing Board, 2004) pushes the definition for proficiency even further. For example, students will be expected to read comfortably across genres within fiction, nonfiction, procedural texts, and poetry. They will be required to successfully answer questions, 70% to 80% of which call for the integration, interpretation, critique, and evaluation of texts read independently. Traditional questions that simply require readers to locate and recall information will constitute only a third to a fourth of the questions that students will face. Over half of

Reprinted from Raphael, T.E., & Au, K.H. (2005). QAR: Enhancing comprehension and test taking across grades and content areas. *The Reading Teacher*, 59(3), 206–221.

the higher level questions will require students to provide a short or extended written response rather than simply to select from multiple-choice options. To be judged as proficient in reading fiction, students must demonstrate that they can think deeply about and write in response to questions that address themes and lessons, elements of plot structures, and multiple points of view. To demonstrate high levels of literacy when reading nonfiction, students will need to draw on their knowledge of text organization (e.g., description, causal relationships, logical connections) and be able to identify important details in texts, graphs, photos, and other materials.

The kind of strategic knowledge assessed on national and state tests, now and in the future, is central to the achievement of high levels of literacy. In this context, the gap between the literacy achievement of mainstream students and students of diverse backgrounds must be a central concern (Au, 2003). Students of diverse backgrounds differ from mainstream students in terms of their ethnicity, socioeconomic status, or primary language (Au, 1993). In the United States, for example, students of diverse backgrounds may be African American, Latino American, or Native American in ethnicity; come from low-income families; or speak African American Vernacular English or Spanish as their primary language.

As displayed in Table 1, the existence of an achievement gap between students of diverse backgrounds and mainstream students is underscored by 2002 reading results (Grigg, Daane, Jin, & Campbell, 2003). These results show that, as a group, students of diverse backgrounds have fallen four years behind their mainstream peers in reading achievement by the time they reach grade 12. The average 12th-grade black student's score (267) is at the same level as the average 8th-grade Asian/Pacific Islander student (267), and slightly below that of the average 8th-grade white student (272). Similarly, an average 12th-grade Hispanic student's score (273) is only 1 point above that of an average 8th-grade white student. This gap is present as students move through the elementary grades, and it only becomes worse.

Table 1
Average 2002 NAEP Reading Scores

Ethnicity	Grade 4	Grade 8	Grade 12
White	229	272	292
Black	199	245	267
Hispanic	201	247	273
Asian/ Pacific Islanders	224	267	286

Many theories have been proposed to explain the literacy achievement gap, identifying factors within and beyond the purview of the classroom teacher. We focus here on an area that falls within the control of individual classroom teachers and their school colleagues: diverse students' currently limited opportunities for high-quality instruction in reading comprehension. Research shows that, in comparison to their mainstream peers, students of diverse backgrounds tend to receive a great deal of instruction in lower level skills and little instruction in reading comprehension and higher level thinking about text (Darling-Hammond, 1995; Fitzgerald, 1995). This emphasis on lower level skills frequently results from lowered expectations for the achievement of students of diverse backgrounds, reflecting the mistaken belief that these students are less capable of higher level thinking than mainstream students (Oakes & Guiton, 1995). Using this misguided logic leads to the erroneous conclusion that instruction in lower level skills is a better match to the abilities of students of diverse backgrounds.

These stereotypes of students of diverse backgrounds are especially harmful at a time of rising standards for reading performance. As noted earlier, a high proportion of test questions—within the next five years, approximately three quarters to four fifths of questions on the NAEP reading assessment—require students to use higher level thinking, such as making reader–text connections or examining the content and structure of the text (National Assessment Governing Board, 2004; Donahue et al., 2003). As indicated above, studies suggest that many students of diverse backgrounds are not receiving the kind of comprehension instruction that would prepare them to perform well on assessments that are increasingly oriented toward higher level thinking with text. It is clear from research that all students need instruction in reading comprehension, especially the kind that focuses on the strategies required to answer and generate challenging questions (Taylor, Pearson, Peterson, & Rodriguez, 2003).

In our work with schools enrolling a high proportion of students of diverse backgrounds, we find that teachers often experience difficulty making the desired changes to instruction. Typically, these teachers have become accustomed to instruction focused on lower level skills rather than on higher level thinking and reading comprehension. Or they are unsure of how to teach different comprehension strategies in a way that allows students to see how the strategies work together to facilitate an understanding of the text. The consequences of weak instruction for all students, but particularly for those of diverse backgrounds, may extend far beyond testing, likely limiting their opportunities for higher education, employment, and overall advancement in society.

In summary, current practice and future trends place increasingly heavy demands on teachers to ensure that all of their students achieve high levels of literacy. Teachers may feel overwhelmed by the challenges of bringing students to these high levels of literacy, due to uncertainty about how to teach reading comprehension strategies to foster the integration, interpretation, critique, and evaluation of text ideas. The challenges are compounded by the fact that students of diverse backgrounds often enter classrooms reading far below grade level.

We believe QAR provides a framework that offers teachers a straightforward approach for reading comprehension instruction with the potential of eventually closing the literacy achievement gap. QAR can serve as a reasonable starting point for addressing four problems of practice that stand in the way of moving all students to high levels of literacy:

- The need for a shared language to make visible the largely invisible processes underlying reading and listening comprehension.
- The need for a framework for organizing questioning activities and comprehension instruction within and across grades and school subjects.
- The need for accessible and straightforward whole-school reform for literacy instruction oriented toward higher level thinking.
- The need to prepare students for high-stakes testing without undermining a strong focus on higher level thinking with text.

Two decades ago, research showed that QAR could reliably improve students' comprehension (Raphael & McKinney, 1983; Raphael & Pearson, 1985; Raphael & Wonnacott, 1985). In the two decades since, literacy educators in a broad range of settings have demonstrated its practical value and shared their experiences in professional journals (e.g., Mesmer & Hutchins, 2002), textbooks (e.g., Leu & Kinzer, 2003; Reutzel & Cooper, 2004; Roe, Smith, & Burns, 2005; Vacca et al., 2003), and on the World Wide Web (e.g., www.smsd.org/schools/diemer/ and http://gallery.carnegiefoundation.org/yhutchinson). In the remaining sections of this article, we discuss the reasons underlying the "staying power" of QAR and its usefulness across a variety of settings. We frame our discussion in terms of the four problems of practice the QAR framework can address.

Making the Invisible Visible Through QAR

The vocabulary of QAR—In the Book, In My Head, Right There, Think & Search, Author & Me, and On My Own—gives teachers and students a language for talking about the largely invisible processes that constitute listening and reading comprehension across grades and subject areas. Teachers know the value of modeling and thinking aloud to make visible the thought processes involved in higher levels of thinking, but it can be frustrating trying to convey complex ideas without a shared vocabulary. Thus, QAR first and foremost provides teachers and students with a much-needed common language.

How many times and in how many classrooms have conversations (such as the one that follows) taken place when students answer questions after reading or listening to text? In this fifth-grade classroom, students have read and are now writing answers to questions about *Hatchet* (Paulsen, 1987). Brian, the main character, is the lone survivor of a plane crash. He has as his only tool a hatchet. The teacher, Ms. Bendon, notices Alex looking upset as he reads and rereads the text. (Pseudonyms are used for teachers and students.)

Ms. Bendon: Alex, you look like you might need help. What can I do for you?

Alex: I don't get it.

Ms. Bendon: Can you tell me what it is that you don't get?

Alex: I don't know. I just don't get it.

Ms. Bendon: Can you tell me the question you are having trouble with?

Alex: [Turns to the page of questions sitting to the side, and points to the question, "How do you think Brian's hatchet might come in handy?"]

Ms. Bendon: OK, let's think about this. What could you do to help answer this question?

Alex: [shrugs]

Ms. Bendon: [taking the book from Alex] I think you know a lot to help you answer this question. Just think about this some more and I'm sure you'll be able to think of some reasons.

Alex: OK.

Ms. Bendon knew that Alex had background knowledge about hunting, survival strategies, and the use of hatchets and other tools. Thus, she walked away believing that Alex would be fine, because she had cued him to reflect on his background knowledge rather than refer to the text. But instead we see Alex move the question page aside and go back to his already frustrating rereading strategy; to him, the process of answering the question remains mysterious. He may believe the right answer is found only in the text. He may not want to take risks by using his own knowledge and experience. He may not realize the importance of using his background knowledge in question-answering activities. There are many possibilities for why he "doesn't get it," but they remain unidentified and unarticulated in the absence of a language framework to talk about questioning and related strategies. The original articles written to introduce QAR explained the common vocabulary, but they did not provide guidance about the best approach for introducing this language. Over the years, it has become increasingly clear that there are advantages to introducing QAR language in terms of three binary comparisons: In the Book versus In My Head, Right There versus Think & Search, and Author & Me versus On My Own.

Too often, students of diverse backgrounds are denied access to the language needed to discuss strategies and questions, because the lessons they receive focus largely on lower level skills. We have observed that lessons in the reading programs often used in these classrooms tend to be based on texts that do not challenge or interest students. Questions tend to be limited to the Right There category, and students are not taught strategic or critical thinking. The classroom examples that follow show how teachers can move away from these limitations to provide more effective instruction, especially for students of diverse backgrounds.

Developing QAR's Shared Language

In QAR classrooms during the first few days of school, Ms. Bendon and other teachers introduced students to the basic principle underlying QAR: that generating and answering questions draws on two core sources of information. As illustrated in Figure 1, these sources are the texts that we read and our background knowledge and experiences; or, in the language of QAR, information that is In the Book or In My Head,

Figure 1
The QAR Framework as a Developmental Progression

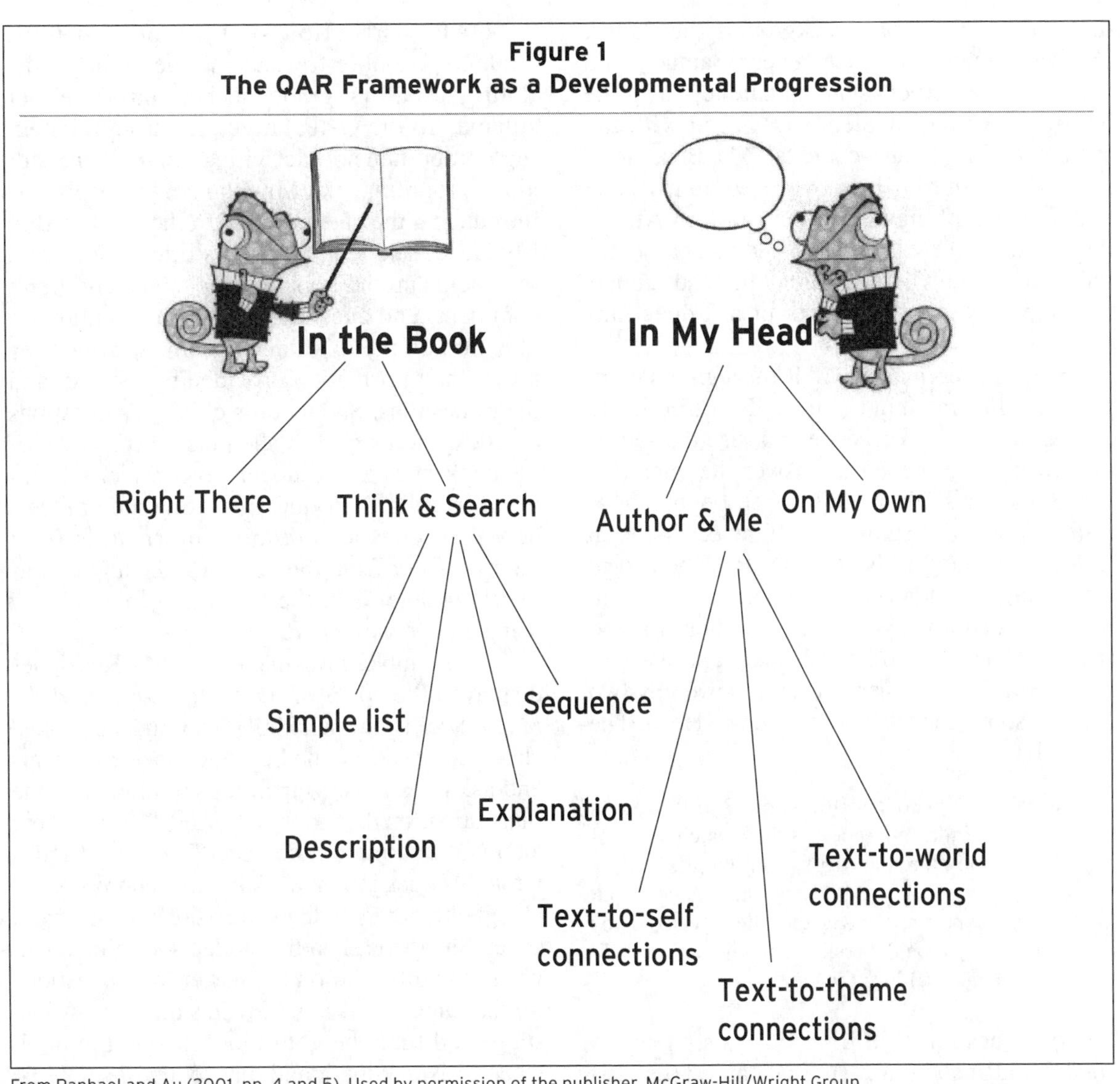

From Raphael and Au (2001, pp. 4 and 5). Used by permission of the publisher, McGraw-Hill/Wright Group.

respectively. Teachers use QAR language as they emphasize the importance of both sources of information. Furthermore, teachers use QAR language to help students learn to use strategies effectively. For example, they explain how skimming or scanning might lead to details for an In the Book QAR (a typical locate/recall strategy) or how using clues from the title and chapter headings can point to relevant background knowledge for answering an In My Head QAR (a relatively simple interpret/integrate/infer task).

Students like Alex may still say, "I don't get it," but they are more able to describe the strategies they've used and the kind of help they need. For example, Alex could explain that he has tried three In the Book strategies—rereading, skimming, and scanning—but can't find an answer explaining how a hatchet could help. Ms. Bendon could convey that this is an In My Head QAR and, thus, there are more effective strategies to use for this particular question. Once freed from his focus on the text, Alex could be directed to consider his background knowledge. Furthermore, he could help a peer, Samuel, who has never used tools such as hatchets or gone hunting with family members. Faced with the same question, Samuel could tell Ms. Bendon, "I know it's an In My Head but I went to my head and there's nothing there. Can I talk to Alex?" Armed with QAR language, students can communicate about what they are doing and request the help they need to answer or ask questions effectively.

Students learn about QAR through the comparisons illustrated in Figure 1. To differentiate among the QARs, teachers emphasize the source of information needed to answer the question. Mr. Blanco, a sixth-grade teacher, begins QAR instruction by analyzing the differences between In the Book and In My Head QARs. The text in the lesson is an adapted newspaper article about a heroic gorilla who rescued a toddler at a zoo (Bils & Singer, 1996). Mr. Blanco and his students read short segments, each followed by two questions, one In the Book, one In My Head. The article begins,

> A crowd of visitors at Brookfield Zoo looked on in horror Friday afternoon as they watched a toddler tumble more than 15 feet into a pit, landing near seven gorillas. But as zoo patrons cried out for help, expecting the worst for the 3-year-old boy lying battered on the concrete below, an unlikely hero emerged. (Bils & Singer, p. 1)

The two questions Mr. Blanco asks students to answer and analyze are (1) What caused the visitors to look on in horror? and (2) What do you think makes a hero an unlikely one?

Answering the first question requires readers to use the information in the first two sentences of the text, that a toddler fell 15 feet into a gorilla pit. The horror might be attributed to the length of the fall, the toddler landing in the midst of the gorillas, or the toddler lying battered, but the limited information relevant to answering the question is in the text. In contrast, answers to the second question will vary considerably, depending on the background knowledge and experiences of the reader.

QAR instruction should not wait until students are able to read independently. Ms. Rodrigues, a first-grade teacher, introduces her students to the QAR language through listening comprehension activities during her read-aloud program. Like Mr. Blanco, she begins by introducing the categories of In the Book and In My Head. She reads a book's title to her class, then holds up the book and fields the children's comments and questions. She focuses children's attention on the relationships among what they know, the information provided by the text, and their questions. She records children's questions on sticky notes, which she puts on the cover of the book, then asks students to consider sources for answering their questions. She then models how their questions require information from their heads or from the text, introducing the formal language of In the Book and In My Head using a large wall chart.

For example, early in the year, Ms. Rodrigues displayed the cover of the text, *Anansi and the Magic Stick* (Kimmel, 2001). The students looked closely at the cover and began to make comments and ask questions. Martin looked closely at the illustrations on the cover and asked, "Why is there a tomato floating on the water?" Ms. Rodrigues wrote his question on a sticky note and placed it, along with other students' questions, on the front cover. She then asked the students to think about where the information to answer their questions might come from. For Martin's question, Viola suggested that "he could look inside the book when he is reading it and maybe it will say." Ms. Rodrigues reinforced that as one possibility, then asked, "What if you finish reading the book, and you still don't really have an answer? What if the book doesn't exactly tell you?" In this way she introduced the possibility that not all questions may be answered in the text. The students then read the story and paused to talk about relevant information for answering their questions. Following the reading, Ms. Rodrigues created a two-column chart, with In the Book and In My Head each heading a column. She modeled how to think about the questions they had asked in terms of the source of information needed for answers, placing a sticky note for each question in the appropriate column on the chart.

Regardless of grade level and whether students read independently or participate in shared readings or read alouds, teachers introduce students to the language of QAR by analyzing the differences between questions with answer sources in the book and those where the answer source is students' own heads. Shorter texts work quite effectively for characterizing basic differences between these two information sources, but as students become more experienced with QARs, this simple distinction is not sufficient to capture the range of strategies used to answer and generate questions related to text. Thus, teachers build on In the Book and In My Head by introducing the four core QARs.

Once students are confidently and accurately identifying In the Book QARs, teachers introduce its subcategories, Right There and Think & Search. Similarly, when students are confident and accurate with In My Head QARs, teachers introduce its subcategories, Author & Me and On My Own (see Figure 2 for definitions of each).

Longer passages (e.g., 3–5 paragraphs) are used for this instruction so that students can more easily see the differences between Right There and Think & Search, as well as between Author & Me and On My Own responses.

Mr. Blanco conducted QAR instruction within a unit on immigration. For these QAR lessons, he used the following passages from a short biography of Cesar Chavez, displayed on an overhead transparency:

Figure 2
The Core Question Answer Relationships

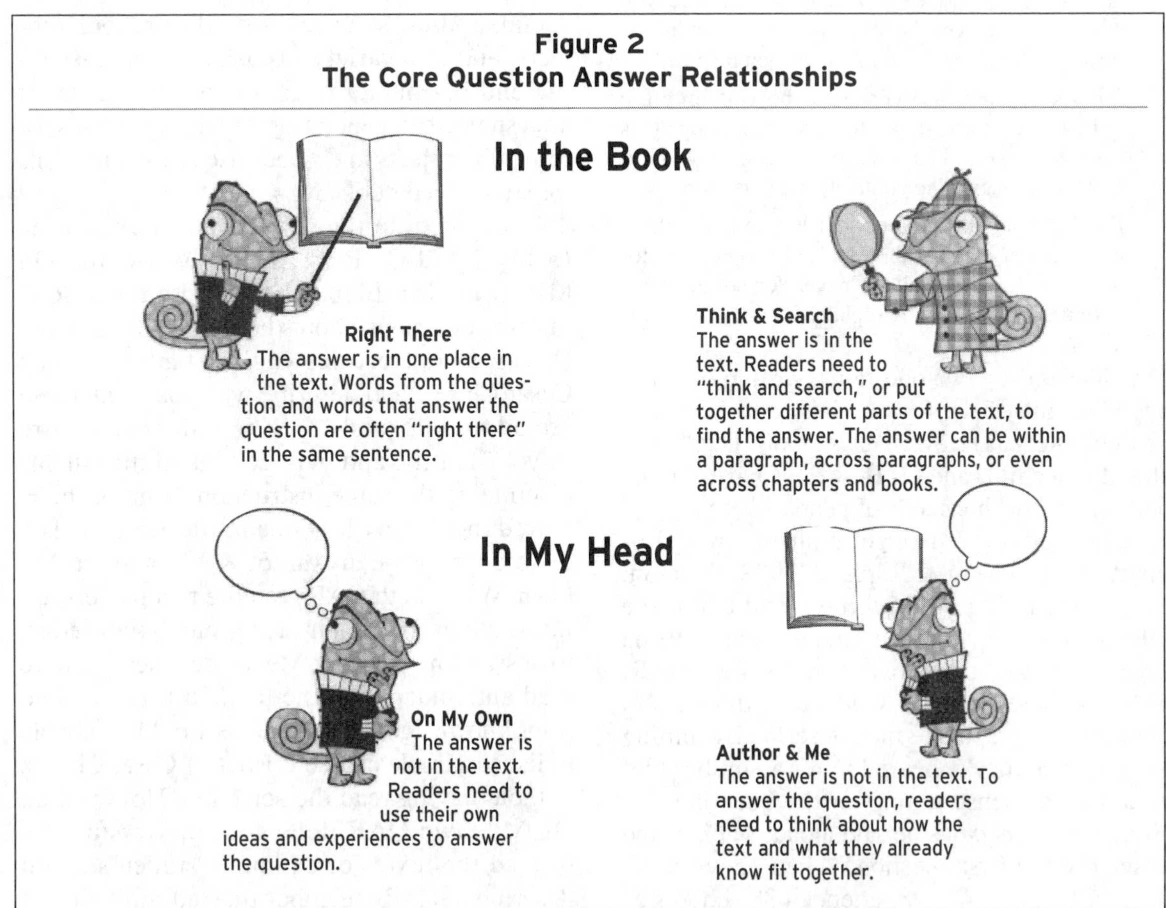

In the Book
Right There
The answer is in one place in the text. Words from the question and words that answer the question are often "right there" in the same sentence.
Think & Search
The answer is in the text. Readers need to "think and search," or put together different parts of the text, to find the answer. The answer can be within a paragraph, across paragraphs, or even across chapters and books.
In My Head
On My Own
The answer is not in the text. Readers need to use their own ideas and experiences to answer the question.
Author & Me
The answer is not in the text. To answer the question, readers need to think about how the text and what they already know fit together.

From Raphael and Au (2001, pp. 4 and 5). Used by permission of the publisher, McGraw-Hill/Wright Group.

> Cesar Chavez moved from Arizona to California with his family when he was ten years old. He and his family worked as migrant farm laborers. Chavez attended more than thirty-eight schools during his childhood. After eighth grade, he worked full-time to help his family until he left home to fight in World War II.
>
> When he returned home after the war, Chavez learned all he could about labor law and worked at organizing protest marches for the rights of farm laborers. In 1962 he organized the National Farm Workers Association, called *La Causa*, in Fresno, California. *La Causa* wanted to stop using dangerous chemicals in the fields. "Our belief is to help everybody, not just one race," Chavez said.
>
> Most farm owners refused to negotiate with *La Causa*. Some reacted with violence, and local police usually supported the owners. Chavez urged protesting workers to leave their guns and knives at home. "If we used violence, we would have won contracts long ago," he said, "but they wouldn't be lasting because we wouldn't have won respect."
>
> *La Causa* called for Americans to boycott, or refuse to buy, lettuce and grapes to show their sympathies for the workers. The boycotts were so successful that owners agreed to contracts with the workers.
>
> By the time Chavez died in 1993 he had helped create better lives for thousands of people. Senator Robert F. Kennedy called Chavez "one of the heroic figures of our time." (Raphael & Au, 2001, p. 15)

Mr. Blanco used two questions, written on chart paper, to introduce Right There and Think & Search QARs: (1) How many schools did Chavez attend as a child? and (2) How did Chavez create better lives for thousands of people?

He used a "transfer of control" model of instruction (see Au & Raphael, 1998; Pearson, 1985), beginning by thinking aloud about the information source for the first question. While saying he thought this was an In the Book QAR, he highlighted the words *schools* and *attended* in the first paragraph. He then described scanning the sentence they appeared in for a number that would make sense to answer the question. He circled *thirty-eight* as he said aloud, "This is the answer to the first question." Then he wrote on the chart paper, "Chavez attended 38 schools as a child." He used a similar process of modeling, highlighting, and displaying an answer to the second question, highlighting better working conditions, getting higher pay, and learning to use boycotts rather than violence.

Mr. Blanco then spoke about his own analysis of the differences in what it took to answer the two questions, drawing on the definitions in Figure 2 (Raphael & Au, 2001). He talked about how much more difficult a Think & Search QAR can be for many reasons. Think & Search QARs require that readers find *all* the information that is relevant to the question and then integrate that information into one coherent answer. This is more challenging than finding a detail in the text to respond to a Right There question. Over time and through many examples, Mr. Blanco's students learned to apply the heuristic that their teacher had taught them to reading, social studies, science, and other school subjects, and to a variety of tasks—from answering end-of-chapter questions in their content area subjects to generating inquiry questions for research projects and good discussion questions for student-led book clubs.

To illustrate the differences between the In My Head QARs—Author & Me and On My Own—Mr. Blanco began with the following two questions about the Chavez biography: (1) List characteristics you most admire about Cesar Chavez and describe why you think these are admirable, and (2) Whom do you admire in your family, and why do you admire them? Continuing the same instructional approach, he paired these two questions to illustrate the key difference between Author & Me and On My Own. While both QARs require that readers use information from their background knowledge, to answer an Author & Me, readers need to have read and understood the text. Unless they had prior knowledge, most students would be unable to list admirable characteristics of Cesar Chavez without having read the selection. However, an On My Own QAR does not require students to read the text. For example, students could describe a family member they admire without reading or understanding the biography.

Organizing Comprehension Instruction Through QAR

QAR instruction can be adjusted for use across grade levels and content areas because of the way the categories form a progression of difficulty. This provides an opportunity to coherently frame specific instruction in QAR, as well as more general instruction in the range of high-level comprehension strategies students learn across grade levels.

The use of QAR as a framework for comprehension across the grades and school subjects may be particularly helpful in schools serving many students of diverse backgrounds. Often, under the pressure to raise test scores, teachers in these schools have been implementing highly structured programs focusing on lower level skills. Teachers usually report that they see gains in lower level skills, such as word identification, but not in comprehension and higher level thinking. QAR provides a means for teachers to gain or regain a focus on instruction in comprehension strategies in their classrooms.

Initially, teachers introduce In the Book and In My Head QARs. In early primary grades, some teachers may use only these two categories and may depend on teachers in later grade levels to introduce the next level of categories. Others may begin with the two categories but choose to introduce the next level once certain students understand the two sources well. Research has shown that by second grade, students comfortably learn to distinguish between Right There and Think & Search QARs (Raphael & McKinney, 1983). Further, research studies have demonstrated that fourth graders understand the differences among the four core QARs (e.g., Raphael & Wonnacott, 1985). Introduction of the core categories varies depending on the knowledge of the teacher as well as the progress of students. However, anecdotal data from teachers such as Ms. Rodrigues suggest that, with appropriate instruction, even young students are able to talk about all four QARs.

Across grade levels and subject areas, teachers continue to use the QAR categories to frame listening and reading comprehension strategy instruction (see Table 2). Although there are

Table 2
Using QAR to Frame Comprehension Strategy Instruction

QAR	Sample comprehension strategies
On My Own	1. Activating prior knowledge (e.g., about genre, experiences, authors) 2. Connecting to the topic (e.g., self-to-text)
Right There	1. Scanning to locate information 2. Note-taking strategies to support easier recall of key information 3. Using context clues for creating definitions
Think & Search	1. Identifying important information 2. Summarizing 3. Using text organization (e.g., comparison/contrast, problem/solution, list, explanation) to identify relevant information 4. Visualizing (e.g., setting, mood, procedures) 5. Using context to describe symbols and figurative language 6. Clarifying 7. Making text-to-text connections 8. Making simple inferences
Author & Me	1. Predicting 2. Visualizing 3. Making simple and complex inferences 4. Distinguishing fact and opinion 5. Making text-to-self connections

exceptions (e.g., reciprocal teaching, transactional strategy instruction, Questioning the Author), many approaches to comprehension instruction are based on teaching individual strategies. However, readers functioning at high levels of literacy use strategies in combination and apply different approaches to strategic thinking, depending on the genre or difficulty of the texts. Understanding how strategies interrelate can be quite abstract for students faced with the need to apply several strategies, as well as quite demanding for teachers in terms of providing effective instruction. Table 2 conveys how QAR can be used to help students see the relationships among the strategies they are learning and the task demands represented by different questions. Table 3 shows how questions asked typically vary across the reading cycle.

Thinking about QAR in this way provides a framework that students can use to link strategies at appropriate points in the reading cycle—whether during their language arts instruction or in other school subjects. Furthermore, the framework guides teachers' modeling of question-asking practices before (e.g., eliciting relevant background knowledge), during (e.g., focusing on important information, locating key terms, making inferences about key plot events or character motivation), and after reading (e.g., considering themes, building arguments about author intent supported by text evidence). Understanding and control of strategies learned helps readers engage in the high levels of literacy for which they are accountable in their day-to-day classroom literacy activities and in high-stakes assessments at the district, state, and national levels.

Table 3
Using QAR to Frame Questioning Within the Reading Cycle

Before reading	On My Own • From the title or the topic, what do I already know that can connect me to the story or text? Author & Me • From the topic, title, illustrations, or book cover, what might this story or text be about?
During reading	Author & Me • What do I think will happen next? • How would I describe the mood of the story and why is this important? Think & Search • What is the problem and how is it resolved? • What role do [insert characters' names] play in the story? • What are the important events? (literary, informational) Right There • Who is the main character? (literary) • Identify the topic sentence in this paragraph. (informational) • What are some words that describe the setting? (literary)
After reading	Author & Me • What is the author's message? • What is the theme and how is it connected to the world beyond the story? • How can I synthesize the information with what I know from other sources? • How well does the author make his or her argument? • How is the author using particular language to influence our beliefs? Think & Search • Find evidence in the text to support an argument.

Whole-School Reform Through QAR

The efforts of an individual teacher to provide effective comprehension strategy instruction can certainly contribute to improvements in students' achievement. However, more than one year of instruction by an individual teacher is usually required to bring students of diverse backgrounds to high levels of literacy and to ensure their continued success as readers. There has been increasing recognition that to have the strongest effect on students' literacy development, we should look to the school as the unit of change (Cunningham & Creamer, 2003) and organize professional development to promote teacher learning that leads to a coherent, schoolwide approach to literacy instruction. Coherence is central to students' literacy success on informal and high-stakes assessments (Newmann, Smith, Allensworth, & Bryk, 2001; Taylor et al., 2003). Coherent efforts are particularly needed for increasing the access of students of diverse backgrounds to the kind of reading comprehension instruction that will close the literacy achievement gap.

In the United States, under the influence of the federally funded Comprehensive School Reform program of 2001, many schools—enrolling considerable numbers of students of diverse backgrounds—purchased packaged programs that emphasized lower level skills (Viadero, 2004). The problem with reform efforts based on packaged programs is that they do not foster the kinds of conversations among teachers within and across grades that can lead to coherent and cohesive literacy instruction. Research (e.g., Anders & Richardson, 1991; Duffy, 2004; Taylor, Pearson, Peterson, & Rodriguez, 2005) suggests that a schoolwide approach based on collaboration and long-term commitment is more effective than top-down models or packaged programs designed as a "quick fix." Our observations suggest that schools serving students of diverse backgrounds often prefer to rely on packaged programs rather than undertaking the long-term professional development efforts that are likely to be more effective. The reasons that such schools favor packaged programs include large numbers of inexperienced teachers, high rates of teacher turnover, and a lack of the expertise or funding needed to carry out systematic, multiyear professional development.

As a framework that is relatively simple and straightforward, yet applicable across grade levels and subject areas, QAR has potential for schoolwide professional development. The QAR framework helps organize comprehension instruction within and across grade levels and serves as a bridge between study of the language arts and other subjects. The application is clear for both day-to-day classroom activities as well as high-stakes assessments. In addition, it is not based on a particular ideology (e.g., it can be applied within basal reading instructional programs or literature-based instruction or content area instruction). The QAR framework can be a starting point for conversations that lead teachers to think deeply about reading comprehension instruction to promote sustained changes in practice.

For example, teachers at one of the largest elementary schools in Hawaii use QAR to frame comprehension instruction in their ongoing efforts to improve their students' reading achievement. To implement a schoolwide focus on reading comprehension, teachers mapped their end-of-year targets for student learning in terms of grade-level benchmarks related to state standards. The QAR framework laid out in Figure 1 helps a school with such mapping. In this case, the first-grade teachers agreed to teach In the Book and In My Head QARs. The third-grade teachers agreed to teach their students all four of the core categories. Teachers in the fourth through sixth grades agreed to emphasize Think & Search, which students could use with both fiction and nonfiction texts.

At this school, teachers in special education as well as in general education use the language of QAR. One of the special education teachers developed approaches for teaching her students about QARs by drawing on multiple modalities. She created rhythmic chants for In the Book and In My Head. She used sentence strips so that students could physically match questions and answers. She created charts for each category to help students better understand the meaning of "sources of information." As shown in Figure 3, one of the charts was developed as students brainstormed places that information comes from before it eventually ends up in our heads. She then helped students identify which of these information sources could be read, putting an *R* in the box by the source.

Having the common language of QAR can help teachers know how to proceed when they are seeking to improve comprehension instruction. For example, when examining the results of their classroom-based assessments, the first-grade teachers at this school noticed that their students had trouble making inferences. As they discussed the problem, one of the teachers had an idea. She explained to the other teachers that the problem might lie in the fact that they had been teaching only the QAR categories of In the Book and In My Head. However, to answer questions requiring inferences, children needed to know the category of Author & Me. At the time, Author & Me was being introduced to students in later grades, but the first-grade teachers decided that they should begin teaching it.

Figure 3
Information source chart

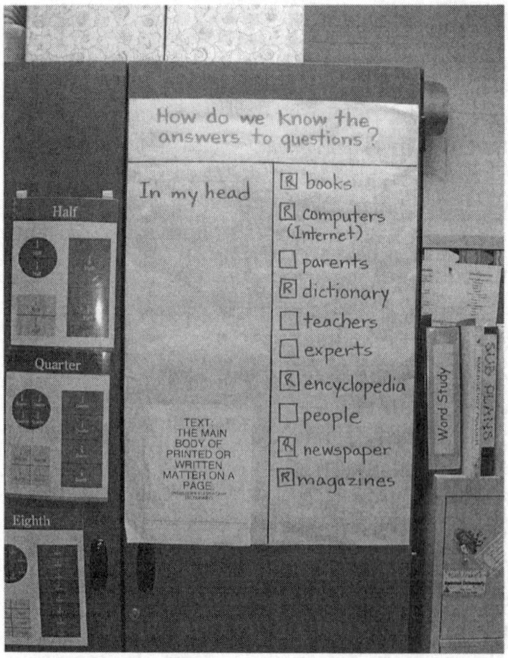

Photograph by the authors.

Consistent QAR instruction across the grades and school subjects establishes the foundation for improved reading and listening comprehension. By the time students are in intermediate grades, those who have received consistent QAR instruction develop sophisticated strategies to analyze questions and use appropriate strategies and language for formulating good answers. For example, Kathy Highfield documented students' use of QARs from third through fourth grade (Highfield, 2003). She found several examples of students' theorizing about how questions work as well as appropriate strategies for answering questions. For example, students in her classroom discovered that the word you may signal that the question is either an On My Own or Author & Me, while they also recognized that this is not always the case.

Highfield (2003) found that students learned to value skimming or rereading strategies to locate specific information in the text for Right There QARs (and the occasional Think & Search), while simultaneously recognizing the role of their prior knowledge in answering questions. They even began to debate individual differences in the way QARs might apply as they read and responded to questions. Toward spring of fourth grade, Highfield eavesdropped as two students debated whether a question represented a Right There or an On My Own QAR. After the debate had gone on for a few minutes, one student explained that for her, it was an On My Own because she already knew the information to answer the question, but for her peer, it was a Right There, because she didn't already have the information and had to get it from the book. Such metacognitive knowledge about questioning and related strategies supports students in their day-to-day work with text, as well as when they must take a high-stakes test.

Accountability and Test Preparation Through QAR

Educators in U.S. schools are under increasing pressure to improve students' reading performance, as measured by scores on standardized and state reading tests. This pressure is greatest in schools with histories of low test scores, and these are schools that often have high proportions of students of diverse backgrounds. In their attempts to raise test scores, these schools inadvertently lower the quality of educational experiences. For example, one common response is to narrow the curriculum to focus on tested subjects such as reading and math, to the exclusion of subjects such as science, social studies, the arts, and physical education (Smith, 1991). Another common response, often months prior to spring testing, is to spend the bulk of instructional time on test preparation.

Test preparation typically takes the form of having students complete workbook exercises with items of a form and content ostensibly similar to those on upcoming tests. In general, students practice by reading short passages and responding to multiple-choice items. Most test preparation packages involve little or no instruction by the teacher. The problem with practice-only activities is that students who have not already acquired reading comprehension strategies gain little or nothing from the large amounts of time spent on these activities. Some students will muddle through as best they can, using the coping techniques at their disposal, while other students simply quit trying altogether. Teachers in schools following these practices have reported to us that many students of diverse backgrounds experience burnout and discouragement. These students lack motivation by the time large-scale testing actually occurs. For these reasons, practice-only test preparation activities cannot be expected to improve the test scores of most students of diverse backgrounds, much less help them to become better readers and thinkers.

With QAR as the framework for teaching listening and reading comprehension strategies, within a rich curriculum in language arts and other school subjects, teachers can help students be strategic when faced with the texts and tasks on high-stakes tests. As we described earlier, the trend in national assessments is toward ever higher levels of literacy, moving away from a heavy emphasis on locating and recalling information to require that students integrate ideas across texts, draw inferences, critique, and evaluate.

To illustrate this trend, we present an analysis of the 12 questions on a fourth-grade NAEP reading selection, "Watch Out for Wombats!" (Donahue et al., 2003). An overview of the questions and their characteristics is presented in Table 4. There are 6 multiple-choice questions, 5 short constructed responses, and 1 extended constructed response. For 4 of the multiple-choice questions, the QAR is Right There. For 1 of the remaining multiple-choice questions, the QAR is Author & Me, and for the other, Think & Search. Thus, even multiple-choice questions on the NAEP may go beyond simple forms of comprehension. With the 5 short constructed response items, 3 reflect the Think & Search QAR, while 1 is an Author & Me and the other a Right There. For the extended constructed response, the QAR is Author & Me. In total, students are required to answer 5 Right There items, 3 Author & Me items, and 4 Think & Search items. This analysis shows the shift toward higher level comprehension in current assessments and also highlights the fact that there is not a simple one-to-one correspondence between question format and QAR in current reading assessments. Specifically, multiple-choice questions do not always have a QAR of Right There. It is clear that teachers who want their students to perform well on reading tests would be wise to provide instruction in all the QARs and the reading strategies associated with them, as listed in Table 2. Instruction should foster students' independence in the application of QARs and reading strategies, as well as a mindset toward critical evaluation.

Through QAR instruction, teachers do not need to teach to a particular test but instead are able to unpack the task demands of different types of questions and alert students to these demands as appropriate to the different tests students face. For example, in 2003 on the Illinois State Achievement Test, many students were not successful when required to write an extended response. The state's definition for success required that students meet the following criteria:

- Demonstrate an accurate understanding of important information in the text by focusing on the key ideas presented explicitly or implicitly.

Table 4
Analysis of NAEP Sample Passage Questions

Question	Format	QAR and Strategies
1. This article mostly describes how....	Multiple choice	Think & Search: • Identifying important information • Summarizing • Making simple inferences
2. Where do wombats live?	Multiple choice	Right There • Scanning to locate information
3. Describe one way in which wombats and koalas are similar and one way in which they are different.	Short constructed response	Think & Search • Visualizing • Identifying important information • Using text organization to identify relevant information • Summarizing
4. Use the information in this passage to describe marsupials.	Short constructed response	Think & Search • Visualizing • Identifying important information • Using text organization to identify relevant information • Summarizing
5. Where do wombats usually live?	Multiple choice	Right There • Scanning to locate information
6. Choose an animal, other than a koala, that you know about and compare it to the wombat.	Short constructed response	Author & Me • Visualizing • Making simple and complex inferences (to compare) • Making text-to-self connections
7. Why are wombats not often seen by people?	Multiple choice	Right There • Scanning to locate information
8. Describe the sleeping area of wombats.	Short constructed response	Right There • Scanning to locate information • Note-taking to support easier recall
9. To get food, the wombat uses its....	Multiple choice	Right There • Scanning to locate information
10. What would a wombat probably do if it met a person?	Multiple choice	Author & Me • Predicting • Making simple and complex inferences
11. Why has Australia set up animal reserves to protect the wombat?	Short constructed response	Think & Search • Identifying important information • Using text organization to identify relevant information • Making simple inferences
12. Give two reasons why people should not have wombats as pets. Use what you learned in the passage to support your answer.	Extended constructed response	Author & Me • Identifying important information • Making complex inferences • Visualizing

Note. Questions retrieved June 14, 2005, from http://nces.ed.gov/nationsreportcard/ITMRLS/search.asp?picksubj=Reading

- Use information from the text to interpret significant concepts or make connections to other situations or contexts logically through analysis, evaluation, inference, or comparison/contrast.
- Use relevant and accurate references; most are specific and fully supported.
- Integrate interpretation of the text with text-based support (Illinois State Board of Education, 2004).

Many students simply wrote a personal response without making explicit connections to the text. Others wrote about the text but did not include any personal connections. Simply writing an extended essay was not sufficient. To be successful, students needed to identify the QAR as Author & Me and compose a written response including both text ideas and a personal connection.

Concluding Comments

We believe QAR addresses four troubling problems of practice today, particularly involving students of diverse backgrounds who often receive little literacy instruction oriented to promoting high levels of thinking about text. First, QAR can help address the lack of a shared language among teachers and students for improving questioning practices, whether in the day-to-day life of the classroom, in students' activities outside of school, or in high-stakes testing situations. Second, QAR can bring coherence to literacy instruction within and across grade levels by providing a framework for a developmental progression for comprehension instruction. As a framework, QAR provides a means for organizing comprehension strategy instruction. Third, QAR provides a focal point to begin sustained efforts for whole-school reform aimed at higher standards for literacy learning and teaching. It is difficult to find points of contact that bring teachers from kindergarten through middle school to the table with the same high levels of interest. Yet all readers at all grades can benefit from learning to think in terms of information sources for answering and asking questions. Fourth, QAR provides a responsible approach to preparing students for high-stakes tests at different grade levels and in a variety of subject areas, without detracting from the high-quality instruction that leads to high levels of literacy.

Using the QAR framework can provide benefits to schools, teachers, and students for a relatively small amount of time and effort. For schools, the benefit comes in the chance to pull the grade levels together around reading comprehension instruction. For teachers, the benefit is found in the opportunity to improve instruction around questioning activities and reading comprehension. For students, the benefit lies in gaining access to reading comprehension and higher level thinking with text—an opportunity often unavailable to those of diverse backgrounds.

References

Anders, P., & Richardson, V. (1991). Research directions: Staff development that empowers teachers' reflection and enhances instruction. *Language Arts*, *68*, 316–321.

Au, K.H. (1993). *Literacy instruction in multicultural settings*. Fort Worth, TX: Harcourt Brace Jovanovich College.

Au, K.H. (2003). Literacy research and students of diverse backgrounds: What does it take to improve achievement? In C.M. Fairbanks, J. Worthy, B. Maloch, J.V. Hoffman, & D.L. Schallert (Eds.), *52nd yearbook of the National Reading Conference* (pp. 85–91). Oak Creek, WI: National Reading Conference.

Au, K.H., & Raphael, T.E. (1998). Curriculum and teaching in literature-based programs. In T.E. Raphael & K.H. Au (Eds.), *Literature-based instruction: Reshaping the curriculum* (pp. 123–148). Norwood, MA: Christopher-Gordon.

Bils, J., & Singer, S. (1996, August 17). *Gorilla saves tot in Brookfield Zoo ape pit*. Chicago Tribune, p. 1.

Cunningham, J.W., & Creamer, K.H. (2003). Achieving best practices in literacy education. In L.M. Morrow, L.B. Gambrell & M. Pressley (Eds.), *Best practices in literacy education* (2nd ed., pp. 333–346). New York: Guilford.

Darling-Hammond, L. (1995). Inequality and access to knowledge. In J.A. Banks & C.A.M. Banks (Eds.), *Handbook of research on multicultural education* (pp. 465–483). New York: Macmillan.

Donahue, P., Daane, M., & Grigg, W. (2003). *The nation's report card: Reading highlights 2003* (NCES 2004-452). Washington, DC: National Assessment of Educational Progress.

Duffy, G.G. (2004). Teachers who improve reading achievement: What research says about what they do and how to develop them. In D.S. Strickland & M.L. Kamil (Eds.), *Improving reading achievement through professional development* (pp. 3–22). Norwood, MA: Christopher-Gordon.

Fitzgerald, J. (1995). English-as-a-second-language reading instruction in the United States: A research review. *Journal of Reading Behavior, 27*, 115–152.

Grigg, W.S., Daane, M.C., Jin, Y., & Campbell, J.R. (2003). *The nation's report card: Reading 2002* (NCES 2003-521). Washington, DC: U.S. Department of Education, Institute for Education Sciences.

Highfield, K. (2003). *QAR and test preparation in a fourth grade classroom.* Unpublished dissertation, Oakland University, Rochester, MI.

Illinois State Board of Education. (2004). *Extended-response reading rubric.* Retrieved June 14, 2005, from www.isbe.net/assessment/readrubric.htm

Kimmel, E.A. (2001). *Anansi and the magic stick.* Ill. J. Stevens. New York: Holiday House.

Leu, D.J., & Kinzer, C.K. (2003). *Effective literacy instruction: Implementing best practice K–8* (5th ed.). Upper Saddle River, NJ: Pearson Education.

Mesmer, H.A.E., & Hutchins, E.J. (2002). Using QARs with charts and graphs. *The Reading Teacher, 56*, 21–27.

National Assessment Governing Board. (2004). *Reading Framework for the 2009 National Assessment of Educational Progress* (Contract No. ED-02-R-0007). Washington, DC: American Institutes for Research.

Newmann, F.M., Smith, B.S., Allensworth, E., & Bryk, A.S. (2001). Instructional program coherence: What it is and why it should guide school improvement policy. *Education, Evaluation, and Policy Analysis, 23*, 297–321.

Oakes, J., & Guiton, G. (1995). Matchmaking: The dynamics of high school tracking decisions. *American Educational Research Journal, 32*, 3–33.

Paulsen, G. (1987). *Hatchet.* New York: Puffin Books.

Pearson, P.D. (1985). Changing the face of reading comprehension instruction. *The Reading Teacher, 38*, 724–738.

Pressley, M. (2002). Comprehension strategies instruction. In C.C. Block & M. Pressley (Eds.), *Comprehension instruction: Research based best practices* (pp. 11–27). New York: Guilford.

Raphael, T.E., & Au, K.H. (2001). *SuperQAR for testwise students: Teacher resource guide, Guide 6.* Chicago: McGraw-Hill/Wright.

Raphael, T.E., & McKinney, J. (1983). An examination of 5th and 8th grade children's question answering behavior: An instructional study in metacognition. *Journal of Reading Behavior, 15*, 67–86.

Raphael, T.E., & Pearson, P.D. (1985). Increasing students' awareness of sources of information for answering questions. *American Educational Research Journal, 22*, 217–236.

Raphael, T.E., & Wonnacott, C.A. (1985). Heightening fourth-grade students' sensitivity to sources of information for answering comprehension questions. *Reading Research Quarterly, 20*, 282–296.

Reutzel, D.R., & Cooper, R.B. (2004). *Teaching children to read: Putting the pieces together* (4th ed.). Upper Saddle River, NJ: Pearson Education.

Roe, B.D., Smith, S.H., & Burns, P.C. (2005). *Teaching reading in today's elementary schools* (9th ed.). Boston: Houghton Mifflin.

Smith, M.L. (1991). Put to the test: The effects of external testing on teachers. *Educational Researcher, 20*, 8–11.

Snow, C.E. (2002). *Reading for understanding: Toward an R&D program in reading comprehension.* Santa Monica, CA: RAND.

Sweet, A.P., & Snow, C.E. (Eds.). (2003). *Rethinking reading comprehension: Solving problems in teaching of literacy.* New York: Guilford.

Taylor, B.M., Pearson, P.D., Peterson, D.P., & Rodriguez, M.C. (2003). Reading growth in high-poverty classrooms: The influence of teacher practices that encourage cognitive engagement in literacy learning. *The Elementary School Journal, 104*, 3–28.

Taylor, B.M., Pearson, P.D., Peterson, D.P., & Rodriguez, M.C. (2005). The CIERA school change framework: An evidenced-based approach to professional development and school reading improvement. *Reading Research Quarterly, 40*, 40–69.

Vacca, J.L., Vacca, R.T., Grove, M.K., Burkey, L., Lenhart, L., & McKeon, C. (2003). *Reading and learning to read* (5th ed.). Boston: Allyn & Bacon.

Viadero, D. (2004, April 21). Reform programs backed by research find fewer takers. *Education Week*, 1–5.

Questions for Reflection

- This article demonstrates that QAR instruction can be adjusted for use across grade levels and content areas because of the way the categories form a progression of difficulty. Which of the core categories would it be most appropriate to teach at your grade level and why? How would this differ in other grade levels?
- Think about the questions that are included on the high-stakes tests or standardized assessments used in your school. How can you use QAR to "unpack the task demands of different types of questions and alert students to these demands"? If you analyzed these questions, as the authors of this article have done in Table 4 in their analysis of NAEP sample passage questions, which QAR strategies could be used to help students answer these questions?

Tile Test: A Hands-On Approach for Assessing Phonics in the Early Grades

Kimberly A. Norman and Robert C. Calfee

The goal of early reading instruction is to help students move as quickly as possible toward independent comprehension of a broad range of texts. Phonics instruction is one gateway toward this goal by providing students with the skills to decode unfamiliar words encountered in new and challenging passages. All children should possess independent reading skills like the young reader who imagines fish being pulled by an invisible thread while reading *Swimmy* (Lionni, 1973). The challenge for growth in comprehension, sometimes referred to as the "fourth-grade slump" (Hirsch, 2003), is to promote in students a willingness—indeed, an enthusiasm—to move beyond known words and safe passages. The foundation for such progress lies in the acquisition of skills, strategies, and confidence in taking risks with print.

Increased attention to "proven practice," particularly in the area of phonics, has led to a call for increases in the amount of time devoted to phonics instruction in the primary grades (National Institute of Child Health and Human Development, 2000). The past three decades of cognitive research have revealed that *understanding* is critical to apply knowledge and strategies in new settings (Bransford, Brown, & Cocking, 2000). However, instruction in phonemic awareness and phonics typically relies on opportunities for practice rather than experiences that promote understanding. How do we help children develop strategic knowledge about the orthographic system and apply that knowledge? How can we assess strategic knowledge of the sort that will enable students in the later grades to independently access text?

In this article, we present an approach for thinking about assessment in a strategic manner. Imagine an ideal setting where you can sit with individual students and engage in a conversation designed to reveal a picture of what they know and can do. The Tile Test is designed to do just that; in a reasonable amount of time, you can examine students' understanding of the English orthographic system. It provides a hands-on interactive experience with letters and sounds for teachers who want to delve more deeply into students' underlying thinking. The test has four distinctive features. First is *efficiency*; much can be learned in a minimum amount of time (5–15 minutes) because you assess the fundamental concepts. The second feature is *flexibility*; the test is composed of individual modules of reading components so you can present the relevant sections to your students. Because it serves as a "shell," teachers can create new versions of the test that focus on the concepts they select. Third, the Tile Test offers rich *clinical opportunities*. Carefully constructed assessment activities allow you to see and hear what students know and how they know it. Finally, it provides the feedback needed to guide instruction.

Understanding Is Essential

We noted earlier that many programs do not emphasize understanding or strategic learning. Consequently, students are presented with isolated objectives that take time to learn and have limited transfer. Some might question whether there is more to phonics than a basic skill, and we have argued that understanding is essential

Reprinted from Norman, K.A., & Calfee, R.C. (2004). Tile Test: A hands-on approach for assessing phonics in the early grades. *The Reading Teacher, 58*(1), 42–52.

to promote rapid and transferable learning. Over the past decade we have examined ways to teach phonics for understanding and have developed tools that reveal students' knowledge and strategies for approaching words (Calfee, Norman, Trainin, & Wilson, 2001). Word Work (Calfee, 1998), a decoding-spelling framework, is an approach to teaching phonics that fosters students' exploration of the system and scaffolds students as they explain their thinking. The Word Work strategy builds on the historical and morphophonemic structure of English orthography (Venezky, 1999). Students in the primary grades need to rapidly master words from the Anglo-Saxon layer of English; Word Work focuses on the most productive letter–sound correspondences from this layer, with a particular emphasis on the central importance of vowels as the "glue" that connects consonants (Venezky).

Students begin with phonemic awareness by turning their attention to how they articulate or produce sounds in their mouths. *Articulatory phonemic awareness* draws upon principles from the motor theory of speech perception (Liberman & Mattingly, 1985) to guide students to examine the features of consonant production (manner, place, and voicing). As first graders attend to their speech, they explain that "the air comes out really fast—it explodes" when producing the popping sounds (plosives) *p*, *t*, and *k*. For the hissing sounds (fricatives), students' explorations of *f* and *s* lead to comments that "the air is coming out kind of slow" and "soft on your hand."

Once familiar with a small collection of consonants, students begin to use vowels (glue letters) to build words. The word *pat* is built by "putting your lips together and popping, gluing in the /a:::/ sound, and then tapping your tongue to the roof of your mouth." As students explain how they build words in this fashion, they use the *metaphonic principle*, learning to decode and spell by understanding the system rather than through rote memorization. Therefore, the teacher continually asks students to explain. For example, *dime* is pronounced that way because the final *e* tells the *i* to say its name. Notice that the system integrates decoding and spelling in a single process. Students' reflective talk supports conceptual understanding of English orthography because the talk mirrors their understanding—students become aware of what they know. This, in turn, facilitates the application of their knowledge and strategies to reading and writing across the curriculum (Vygotsky, 1978). (For a discussion of the research findings that support the promotion of metacognitive discussions in primary-grade classrooms, see Calfee & Norman, 2003; Trainin, Calfee, Norman, & Wilson, 2002.)

Determining Understanding

How can you as a teacher, whatever phonics program you are using, determine your students' understanding? First, you have to actively engage the students in working with the code so they can reveal what they know. Second, you need to study how students think about letter–sound correspondences and apply this knowledge. Both can be accomplished by having students work with letter tiles to construct words. Hands-on manipulation of letters reveals their ability to identify and represent phonemes, what they know about the role of vowels in words, and their application of decoding and spelling strategies. Third, you need to scaffold students' talk in order to understand what they know. For instance, how do students approach an unfamiliar word when decoding or spelling? Because metacognitive awareness is important for children to apply their knowledge in different contexts, answers to these questions are important to teachers. The Tile Test is built on these learning principles (Bransford et al., 2000).

In the next section, we present a comprehensive description of the tool, followed by directions for administering it with young children. In later sections we discuss how to analyze and interpret the results, use the information to plan instruction, and adapt the tool to fit your classroom context and curriculum.

Description of the Tile Test

The Tile Test is an individually administered diagnostic assessment designed to quickly evaluate early readers' and writers' understanding of letters, sounds, words, and sentences. A complete description and assessment materials are available online at www.metaphonics4kids.com. The skills tested include several of those generally accepted as necessary for successful beginning reading and spelling: phoneme awareness, letter and sound correspondences, decoding and spelling of words, sight-word reading, and the application of decoding and spelling in sentences. Additional activities have students respond to metalinguistic questions to assess the level of problem-solving strategies known and applied when using English orthography.

The Tile Test is intended for use with students in midkindergarten through first grade, although it may be used with students of any age or language background who are learning the building blocks of English orthography. An expanded version of the Tile Test assesses orthographic concepts extending through second grade and is described later. The entire test can be administered in one session of about 10–15 minutes. It is efficient because it quickly assesses fundamental concepts rather than testing everything. We have intentionally chosen consonants that are highly productive and vowels that are very distinctive. Complicating factors, such as r and l and vowel digraphs, are not included. For present purposes, we do not examine consonant blends or digraphs. We focus on the very core essentials that allow children to demonstrate that they understand the basic principles of English orthography.

Areas of knowledge tested in the first segment of the Tile Test include identification of letters' names and sounds, decoding and spelling of monosyllabic words (consonant–vowel–consonant units), and sight-word reading.

Letters and Sounds

The first section of the Tile Test focuses on the most basic decoding and spelling information—letter–sound correspondence. Using eight letters—two vowels (a, i) and six consonants (p, m, n, s, d, t), teachers can quickly gauge students' general knowledge of letter names and sounds when given visual and auditory stimuli. Letter inversions (p, d) and confusions (m, n) can also be noted in student responses.

Words

Decoding. This section of the test begins with reading simple consonant–vowel–consonant (CVC) words, built with lowercase letter tiles. The progression of the first three words of the series focuses on changes from the previous word of either the initial or final consonant (pat® sat® sam) to quickly assess students' processing and functional use of single letter–sound correspondences. The next five words require manipulation of more than one consonant or the vowel.

Spelling. The next section consists of building the progression of words with initial or final consonant variations followed by vowel variations. These tasks gauge students' ability to employ phonemic awareness of individual and blended sounds when spelling, as well as assess their knowledge of applying the vowel system in words. The students use individual, lowercase letter tiles for word building, eliminating the possible confounding that handwriting may introduce.

Metalinguistic Questions. During both the decoding and spelling sections, questions are asked to further clarify students' thinking and problem solving when working with words. To assess their knowledge of underlying principles the students are asked to explain *why* they gave their answers. For example, a student replied that she knew how to spell the word *sip* that way because she could "feel her tongue behind her lips" at the beginning of the word. Her response reveals an awareness of not only the sound of the letter but also how the letter is produced or feels—an effective skill when approaching unfamiliar words. By embedding the metalinguistic questions in the decoding and spelling activities, even the youngest students are capable of reflecting on and explaining their thinking processes.

Sight Words. This section assesses students' automaticity in reading 17 phonetically regular (e.g., cat, run) and irregular (e.g., the, me) words. Each word is presented on individual word tiles. Words used to begin sentences in the next segment of the test are presented with their initial letter capitalized, and if the word is also found within the sentence, it is presented a second time in lowercase format. Because the word *the* is used twice in one sentence, two word tiles are required.

Sentences

Areas of knowledge tested in the second segment of the Tile Test include the reading and building of sentences. Each sentence is constructed from the sight-word tiles used previously. In the first section, students are asked to read sentences ranging from three to seven words. The test administrator constructs each sentence. Because words such as *sit*, *sat*, *cat*, and *can* are included, some weaknesses in students' word reading strategies can be identified. In the final section of the test, students are asked to build sentences read to them by the test administrator. Students are asked to read the sentences after building, which allows for self-correction. In addition to word recognition, this activity demonstrates students' ability to hold sentences of varying lengths in working memory.

Validity and Reliability of the Tile Test

The Tile Test's validity was tested by examining the relationship of performance on the Tile Test with measures of early reading commonly used in schools. The data show that there is a high degree of agreement (concurrent validity) between the Tile Test and the Developmental Reading Assessment (Celebration Press, 1997), a measure of reading fluency and accuracy ($r = .74$, $p < .001$), suggesting both instruments measure similar constructs. In addition, we found moderate to strong relationships with performance on the Scholastic (1997) Phonemic Awareness Test ($r = .60$, $p < .001$), spelling performance in writing samples ($r = .65$, $p < .001$), and writing assessed with a holistic rubric ($r = .70$, $p < .001$). These data provide further evidence of the relationship between performance on the Tile Test and tasks used to measure students' ability to decode and spell in reading and writing tasks.

The Tile Test has been shown to be a reliable measure of basic decoding and spelling skills. Reliability addresses the trustworthiness of all facets of the test. Cronbach's (1951) alpha, a statistic used to measure the internal consistency of an instrument, was calculated at kindergarten and first grade. These coefficients were .93 for the kindergarten sample and .98 for first grade, indicating that it can be appropriately used in the assessment of individuals. Another index of consistency, test–retest reliability, produced a coefficient alpha of .87–.97.

Administering the Tile Test

This section describes the preparation of assessment materials and provides general guidelines for assessing students. As noted previously, the materials are available online or can be easily created (see the recording sheet in Figure 1 for required materials). (Tip: The Century Gothic font presents *a* and *g* in a format familiar to young students.)

Preparing for the Assessment

Materials. Our usual practice is to use lowercase letter tiles with a horizontal line across the bottom to support students' directionality (see Figure 2). The vowels are distinguished from the consonants by the thickness of the directional line—thick line for vowels, thin line for consonants. Our website includes separate sets of vowels and consonants allowing the vowels to be printed on a colored background, thus offering another distinguishing feature.

Environment. Select a work area large enough to allow the student to easily manipulate the letter tiles in front of him or her. The test administrator should also be able to reach the tiles

Figure 1
Tile Test Recording Sheet

Student ______________________________ Date__________

Letters and sounds: Display letter tiles m, a, p, i, s, t, d, n.
"Here are some letters. I'll say the name of a letter and ask you to point to the letter. Point to the card that has the letter *m*." (Record. Continue procedure with each letter.)

"Now, I'll point to a tile and you'll tell me two things about the letter. First, the *name* of the letter and, second, the *sound* that it makes." (Record.)

	Identification	Name	Sound		Identification	Name	Sound
m				s			
a				t			
p				d			
i				n			

Words: Add letter tiles f, b.
Decoding. "Now let's put some letters together to make words. I'll go first and make a word, then I'll ask you to read it for me." (Manipulate only necessary letters. Stop after *sat* and ask the first metalinguistic question.)

pat ______________ fin ______________
sat* ______________ pit ______________
sam ______________ tab ______________
fan ______________ mid ______________

*Metalinguistic question: "How did you know to say *sat* (or other pronunciation) that way?" ______________

Metalinguistic question: Rebuild the word that the student had the most difficulty with but decoded correctly. "How did you know to say ______________ that way?" ______________

Spelling. "Now, I'll say a word, and you'll build it for me." (As you dictate, clearly articulate by "stretching and exaggerating." Example: tan = /ta:::n:::/. Stop after *tad* and ask the first metalinguistic question.)

tan ______________ sip ______________
tad* ______________ tin ______________
mad ______________ pad ______________
sap ______________ fit ______________

*Metalinguistic question: "How did you know to build (spell) *tad* that way?" ______________

Metalinguistic question: Rebuild the word that the student had the most difficulty with but built correctly. "How did you know to build ______________ that way?" ______________

Sight-word reading. Lay out the collection of word cards. "I'll show you some words, and you read each one." (Record.)

I		me		the		a	
is		at		look		dog	
cat		big		map		can	
sat		fat		sit		on	
run							

(continued)

Figure 1 *(continued)*
Tile Test Recording Sheet

Sentences:
Reading. "I'll make a sentence with some words, and you'll read the sentence for me."

I can run.__________
Look at me.__________
I sat on the cat.__________
The map is big.__________
I can look at the dog.__________
Sit the dog on the fat cat.__________

Building. "Now I'll say a sentence, and you'll build it for me." (Ask the student to read the sentence after building it. Record the sentence built and the student's read of it.)

I can sit.__________
The dog is fat.__________
Look at the map.__________
A dog can look at me.__________
The big cat sat on the dog.__________

General observations:__________

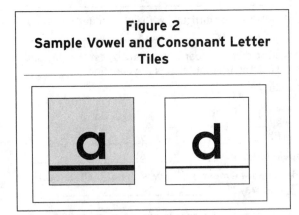

Figure 2
Sample Vowel and Consonant Letter Tiles

a d

comfortably in order to manipulate the tiles at several points during the assessment.

Assessing Students

The first few minutes of the session can be used to build rapport, share the purpose of the session, and help the student to relax. Most find the Tile Test to be an enjoyable experience. We encourage you to approach the situation with an attitude of curiosity; the conversations that ensue from active construction of words and sentences should be fueled by your genuine interest in the student's knowledge and strategies. Because finding the student's best performance is the goal of the Tile Test, allow for conversation and use the probing questions provided.

Letters and Sounds

Begin by laying out the eight individual letter tiles and tell the student that you will say the name of a letter and that he or she should point to that letter. If the student responds correctly, place a check or plus under the "identification" heading on the recording sheet. If incorrect, record the student's response. Continue this process with each letter. The order is not important; you may choose to begin with a letter that you are confident the student will know in order to build early success. Then, explain that you will point to a letter tile and ask the student to respond by saying the name of the letter and the sound that it makes. Check the correct responses and write in the incorrect responses. Restate directions as appropriate. For example, if the student says the name of a letter only, say, "What sound does that letter make?"

Words

Decoding. Add the second collection of letter tiles to the eight used in the previous section. Check that both you and the student can easily reach the tiles and that there is enough space directly in front of the student to build words. To begin, explain that you will put some letters together to make words and that you will ask the student to read them for you.

Build the first word, *pat*, and ask the student to read it to you. Correct responses are marked with a check or plus. For incorrect responses, record the student's exact pronunciation and behaviors, including self-corrections (recorded as SC). You may use the phonetic transcription or your own system. Segmented words read without blending sounds will be marked with slashes between sounds (e.g., /t/ /a/ /p/).

As you build the second word, *sat*, manipulate only the necessary letter tiles. In this case, exchange only the initial consonant, leaving the *-at* in place. After the student decodes *sat* (identified by an asterisk on the recording sheet), ask the first metalinguistic question to tap into the student's understanding of his or her decoding strategy: "How did you know to say *sat* that way?" Record student responses. Use probes as necessary to tap into the full response of the student. For example, if the student provides a limited response or a shrug or says, "I don't know," ask, "What were you thinking or looking at?" "How did you know how to say *sat* instead of *mat*?" (Note: If the student pronounces *sat* differently [e.g., *sam*], use the student's pronunciation when asking the metalinguistic question "How did you know to say *sam* that way?")

Continue through the word list exchanging the minimum number of letters required to progress from one word to the next. At the end of the word decoding section, ask the second metalinguistic question. First, rebuild the word that the student had the most difficulty with but sounded out correctly. Then say, "This word was kind of hard. You were right when you said (word) for this word. How did you know to say it that way?" If the student is reluctant to answer, provide and document probing questions. If the student reads all words with equal ease, select one that required manipulation of the vowel (e.g., *sit*). Because valuable information can also be gained from students' incorrect attempts, if none of the words are read correctly, select one that is of interest to you.

Spelling. In this activity, the student becomes the word builder—a role that most are eager to assume. Tell the student that you will say a word and that he or she will use the letter tiles to spell the word. When dictating the words, articulate clearly by stretching and exaggerating so the student can attend to each sound (e.g., /ta:::p/, /s:::a:::t/) but do not break the word into individual sounds (/t/ /a/ /p/). Plosives (t, p, k) cannot be stretched, but they can be exaggerated; other consonants, including fricatives (s, v, f) and nasals (m, n), can be stretched by continuing the airflow.

Say the first word, *tan*, and ask the student to build it for you. Once built, ask the student to read the word or "check it." Record the word exactly as the student builds it, noting any self-corrections made along the way. Move to the next word, *tad*, by stating, "If this word says *tan* (previously built word) what would you have to do to make it say *tad*?" Encourage the student to listen to the entire word before building. After the child builds *tad*, ask the first metalinguistic question (denoted by an asterisk in Figure 1): "How did you know to build *tad* that way?" If necessary, draw from and document the use of the following probes: "What were you thinking when I said the word?" "How did you know to add the *d* instead of a *p*?" "I noticed your mouth moving. How did that help you?"

If the student gives an incorrect response on a particular item, record the response (including behavior and language) and then go to the next word. Do not correct the student in the sense of making the change. For example, if the student spelled *tan* as *fat*, you would not say, "That's not *tan*, that's *fat*." Rather, you would say, "You built the word *fat*. What would you have to do to spell the word *tad*?" When recording students' responses, also note their building strategies (e.g., manipulates all tiles or the minimum required).

At the end of the spelling section, ask the second metalinguistic question. Rebuild the word that the student had the most difficulty with but spelled correctly. Say, "You were right when you built (word) that way. How did you know to spell it that way?" If few words are spelled correctly, you may want to ask the metalinguistic question of an incorrect attempt.

Sight Words. Set the letter tiles aside to begin the sight-word reading section. Lay out the collection of word tiles in front of the student and ask him or her to read the words. If the student looks over the words and does not respond, point to a word that you anticipate he or she would know (e.g., I, the, a, cat) in order to build success. Ask, "What is this word?" Once the student has gained momentum, support by saying, "Find other words you know and read them to me." You can support a situation that may be overwhelming for a young reader.

Sentences

Use the sight words from the previous activity to read and build sentences. To begin, build the first sentence and ask the student to read the sentence to you. Record the student's response, including self-corrections and decoding strategies. Continue this process with each of the sentences or until the student is unable to attempt working with the words. Then, move to the building section and have the student become the sentence builder. Say the sentence and ask the student to make it for you. We recommend that the student read the sentence after building to allow for self-correction and to provide additional assessment information. As you continue this process, dictate each sentence slowly and encourage the student to listen to the entire sentence before building. You may choose to read each sentence twice, but in order to assess short-term memory, do not dictate one word at a time.

Decision Rules and Scoring

The purpose of the Tile Test is to assess student performance and feed that information into instruction. Therefore, it is not intended that the administrator instruct students on the concepts of the tool. Students are not provided specific feedback, whether correct or incorrect. General responses should be positive: "You're doing a great job, let's move to the next activity." The two criteria used to decide when to stop are accuracy and speed. If the students' responses are incorrect, even if they are moving through the activities quickly, you probably do not want to continue. In addition, if they struggle with an activity and take a long time then you probably should not continue the specific activity. If students have difficulty in one section (e.g., decoding words), stop the assessment in that section and move to the next section. There are two reasons for attempting each section of the test. First, knowledge in one area may not be indicative of knowledge in another; for example, a student may build words more easily than decode words. Second, the Tile Test was designed around a particular curriculum, and students may have been through a different set of curriculum experiences.

The total score and subsection scores make it possible to monitor growth over time. The total possible points for each subsection are located in Table 1. When scoring, award credit for self-corrections. No partial credit is given.

The metalinguistic questions are scored against the rubric in Table 2. Consider the student's responses to the two decoding and two spelling items when making decisions. To score the sentence reading and building sections, assign 1 point for each complete sentence read (or built) correctly.

Table 1
Scoring Totals

Test section	Total points
Letters and sounds	
Letter identification	8
Letter name	8
Letter sound	8
Words	
Decoding	8
Spelling	8
Metalinguistic	6
awareness	17
Sight-word reading	
Sentences	
Reading	6
Building	5

Table 2
Tile Test: Metalinguistic Rubric

0	No response. "I don't know."
1	"I know it." "My mom taught me." "I'm smart."
2	Recognition of letters (e.g., "I looked at the letters").
3	Recognition of sounds (e.g., "I sound it out," "I listen to the sounds").
4	Partial linking sounds to letters (e.g., "It starts with a p /p/, then /l/") or partial analogy (e.g., "Pat is like cat").
5	Explains the spelling of each sound or full analogy (e.g., "Pat is like cat, but it starts with a /p/").
6	Explains how sounds are articulated. "It starts with /p/ my lips are together and the air pops out, my tongue is resting in the middle of my mouth...."

Instructional Decisions

The results of the Tile Test can be used to help teachers identify the level of understanding students have about letters, sounds, words, and sentences, as well as the strategies they employ and their awareness of strategy use. Students' responses provide valuable qualitative information that immediately informs instruction. For example, Anthony (all student names are pseudonyms), a kindergarten student, could identify the eight letters in the Tile Test when asked to point to each and provided the name and sound of the six consonants presented in isolation (no vowels). However, when asked to use the letters at the word level, he was unable to link the sounds to the letters when decoding (see Table 3) and had minimal representation of consonants when spelling. When spelling, Anthony identified individual sounds in speech and represented them with letters.

Irvin also identified each of the eight letters in the Tile Test and correctly provided the names and sounds of the consonants and the vowel *a* (short pronunciation) in isolation. He responded that the name of the letter *i* is *e* and is pronounced as /e/

Table 3
Students' Word Decoding and Spelling

	Anthony	Irvin
Decoding		
pat	p-a-t	/p/ /t/
sat	[no attempt]	/s/ /t/
sam		/s/ /f/
fan		/f/ /h/
sit		/s/ /n/
Spelling		
tan	n t	tan
map		/ma/, map
sip		/sa/, sp
fin		/p/ /a/, fn
sap		/s/ /ap/ /a:::p/,sap

(long pronunciation). When decoding (see Table 3), he identified initial and final consonant sounds but was unable to blend the sounds to form a word. Although he knew the sound for *a* when presented in isolation, he did not identify the vowel in the context of words. When building words with the vowel *a*, Irvin represented each sound with a letter tile. When responding to the metalinguistic question of how he knew to spell *sip* that way (as *sp*), he referenced the vowel stating, "It's not an *a*."

Both these students would benefit from instruction that includes opportunities to manipulate letter tiles to build and decode words. Because Anthony demonstrated letter–sound correspondence for a collection of consonants, he is ready to study vowels and their function in words: The vowel a glues the consonants together to create a word. Prompts to "stretch and exaggerate" when articulating words will help Anthony attend to each and every sound and will help Irvin blend rather than separate sounds. Many children, in our experience, when taught to separate phonemes to decode a word (e.g., /c/-/a/-/t/), must then be taught to blend. Therefore, we never ask a child to break a word into its individual phonemes, so they do not have to be taught to blend the phonemes. Finally, prompts to explain their thinking while working with words will facilitate their application of letter–sound knowledge during phonics instruction and when reading and writing throughout the day.

Use of the Tile Test

The Tile Test can be used to collect information before, during, and after instruction to check students' prior knowledge and progress and to plan for future instruction. We suggest that the teacher begin by administering it to a few students.

After you have gained some familiarity with the test, you will find that you can adapt the test for your own needs. One adaptation that takes advantage of the distinct segments that assess different orthographic concepts is to use portions of the test to follow up instruction with all of your students or six to eight focal students. Consider reading ability, language background, gender, and other important factors in your context when selecting students so you gain information regarding the full range of your class.

A second adaptation is to use the Tile Test with small groups of four to six students. You should have a reasonable degree of comfort with the test in order to scaffold students' metaphonic responses. Because there is not always time to assess each student individually, the group administration is well worth the effort. Sample "group assessments" are available on our website.

The third option is to adapt the test to a whole-class administration once students understand the format of the test, have worked with tiles, and have become accustomed to questions that prompt them to talk about the strategies they use when decoding and spelling words. Each student (or pair) has a collection of tiles. As you give a task (e.g., to build the synthetic word *wembick*), walk around and ask students to explain their problem-solving strategies (use the metalinguistic questions and probes presented earlier). Careful note-taking of your observations can guide your instructional planning.

The Tile Test also serves as a shell for incorporating a broad range of orthographic patterns so that you can adapt the test to your curriculum content. After the initial administration, assess different collections of letters and select words to decode and spell that are based on orthographic concepts being studied. For example, when instruction focuses on students' ability to work with the entire collection of short vowels, make the appropriate substitutions in the decoding and spelling segment. Item selection should be made in a principled way. For example, be careful about items like *r*, *l*, and *w*, which influence the vowel pronunciation (include intentionally when appropriate). An expanded version of the Tile Test is available on our website to provide guidance in creating your own versions and to provide a tool for assessing more complex orthographic concepts (appropriate for use with students through second grade). This version includes the use of

Figure 3
Decoding Real and Synthetic Word Activity From the Expanded Version of the Tile Test

pat__________	vute__________
sat __________	flass __________
sam__________	lodded __________
hin __________	wembick__________

individual real and synthetic words (see Figure 3). The synthetic word series assesses knowledge of the basic consonant–vowel–consonant building blocks in monosyllabic and polysyllabic words and includes consonant blends and the long vowel marking system. Synthetic words are included in both the decoding and spelling activities to place the emphasis on sound–symbol relationships. This rationale is supported by research (Felton & Wood, 1992) showing that synthetic word reading is correlated with reading success more highly than verbal IQ. Additional activities have students respond to metalinguistic questions to assess the problem-solving strategies known and applied. Finally, phoneme awareness is tapped by questions about the articulation of consonant sounds in real and synthetic words.

The Tile Test Is Effective and Flexible

The Tile Test provides teachers with an efficient and effective tool for assessing young students' understanding of the English orthographic system. Their problem-solving strategies and awareness of strategy use when decoding and spelling new or unfamiliar words surface through the metaphonic discussions. The flexibility of the tool provides teachers with multiple ways to adapt it for classroom use. Its structure and the ability to match items to the curriculum help teachers think about what is important to know and how to assess the different constructs of literacy. Careful analysis of the students' responses to the activities and metalinguistic questions, coupled with observations of student behaviors in various classroom literacy contexts, can help teachers identify student knowledge before instruction, monitor the impact of instruction, and guide future instruction.

References

Bransford, J.D., Brown, A.L., & Cocking, R.R. (Eds.). (2000). *How people learn: Brain, mind, experience, and school.* Washington, DC: National Academy Press.

Calfee, R.C. (1998). Phonics and phonemes: Learning to decode and spell in a literature-based program. In J.L. Metsala & L.C. Ehri (Eds.), *Word recognition in beginning literacy* (pp. 315–340). Mahwah, NJ: Erlbaum.

Calfee, R.C., & Norman, K.A. (2003, April). *Decoding and spelling instruction: Which factors matter most?* Paper presented at the annual meeting of the American Educational Research Association, Chicago, IL.

Calfee, R.C., Norman, K.A., Trainin, G., & Wilson, K.M. (2001). Conducting a design experiment for improving early literacy: What we learned in school last year. In C.M. Roller (Ed.), *Learning to teach reading: Setting the research agenda* (pp. 166–179). Newark, DE: International Reading Association.

Celebration Press. (1997). *Developmental reading assessment.* Glenview, IL: Addison-Wesley.

Cronbach, L.J. (1951). Coefficient alpha and the internal structure of tests. *Psychometrika, 16,* 297–334.

Felton, R.H., & Wood, F.B. (1992). A reading level match study of nonword reading skills in poor readers with varying IQ. *Journal of Learning Disabilities, 25,* 318–326.

Hirsch, E.D. (2003). Reading comprehension requires knowledge—of words and the world: Scientific insights into the fourth-grade slump and the nation's stagnant comprehension scores. *American Educator, 27*(1), 10–48.

Liberman, A.M., & Mattingly, I.G. (1985). The motor theory of speech perception revised. *Cognition, 21,* 1–36.

Lionni, L. (1973). *Swimmy.* New York: Pantheon.

National Institute of Child Health and Human Development. (2000). *Report of the National Reading Panel. Teaching children to read: An evidence-based assessment of the scientific research literature on reading and its implications for reading instruction* (NIH Publication No. 00-4769). Washington, DC: U.S. Government Printing Office.

Scholastic. (1997). *Literacy place: Kindergarten test of phonemic awareness.* Jefferson City, MO: Author.

Trainin, G., Calfee, R.C., Norman, K.A., & Wilson, K. (2002, April). *Supporting metacognitive development: The impact of teacher practice.* Paper presented at the annual convention of the International Reading Association, San Francisco, CA.

Venezky, R.L. (1999). *The American way of spelling: The structure and origins of American English orthography.* New York: Guilford.

Vygotsky, L.S. (1978). *Mind in society: The development of higher psychological processes* (M. Cole, V. John-Steiner, S. Scribner, & E. Souberman, Eds. & Trans.). Cambridge, MA: Harvard University Press. (Original work published 1934)

Questions for Reflection

- As described in the article, the Tile Test can be modified to incorporate a broad range of orthographic patterns so that you can adapt the test to meet the needs of your classroom. How would you go about adapting the Tile Test so that it more specifically applies to your curriculum content? Because it serves as a "shell," what new versions of the test could you create to focus on specific concepts—and on which concepts do you think it's important to focus?
- The authors suggest that when first starting out with the Tile Test, teachers should begin by administering it to six to eight focal students. How would you go about selecting these students for the initial Tile Tests?

Assessing Adolescents' Motivation to Read

Sharon M. Pitcher, Lettie K. Albright, Carol J. DeLaney, Nancy T. Walker, Krishna Seunarinesingh, Stephen Mogge, Kathy N. Headley, Victoria Gentry Ridgeway, Sharon Peck, Rebecca Hunt, and Pamela J. Dunston

Interviewer: How much time do you spend on the computer a day?

Adolescent: Two hours every day.

Interviewer: What do you usually do?

Adolescent: Search and play games on the Internet. I go to Ask Jeeves and ask questions. Draw things and write e-mails, print them out and hang them up. Shop for my mother so she can go to the store and buy things. Read about things that are going on around the world. I read magazines and music on the Internet and about getting into college and things.

(The adolescent was a sixth grader in an urban public school when interviewed.)

How to increase students' motivation to read has long been a priority in what teachers want to know. This inquiry usually starts with the question "Do adolescents read?" Recent studies have suggested that few adolescents choose to read on their own (Strommen & Mates, 2004). Gambrell, Palmer, Codling, and Mazzoni (1996) developed and standardized the Motivation to Read Profile (MRP) to aid elementary teachers in assessing the motivation of their students. In the study described in this article, 11 researchers worked as a team to revise the Motivation to Read Profile to be used with adolescents and then assess students using the Adolescent Motivation to Read Profile (AMRP) at eight sites in the United States and Trinidad. Our work suggests that teachers need to ask different questions of adolescents than of younger children. Some of the questions that we found ourselves asking were the following: How do teachers define reading? What kinds of reading will motivate adolescents today? How can these types of reading be incorporated into secondary classrooms?

Motivation to Read: The Roles of Engagement, Self-Efficacy, and Purpose for Reading

According to Guthrie and Wigfield (1997), motivation is defined in terms of "beliefs, values, needs and goals that individuals have" (p. 5). Thus, the closer that literacy activities and tasks match these values, needs, and goals, the greater the likelihood that students will expend effort and sustain interest in them. When some students judge reading and literacy activities to be unrewarding, too difficult, or not worth the effort because they are peripheral to their interests and needs, they can become *nonreaders* (Strommen & Mates, 2004) or *aliterate adolescents* (Alvermann, 2003) who are capable of reading but choose not to do so.

Generally, the two strands of research on adolescent motivation to read focus on

(a) adolescents as meaning-makers in out-of-school contexts that meet their competency needs (Alvermann, 2003;

Reprinted from Pitcher, S.M., Albright, L.K., DeLaney, C.J., Walker, N.T., Seunarinesingh, K., Mogge, S., Headley, K.N., Ridgeway, V.G., Peck, S., Hunt, R., & Dunston, P.J. (2007). Assessing adolescents' motivation to read. *Journal of Adolescent & Adult Literacy, 50*(5), 378-396.

O'Brien, 2001; Strommen & Mates, 2004), and

(b) adolescents as victims of positioning by schools that have devalued literacy activities at which they are literate and competent-such as media-text, electronic games, electronic messaging, and visual productions-and instead have valued primarily print-based, content-area texts (Alvermann, 2001b; O'Brien; Smith & Wilhelm, 2004) that students have difficulty comprehending.

In each case, school practices act as disincentives because they fail to take into account what motivates adolescents to read.

Although school reading is based on traditional textbooks (Alvermann & Moore, 1991), out-of-school reading involves a range of multimedia (Bean, Bean, & Bean, 1999). Traditional texts, according to the New London Group (1996), are "page-bound, official, standard forms of the national language" (p. 61) that limit the possibility for multiple discourses in the classroom. "An expanded concept of 'text' must transcend print-based texts to also include various electronic media and adolescents' own cultural and social understandings" (Phelps, 2006, p. 4).

Thus, motivation to read is a complex construct that influences readers' choices of reading material, their willingness to engage in reading, and thus their ultimate competence in reading, especially related to academic reading tasks. Although much is known about adolescent motivation to read, the existing research can be supplemented by information that contributes to our understanding of motivation to read amongst a sample that is diverse in geography, ethnicity, school type, school system, and gender. This information is pertinent given the range of findings about adolescents' motivation to read.

Revision of the Motivation to Read Profile for Adolescents

Yearly, at the National Reading Conference, attendees have the opportunity to participate in a study group on adolescent reading research. During the 2002 conference, the participants in the study group decided that understanding what motivates teens to read could be the key to improving reading instruction at the secondary level. Many of us were familiar with the Motivation to Read Profile (Gambrell et al., 1996) that was designed to look at motivation of elementary school readers from different perspectives using two different types of instruments. We decided to revise the MRP to provide a flexible instrument for secondary teachers to better understand their students' motivations to read.

The MRP includes two instruments: the reading survey and the conversational interview. The reading survey, a group-administered instrument, consists of 20 items using a four-point scale assessing self-concept as a reader (10 items) and value of reading (10 items). The conversational interview is individually administered with 14 scripted items that are open-ended to encourage free response and assess narrative reading, informational reading, and general reading.

Working with the original MRP and using an e-mail listserv for in-depth conversations, we discussed and revised items for the AMRP using recommendations from adolescent research and our own experience working with teens. We reviewed the research literature and revised the language of the instrument to appeal to teens. Using adolescent research as our guide, we included more questions on the AMRP about using electronic resources (Alvermann, 2001a), schoolwork and projects that students enjoyed (Wasserstein, 1995), and what students choose to read and write on their own (Roe, 1997).

We revised some language in the AMRP reading survey (see Figure 1) to be more adolescent friendly ("When I grow up" was changed to "As an adult"; "When I am in a group talking about stories" was changed to "When I am in a group talking about what we are reading"; and "I would like for my teacher to read books out loud in my class" was changed to "I would like my teachers to read out loud in my classes"). We changed the grades surveyed and added an item on race or ethnicity to help us better understand

Figure 1
Adolescent Motivation to Read Profile Reading Survey

Name:______________________________ Date:________________

Sample 1: I am in ______________.
- ❑ Sixth grade
- ❑ Seventh grade
- ❑ Eighth grade
- ❑ Ninth grade
- ❑ Tenth grade
- ❑ Eleventh grade
- ❑ Twelfth grade

Sample 2: I am a ______________.
- ❑ Female
- ❑ Male

Sample 3: My race/ethnicity is ______________.
- ❑ African-American
- ❑ Asian/Asian American
- ❑ Caucasian
- ❑ Hispanic
- ❑ Native American
- ❑ Multi-racial/Multi-ethnic
- ❑ Other: Please specify ______________

1. My friends think I am ______________.
- ❑ a very good reader
- ❑ a good reader
- ❑ an OK reader
- ❑ a poor reader

2. Reading a book is something I like to do.
- ❑ Never
- ❑ Not very often
- ❑ Sometimes
- ❑ Often

3. I read ______________.
- ❑ not as well as my friends
- ❑ about the same as my friends
- ❑ a little better than my friends
- ❑ a lot better than my friends

4. My best friends think reading is ______________.
- ❑ really fun
- ❑ fun
- ❑ OK to do
- ❑ no fun at all

5. When I come to a word I don't know, I can ______________.
- ❑ almost always figure it out
- ❑ sometimes figure it out
- ❑ almost never figure it out
- ❑ never figure it out

6. I tell my friends about good books I read.
- ❑ I never do this
- ❑ I almost never do this
- ❑ I do this some of the time
- ❑ I do this a lot

7. When I am reading by myself, I understand ______________.
- ❑ almost everything I read
- ❑ some of what I read
- ❑ almost none of what I read
- ❑ none of what I read

8. People who read a lot are ______________.
- ❑ very interesting
- ❑ interesting
- ❑ not very interesting
- ❑ boring

9. I am ______________.
- ❑ a poor reader
- ❑ an OK reader
- ❑ a good reader
- ❑ a very good reader

(continued)

Figure 1 *(continued)*
Adolescent Motivation to Read Profile Reading Survey

Name:______________________________ Date:______________

10. I think libraries are ______________.
- ❑ a great place to spend time
- ❑ an interesting place to spend time
- ❑ an OK place to spend time
- ❑ a boring place to spend time

11. I worry about what other kids think about my reading ______________.
- ❑ every day
- ❑ almost every day
- ❑ once in a while
- ❑ never

12. Knowing how to read well is ______________.
- ❑ not very important
- ❑ sort of important
- ❑ important
- ❑ very important

13. When my teacher asks me a question about what I have read, I ______________.
- ❑ can never think of an answer
- ❑ have trouble thinking of an answer
- ❑ sometimes think of an answer
- ❑ always think of an answer

14. I think reading is ______________.
- ❑ a boring way to spend time
- ❑ an OK way to spend time
- ❑ an interesting way to spend time
- ❑ a great way to spend time

15. Reading is ______________.
- ❑ very easy for me
- ❑ kind of easy for me
- ❑ kind of hard for me
- ❑ very hard for me

16. As an adult, I will spend ______________.
- ❑ none of my time reading
- ❑ very little time reading
- ❑ some of my time reading
- ❑ a lot of my time reading

17. When I am in a group talking about what we are reading, I ______________.
- ❑ almost never talk about my ideas
- ❑ sometimes talk about my ideas
- ❑ almost always talk about my ideas
- ❑ always talk about my ideas

18. I would like for my teachers to read out loud in my classes ______________.
- ❑ every day
- ❑ almost every day
- ❑ once in a while
- ❑ never

19. When I read out loud I am a ______________.
- ❑ poor reader
- ❑ OK reader
- ❑ good reader
- ❑ very good reader

20. When someone gives me a book for a present, I feel ______________.
- ❑ very happy
- ❑ sort of happy
- ❑ sort of unhappy
- ❑ unhappy

Note. Adapted with permission from the Motivation to Read Profile (Gambrell, Palmer, Codling, & Mazzoni, 1996)

the differences and similarities of various populations.

Gambrell et al. (1996) developed and field tested a 14-item conversational interview to be used as a complement to the survey. The MRP authors indicated that the conversational interview flexibly probes for more in-depth understanding and authentic insights on students' reading experiences, attitudes, and motivations. Gambrell et al. further suggested that the instrument could be used by teachers for instructional decision making with individual students and groups of students. The AMRP conversational interview (see Figure 2) continues these emphases. Finally, the MRP authors encouraged teachers and researchers to extend, modify, and adapt the interview for particular needs and, indeed, that is what we did to create the AMRP. Understanding that school reading experiences expand and diversify in junior and senior high school, the group added the following questions:

- In what class do you most like to read?
- In what class do you feel the reading is the most difficult?
- Have any of your teachers done something with reading that you really enjoy?

As an open-ended, free response, semi-structured interview, these questions (as the authors of the original instrument also suggested) likely lead to additional questions such as the following:

- Why?
- What happens in that class?
- Can you give an example?
- How did that make you feel?
- How is that different from ________?

As noted above, recent research on adolescent literacy reveals that adolescents are using literacy for many purposes outside of school that may bear little resemblance to traditional academic literacy purposes. Therefore, the conversational interview was adapted to include questions and prompts to yield responses related to technological, family, and out-of-school literacies.

To learn more about technology uses, we added the following questions:

- Do you have a computer in your home?
- How much time do you spend on the computer each day?
- What do you usually do on the computer?
- What do you like to read on the Internet?

To learn more about literacy practices in home and family life, the following questions were added:

- Do you write letters or emails to friends or family?
- Do you share any of the following reading materials with members of your family: newspapers, magazines, religious materials, games?

To further explore nonacademic adolescent literacy, we added the following questions:

- Do you share and discuss books, magazines, or other reading material (with friends or others)?
- Do you belong to any clubs or organizations for which you use reading and writing?

These questions lend themselves to alteration and follow-up, enabling the interviewer to probe more deeply and broadly in light of adolescents' responses. The interviewer decides whether individual or small-group interviews are appropriate. Individual interviews may yield more open and free responses while group interviews may lead to discussion of popular or emerging literacy practices. The interviewer could also conduct the interview over a few sessions covering some topics in groups and others individually.

We revised the teacher directions for the reading survey (see Figure 3) to reflect the changes we made and used the original teacher directions for the conversational interview (see Figure 4). The original MRP reading survey scoring directions (see Figure 5) and scoring sheet (see Figure 6) are used to score the AMRP. Also see

Figure 2
Adolescent Motivation to Read Profile Conversational Interview

Name ____

A. Emphasis: Narrative text
Suggested prompt (designed to engage student in a natural conversation): I have been reading a good book. I was talking with...about it last night. I enjoy talking about what I am reading with my friends and family. Today, I would like to hear about what you have been reading and if you share it.

1. Tell me about the most interesting story or book you have read recently. Take a few minutes to think about it (wait time). Now, tell me about the book.

   Probe: What else can you tell me? Is there anything else?

2. How did you know or find out about this book?

   (Some possible responses: assigned, chosen, in school, out of school)

3. Why was this story interesting to you?

B. Emphasis: Informational text
Suggested prompt (designed to engage student in a natural conversation): Often we read to find out or learn about something that interests us. For example, a student I recently worked with enjoyed reading about his favorite sports teams on the Internet. I am gong to ask you some questions about what you like to read to learn about.

1. Think about something important that you learned recently, not from your teacher and not from television, but from something you have read. What did you read about? (Wait time.) Tell me about what you learned.

   Probe: What else could you tell me? Is there anything else?

2. How did you know or find out about reading material on this?

   (Some possible responses: assigned, chosen, in school, out of school)

(continued)

Figure 2 *(continued)*
Adolescent Motivation to Read Profile Conversational Interview

Name ____

3. Why was reading this important to you?

C. Emphasis: General reading

1. Did you read anything at home yesterday? What?

2. Do you have anything at school (in your desk, locker, or book bag) today that you are reading?

   Tell me about them.

3. Tell me about your favorite author.

4. What do you think you have to learn to be a better reader?

5. Do you know about any books right now that you'd like to read?

   Tell me about them.

6. How did you find out about these books?

7. What are some things that get you really excited about reading?

   Tell me about....

(continued)

Figure 2 *(continued)*
Adolescent Motivation to Read Profile Conversational Interview

Name ______________________________

8. Who gets you really interested and excited about reading?

   Tell me more about what they do.

9. Do you have a computer in your home?

   If they answer yes, ask the following questions:

   How much time do you spend on the computer a day?

   What do you usually do?

   What do you like to read when you are on the Internet?

   If they answer no, ask the following questions:

   If you did have a computer in your home, what would you like to do with it?

   Is there anything on the Internet that you would like to be able to read?

D. Emphasis: School reading in comparison to home reading

1. In what class do you most like to read?

   Why?

(continued)

Figure 2 *(continued)*
Adolescent Motivation to Read Profile Conversational Interview

Name ____

2. In what class do you feel the reading is the most difficult?

   Why?

3. Have any of your teachers done something with reading that you really enjoyed?

   Could you explain some of what was done?

4. Do you share and discuss books, magazines, or other reading materials with your friends outside of school?

   What?

   How often?

   Where?

5. Do you write letters or email to friends or family?

   How often?

6. Do you share any of the following reading materials with members of your family: newspapers, magazines, religious materials, games?

   With whom?

   How often?

7. Do you belong to any clubs or organizations for which you read and write?

   Could you explain what kind of reading it is?

Note. Adapted with permission from the Motivation to Read Profile (Gambrell, Palmer, Codling, & Mazzoni, 1996)

Figure 3
Adolescent Motivation to Read Profile Teacher Directions: Reading Survey

Distribute copies of the Adolescent Motivation to Read Survey. Ask students to write their names on the space provided.

Directions: Say: I am going to read some sentences to you. I want to know how you feel about your reading. There are no right or wrong answers. I really want to know how you honestly feel about reading. I will read each sentence twice. Do not mark your answer until I tell you to. The first time I read the sentence I want you to think about the best answer for you. The second time I read the sentence I want you to fill in the space beside your best answer. Mark only one answer. If you have any questions during the survey, raise your hand. Are there any questions before we begin? Remember: Do not mark your answer until I tell you to. OK, let's begin.

Read the first sample item: Say:

Sample 1: I am in (pause) sixth grade, (pause) seventh grade, (pause) eighth grade, (pause) ninth grade, (pause) tenth grade, (pause) eleventh grade, (pause) twelfth grade.

Read the first sample again. Say:

This time as I read the sentence, mark the answer that is right for you. I am in (pause) sixth grade, (pause) seventh grade, (pause) eighth grade, (pause) ninth grade, (pause) tenth grade, (pause) eleventh grade, (pause) twelfth grade.

Read the second sample item. Say:

Sample 2: I am a (pause) female, (pause) male.

Say:

Now, get ready to mark your answer.

I am a (pause) female, (pause) male.

Read the remaining items in the same way (e.g., number _______, sentence stem followed by a pause, each option followed by a pause, and then give specific directions for students to mark their answers while you repeat the entire item).

Note. Adapted with permission from the Motivation to Read Profile (Gambrell, Palmer, Codling, & Mazzoni, 1996)

Figure 4
Teacher Directions: MRP Conversational Interview

1. Duplicate the conversational interview so that you have a form for each child.
2. Choose in advance the section(s) or specific questions you want to ask from the conversational interview. Reviewing the information on students' reading surveys may provide information about additional questions that could be added to the interview.
3. Familiarize yourself with the basic questions provided in the interview prior to the interview session in order to establish a more conversational setting.
4. Select a quiet corner of the room and a calm period of the day for the interview.
5. Allow ample time for conducting the conversational interview.
6. Follow up on interesting comments and responses to gain a fuller understanding of students' reading experiences.
7. Record students' responses in as much detail as possible. If time and resources permit you may want to audiotape answers to A1 and B1 to be transcribed after the interview for more in-depth analysis.
8. Enjoy this special time with each student!

Note. Reprinted with permission from the Motivation to Read Profile (Gambrell, Palmer, Codling, & Mazzoni, 1996)

Figure 5
Scoring Directions: MRP Reading Survey

The survey has 20 items based on a 4-point scale. The highest total score possible is 80 points. On some items the response options are ordered least positive to most positive (see item 2 below) with the least positive response option having a value of 1 point and the most positive option having a point value of 4. On other items, however, the response options are reversed (see item 1 below). In those cases it will be necessary to recode the response options. Items where recoding is required are starred on the scoring sheet.

Example: Here is how Maria completed items 1 and 2 on the Reading Survey.

1. My friends think I am __________.
   - ❑ a very good reader
   - ■ a good reader
   - ❑ an OK reader
   - ❑ a poor reader
2. Reading a book is something I like to do.
   - ❑ Never
   - ❑ Not very often
   - ❑ Sometimes
   - ■ Often

To score item 1 it is first necessary to recode the response options so that

a poor reader equals 1 point,
an OK reader equals 2 points,
a good reader equals 3 points, and
a very good reader equals 4 points.

Because Maria answered that she is a good reader the point value for that item, 3, is entered on the first line of the Self-Concept column on the scoring sheet. See below. The response options for item 2 are ordered least positive (1 point) to most positive (4 points), so scoring item 2 is easy. Simply enter the point value associated with Maria's response. Because Maria selected the fourth option, a 4 is entered for item 2 under the Value of reading column on the scoring sheet. See below.

Scoring sheet

Self-concept as a Reader	Value of reading
*recode 1. 3	2. 4

To calculate the Self-concept raw score and Value raw score add all student responses in the respective column. The full survey raw score is obtained by combining the column raw scores. To convert the raw scores to percentage scores, divide student raw scores by the total possible score (40 for each subscale, 80 for the full survey).

Note. Reprinted with permission from the Motivation to Read Profile (Gambrell, Palmer, Codling, & Mazzoni, 1996)

Figure 6
MRP Reading Survey Scoring Sheet

Student name ______________________________

Grade______________ Teacher ______________________

Administration date ______________________________

Recoding scale

1=4

2=3

3=2

4=1

Self-concept as a reader		Value of reading	
*recode	1. ______		2. ______
	3. ______	*recode	4. ______
*recode	5. ______		6. ______
*recode	7. ______	*recode	8. ______
	9. ______	*recode	10. ______
	11. ______		12. ______
	13. ______		14. ______
*recode	15. ______		16. ______
	17. ______	*recode	18. ______
	19. ______	*recode	20. ______

SC raw score: ______/40 V raw score: ______/40

Full survey raw score (Self-concept & Value): ______________/80

Percentage scores

Self-concept ______

Value ______

Full survey ______

Comments: ______________________________

____

____

Note. Reprinted with permission from the Motivation to Read Profile (Gambrell, Palmer, Codling, & Mazzoni, 1996)

the original article by Gambrell et al. (1996) for more guidelines for scoring and interpretation.

The Study

Eleven researchers at eight sites administered the AMRP reading survey and conversational interview to teens from many different school settings including public, charter, alternative, and government-sponsored schools and in a variety of geographic areas of the United States (West, Southwest, Northeast, Midatlantic, and Southeast) and the Caribbean. Surveys were administered to 384 adolescents and approximately 100 were interviewed. Of the 384 students who responded to the survey, approximately 22% identified themselves as African American, 37% were Caucasian, 30% were Afro/Indo-Trini (from Trinidad and Tobago), 10% were classified as "other," and 1% of the respondents did not specify an ethnicity. Additionally, some of the students interviewed identified themselves as Hispanic. Early adolescents (grades 6-8) accounted for 43.8% of the sample, middle adolescents (grades 9-10) comprised 35.2 %, and late adolescents (grades 11-12) comprised 21% of the sample. Fifty-four percent were female; 46% were male.

In sharing the results of this study, often the students' own words are used. In all cases the names are pseudonyms. In some instances the students chose their own aliases.

The AMRP Reading Survey

The reading survey provides scores for both "Self-concept as a reader" and "Value of reading" and takes approximately 10 minutes to administer to a whole class. The multiple-choice format and easy to follow scoring sheet provide a practical instrument that can be used with large groups of students. With only a small time investment, teachers can assess at the beginning of the year how their students feel about reading. This can lead to different choices for different groups. Using the instrument again at intervals can also assess how different instructional approaches (literature circles, choice reading, projects) affect how students value reading and see themselves as readers.

Through this study's surveys, we found some interesting data with implications for how these teens see themselves as readers. Females had significantly ($p = .000$) higher scores on the surveys than males ($p = .012$). Males scored higher on the survey in their early teens but their scores decreased in their later teens. Females across all groups valued reading more than males ($p = .000$). We also found that females' value of reading increased with grade level but males' decreased. African American ($n = 84$) and Afro/Indo-Trini ($n = 115$) adolescents valued reading significantly ($p = .000$) more than Caucasians ($n = 141$) or students from other ethnicities ($n = 39$). There were no significant differences on self-concept between grade level, gender, or ethnic groups.

These interesting trends often seemed puzzling when we considered the data from the interviews. In comparing answers from the surveys and the interviews, we were better able to understand the reasons behind the data above and to ponder more implications for instruction.

The AMRP Conversational Interview

The interviews provided a view of instructional methods that were used in the classrooms and of how teens spent their free time. The main themes that emerged from the interviews were the discrepancies between students' views of themselves as readers in school and out of school, students' use of multiliteracies, the influence of family and friends on reading, the role of teachers and instructional methods, and the importance of choice. These themes are described below and illustrated with comments from students. The grade levels of these students ranged from 6 to 11.

Students' Perceptions of Reading and Readers. We entered the study under the assumption that interviews would add descriptive data to the survey results, and in most cases, our expectations were met. Yet in other instances, discrepancies did exist between survey answers and interview answers. For example, Jason answered on the survey that he "never" likes to read, but when asked in the interview about the most interesting story he had recently read, he talked about a survival story in a hunting magazine. He went on to say that his grandfather was going to help him pay for a subscription to the magazine, because Jason loved to hunt. Similarly, Jared checked that he liked to read "not very often" on the survey, but when asked about something important he'd learned recently outside of school, he mentioned how he'd learned new fishing tactics from *Field and Stream* magazine.

One of the most extreme examples of survey and interview discrepancies arose with Paul, who shared on the survey that he found reading "a boring way to spend time." The interview told a different story when he mentioned spending about 20 hours a week on the Internet reading e-mails, articles, games, and "stuff." Michael, another student from the same school, checked on the survey that he never reads a book, but his conversation during the interview included his reading of magazines, hobby books, and stories written by friends. He and his friends write and share stories on e-mail often. The definition that these boys assigned to the word, "reading," may not have included the reading of magazines, e-mail, games, or other leisure reading for pleasure or information. Additionally, their reading interests did not seem to include any forms of academic reading.

Generally, students' self-concepts as readers and their value of reading coincided with their reading choices and overall enjoyment of reading. Jesse was one of several exceptions. On the survey he selected "poor reader" in the self-concept section, and he checked that he read "not very often" in the value portion. Conversely, when asked about the most interesting book he had read recently, he explained, "The most interesting book I have read was by Michael Crichton. It was about alternate universes, time travel. I first saw this book at a store, read the review, and decided to buy it. I liked it because it involved history, technology, a different perspective on the universe." This student's choice of books, along with his speaking vocabulary, would not have led us to view him as a "poor reader," but he was one of the students enrolled in a summer class after failing English 11. Obviously, in English 11 he was considered a poor reader, a fact that suggests a strong disconnect between academic forms of reading and pleasure reading.

Adolescents' need for connection to a topic was well expressed by Tommy. In answering the survey question of how often he likes to read, Tommy marked "sometimes." When asked during the interview to tell about the most interesting story he had read recently, Tommy replied that it was a book about the U.S. Civil War in which the South won. He added that it was mostly historically correct. In answer to why this story was interesting, Tommy replied that he had Confederate ancestors.

Use of Multiliteracies. Students' use of multiliteracies was overwhelmingly apparent in the interview data. Students talked about reading magazines and, to a lesser extent, newspapers. Favorite topics of magazines chosen by students were teens, cars, sports, fashion, and people.

Electronic literacies were very frequently mentioned as a form of communication and information gathering, and most students discussed using computers in their homes. They regularly sent e-mail and instant messages (IM) to friends and family members. Jenna even made a distinction between e-mail and instant messages. "Friends, I don't really e-mail because I talk to them almost every night on IM, but I do e-mail them sometimes. When asked whether they read informational text, students often talked about Internet sites, and when asked about the computer, they commonly talked about reading informational resources on the Internet. For example, adolescents used it as a "newspaper" (e.g., several talked about reading America Online's front page for the latest news). They also used it for personal purposes to locate information about a topic in which they were interested. Nikki said, "I read, uh, about kittens of course and about other animals and how to take care of things. Like a while back I was looking up about a dog for my sister." Students also used the Internet to find song lyrics, converse in chat rooms, role play, play games on gaming sites, and find game codes. Heidi shared that she gets on the Internet to e-mail family in Hawaii, read and write fanfiction about Harry Potter, and fix up her own website.

Family and Friends. Students' multiliteracies often involved friends and family members, who exerted considerable influence on what these adolescents read and write. These influences occur both through direct recommendations and through informal talk and sharing about books. Friends are recipients and senders of e-mail and IMs, and they recommend and share books with one another. They talk about magazine articles they have read and sometimes about school-assigned readings. According to Carrie, she and her friends discuss magazine articles "at lunch, and like during class when they give us, like, five minutes before class ends to talk or whatever." Jimmy and his friends share magazine and newspaper articles about "sports or stuff we're talking about."

Family members, including mothers, grandmothers, aunts, uncles, and siblings, are influential forces. Students mentioned mothers and grandmothers recommending and buying books and magazines for them. Carrie explained her mother's strategy, "She knows what kind of books I like so she...buys me a bunch of books and she just puts them on my shelves and I just end up reading them anyway." They discuss and share newspaper articles with their mothers and fathers. When asked if he shared any reading materials with family members, John replied, "Yes, I would say my stepfather because we both really like sports, and we look at the...sports section of the newspaper a lot." These adolescents e-mail relatives who live away from them, and some read to their younger siblings.

Teachers and Instructional Methods. Some interesting replies resulted from the question, Have any of your teachers done something with reading that you really enjoyed? There were students who answered, "No." For example, out of 21 summer school students at one site, 19 said no. Of the 2 that said yes, they added that the teacher read aloud.

Surveys and interviews from a small, experimental middle school in an urban setting produced very different findings. Here, students enthusiastically talked about literature circles, sustained silent reading time, and choosing books in literacy centers that were part of a new reading intervention program. Most of the 10 students interviewed at this site shared that they either borrowed from the teachers or went to the library to get books that other students in their class talked about. Across all sites, adolescents' discussion of teacher instruction revealed that the modeling of strategies for comprehending text and finding information has a strong influence on students' views toward academic forms of reading.

In addition to instructional methods, we noted the powerful influence of teacher talk and modeling about books and authors. From interviews, it became clear that teachers' enthusiasm can have a tremendous impact on students' reading habits and attitudes. The interview participants discussed how teachers' excitement about reading, knowledge of various authors, and enjoyment of certain books affected their own reading. Teachers were often sources for book recommendations. Some students reported that they discovered their "most interesting story or book read recently" from a teacher, as in the experimental middle school.

The teens talked a lot about books that were assigned in class. They mentioned reading books such as *Holes*, the Harry Potter series, *The Dark Is Rising*, *The Watsons Go to Birmingham*, *Scorpions*, *Pinball*, and *Dr. Jekyll and Mr. Hyde*, in language arts classes. Enjoying these texts helped make their classes the ones in which they "most like to read." Two dislikers of reading said that the most interesting story or book they had read was in English class—*Lord of the Flies* and *The Great Gatsby*. At one survey site the students talked a lot about reading books in classroom literature circles. Whether the students really enjoyed these books or most recalled them because they were "done" in school, was not clear. The data did show that these assigned readings could also "turn them off" from reading if the book was "too hard" or "boring." Nevertheless, assigned school reading also influenced what was read at home and kept in the school locker. We did not obtain as vivid descriptions about nonfiction books as we did of the traditional novels.

Nick enthusiastically captured the influence of teachers.

> I think that my sixth grade teacher, her name was Miss Sawyer, she was, uh, she was like one of my favorite reading teachers, and I used to go to her classroom everyday to see what books, like, she would be reading...so she could, like, tell me about them so I could check them out to read them, and... we always would read books in her class and she always, she had like a great voice and...she taught reading like more some of the skills I have in reading like very, like, very enthusiastic and stuff like that.

Choice. The final theme was related to both the role of teachers and the discrepancies among teens' views of what counts as reading. Adolescents clearly identified the importance of choice in their literacy lives, an issue long documented in the literature (Ivey & Broaddus, 2001; Oldfather, 1993). When asked if teachers had ever done something with reading that they really enjoyed, several in this study mentioned teachers allowing them to choose a book to read. Students also valued choice in topics and formats for assigned projects. They recognized the need for teachers to assign some readings, but they wanted them to take into account student preferences in these assignments.

Nick explained,

> Yeah, I think that, um, one thing I think that teachers could do with the reading to make things more interesting is teachers could vote on, like, books that interest kids, cause sometimes teachers, they pick, to me they pick the dumbest books. Like, one of the books we're reading right now is called *The Secret Garden*. It's like, really, really boring. It's like the most boring book I think I've ever read in my life.... I think that if teachers could, like, like, take a poll or something, like, on books that kids think that would be better for them to read, that are like school-appropriate kind of books, I think that kids would do better in reading, and, I think that we would make better grades.

Discussion and Implications

A graduate student in literacy made the following connection about teens' multiple literacies:

> In *Princess in Waiting* (Cabot, 2003), the fourth novel in the Princess Diaries series, 14-year-old Princess Mia Thermopolis writes the following in her journal about discovering her secret talent: "And even though I had never really thought about it before, I realized Michael was right. I mean, I *am* always writing in this journal. And I do compose a lot of poetry, and write a lot of notes and e-mails and stuff. I mean, I feel like I am *always* writing. I do it so much, I never even thought about it as being a *talent*. It's just something I do all the time, like breathing" (p. 258–9). Mia is also adept at instant messaging, and she and her friends often send text messages through their cell phones in school. Mia considers herself a writer not because she gets A's in English class, but because she is always writing, usually in out-of-school contexts. This fictional character is similar to real adolescents in the amount of reading and writing they actually do outside of school; however, most teachers wouldn't consider these forms as literacy. (R. Brushingham, personal communication, March 20, 2005)

Like Princess Mia, the adolescents in this study are reading and writing many hours daily in multiple, flexible, and varied ways and formats. They are also talking about what they read and are often enthusiastic about what they are reading and writing, as well. Unfortunately, however, many of these students still do not see themselves as readers and writers. When comparing the interview results with the survey results, it became apparent to us that students often define "reading" as a school-based activity. When asked indirectly about their reading and writing outside of school (by asking about their use of computers or sharing with friends and family), students revealed that they have many literacy-related competencies and motivations. Yet, when asked in a general way on the survey if they consider themselves to be readers and writers, many responded negatively. They revealed a discrepancy between their stated views of themselves as readers and writers and their actual daily practices.

Students may be defining reading and readers only in an academic context, and this context is often not inclusive of the types of reading and writing they are engaging in outside of the classroom; therefore, they may not be viewing their out-of-school literacies as valid reading and writing. This possibility has strong implications for classroom teaching, yet it also brought our attention to a limitation of the study. Not all participants in the survey portion were interviewed, and we do not know how the other students defined reading. Because of this limitation, we wholeheartedly believe that this research needs to be expanded to other populations.

We further recommend, in accordance with suggestions by Gambrell et al. (1996), that researchers and teachers modify the instrument to allow for differing interpretations of the survey.

These findings show us that we need to do the following:

- recognize the multiple literacies in which students are engaging in outside of the classroom and find ways to incorporate them into classroom instruction;
- model our own reading enjoyment;
- embrace engaging activities, such as literature circles and book clubs, into regular instruction in secondary schools;
- include reading materials of varied formats, levels, and topics in the classroom; and
- incorporate elements of choice in readings and projects.

Like Gambrell et al. (1996), we believe that information from the results of the AMRP should be used in planning developmentally appropriate instruction. Adolescents, in particular, could benefit from more "meaningful, motivational contexts for reading instruction" (Gambrell et al., p. 530), because of their tendency to read less frequently as they enter the teen years (Moje, Young, Readence, & Moore, 2000). From the survey results, males in particular seemed to lose interest in reading by late adolescence. Smith and Wilhelm (2004) attributed this decline to feelings of incompetence with school literacy tasks. Yet, as past research indicates, positive attitudes are essential for mastery of a text but are often given less attention than decoding skills and comprehension strategies (Wilson & Hall, 1972). The students themselves, may have been suggested part of the answer to this dilemma during the interviews. While they placed different meanings on reading for pleasure than on reading for academic purposes, each student expressed literacy preferences that closely aligned with interests and specific purposes. A responsive teacher could draw from the preferences of Jason who had enjoyed a survival story in a hunting magazine, or Jared who learned fishing tactics from *Field and Stream*. Having a wide variety of reading materials including electronic resources available on these topics might make school reading a more pleasurable and purposeful experience for these students.

Strommen and Mates (2004) reminded us that if literacy competence can be attained through reading for pleasure, then, "encouraging a child's love of reading is a desirable goal" (p. 199). By acknowledging students' reading interests and building on them, teachers can help students expand those interests to related topics over time. Furthermore, Partin and Hendricks (2002) suggested that teachers broaden their scope of what they consider acceptable reading material. Expanding the notion of text to include popular culture and music, the Internet, magazines, and other alternatives could invite opportunities for adolescents to become critical consumers of texts.

A decline in reading motivation as students progress through middle and secondary school has been blamed on the mismatch between typical reading assignments and student preferences (Ivey, 1998). Because we know that young people reject literacy tasks that are lacking in purpose and interest, we need to become more aware of students' personal uses of literacy and what is important to them. When reading is limited to textbooks and whole-class literature, we limit ourselves as teachers, and our students as readers. Adolescents are, after all, the major stakeholders in their education, and we, the adults, need to listen to what they have to say.

References

Alvermann, D.E. (2001a). *Effective literacy instruction for adolescents: Executive summary and paper commissioned by the National Reading Conference.* Chicago: National Reading Conference. Retrieved October 20, 2006, from http://www.nrconline.org/index.html

Alvermann, D.E. (2001b). Reading adolescents' reading identities: Looking back to see ahead. *Journal of Adolescent & Adult Literacy, 44*, 676–690.

Alvermann, D.E. (2003). *Seeing themselves as capable and engaged readers: Adolescents and re/mediated instruction.* Retrieved October 20, 2006, from http://www.learningpt.org/pdfs/literacy/readers.pdf

Alvermann, D.E., & Moore, D.W. (1991). Secondary school reading. In R. Barr, M.L. Kamil, P.B. Mosenthal, & P.D. Pearson (Eds.), *Handbook of reading research* (Vol. 2, pp. 951–983). New York: Longman.

Bean, T.W., Bean, S.K., & Bean, K.F. (1999). Intergenerational conversations and two adolescents' multiple literacies: Implications for redefining content area literacy. *Journal of Adolescent & Adult Literacy, 42*, 438–448.

Cabot, M. (2003). *Princess in waiting.* New York: HarperCollins.

Gambrell, L.B., Palmer, B.M., Codling, R.M., & Mazzoni, S.A. (1996). Assessing motivation to read. *The Reading Teacher, 49*, 518–533.

Guthrie, J.T., & Wigfield, A. (1997). Reading engagement: A rationale for theory and teaching. In J.T. Guthrie & A. Wigfield (Eds.), *Reading engagement: Motivating readers through integrated instruction* (pp. 1–12). Newark, DE: International Reading Association.

Ivey, G. (1998). Discovering readers in the middle level school: A few helpful clues. *NASSP Bulletin, 82*, 48–56.

Ivey, G., & Broaddus, K. (2001). "Just plain reading": A survey of what makes students want to read in middle school classrooms. *Reading Research Quarterly, 36*, 350–377.

Moje, E.B., Young, J.P., Readence, J.E., & Moore, D. (2000). Reinventing adolescent literacy for new times: Perennial and millennial issues. *Journal of Adolescent & Adult Literacy, 43*, 400–410.

New London Group. (1996). A pedagogy of multiliteracies: Designing social futures. *Harvard Educational Review, 66*, 60–92.

O'Brien, D. (2001, June). "At-risk" adolescents: Redefining competence through the multiliteracies of intermediality, visual arts, and representation. *Reading Online, 4*(11). Retrieved February 7, 2005, from http://www.readingonline.org/newliteracies/lit_index.asp?HREF=/newliteracies/obrien/index.html

Oldfather, P. (1993). What students say about motivating experiences in a whole language classroom. *The Reading Teacher, 46*, 672–681.

Partin, K., & Hendricks, C.G. (2002). The relationship between positive adolescent attitudes toward reading and home literary environment. *Reading Horizons, 43*, 61–75.

Phelps, S.F. (2006). Introduction to Part I: Situating adolescents' literacies. In D.E. Alvermann, K.A. Hinchman, D.W. Moore, S.F. Phelps, & D.R. Waff (Eds.), *Reconceptualizing the literacies in adolescents' lives* (2nd ed., pp. 3–4). Mahwah, NJ: Erlbaum.

Roe, M.F. (1997). Combining enablement and engagement to assist students who do not read and write well. *Middle School Journal, 28*(3), 35–41.

Smith, M., & Wilhelm, J.D. (2004). "I just like being good at it": The importance of competence in the literate lives of young men. *Journal of Adolescent & Adult Literacy, 47*, 454–461.

Strommen, L.T., & Mates, B.F. (2004). Learning to love reading: Interviews with older children and teens. *Journal of Adolescent & Adult Literacy, 48*, 188–200.

Wasserstein, P. (1995). What middle schoolers say about their schoolwork. *Educational Leadership, 53*(1), 41–43.

Wilson, R.M., & Hall, M. (1972). *Reading and the elementary school child: Theory and practice for teachers.* New York: Van Nostrand Reinhold.

Questions for Reflection

- If you presented your students with the survey question "Have any of your teachers done something with reading that you really enjoyed?" what do you think their answer would be? In one school described in this article, students enthusiastically talked about literature circles, sustained silent reading, and choosing books in literacy centers—what literacy practices do you think your students most enjoy?
- Because of the discrepancies between some students' stated views of themselves as readers and writers and their actual daily practices, the authors conclude that students may be defining reading and writing in a strictly academic context. Why do you think this is the case? What ideas do you have for transforming students' perceptions of themselves as readers?

Teacher Questioning as Assessment

Peter Afflerbach

Questions are deeply engrained in the routines of the school day, where they serve a variety of functions. Questions help us understand students' ongoing and summary understanding of text, their metacognitive development, and the manner in which they use what has been learned from reading. By using questions, teachers seek an account of how well students are reading. The form and content of our questions should be informed by our knowledge of students, the curriculum, and our goals for instruction. These questions help us understand what students know and, most important, what they learn from reading. The types of questions we ask of our students can be as broad as our conceptualization of what students learn from reading and how they think. Questions help us model good assessment practice for our students. In each and every case, we must be sure that we are asking the right questions and that we are making full use of the student responses that our questions elicit.

A Brief History of Questioning

Throughout the history of schooling, questioning has been associated with teaching and learning. Beginning in the fourth century BC, Socrates is credited with developing a method of rigorous questioning that serves two purposes: (1) using the question as a guide to inquiry and thinking and (2) using questions to determine what the person who answers the question knows. A teacher poses questions that encourage students to think in new ways and questions that provide the opportunity to assess students' learning from text. For example, after a fifth-grade class reads a textbook chapter on immigration, the teacher uses Socratic questioning to help students focus on their family histories of immigration and then how the reasons for immigrating as described in the chapter apply to these histories. The Socratic method also serves as a challenge: As teachers we should pose questions that assess different types of learning, that provoke thought, and that are worthy of response.

How we think about reading, the purposes of reading instruction, and the development of the students we teach should influence the nature of the questions we ask. Decades ago, behaviorism posited that we read with text as stimulus and comprehension as the response (Watson, 1913). Such a view of reading suggests that verbatim recital of text as the response to questions is a desirable benchmark of the accomplished reader. However, the evolution of our understanding of the mind and reading (Huey, 1908; RAND Reading Study Group, 2002; Thorndike, 1917) should be reflected in an evolution in the types of questions we ask of student readers. Cognitive psychology demonstrates that readers use prior knowledge, combined with skills and strategies, to construct meaning (Pressley & Afflerbach, 1995). We also know that most students are capable of complex thinking. We should ask questions that honor this understanding. Moreover, our increasing understanding of the socially situated nature of cognition and the increasing demands on students to develop complex literacy abilities for success in life should influence our theory and practice of asking questions.

Questions have been the focus of considerable attention over the past century (Bloom, 1956; Guszak, 1967; Pearson & Johnson, 1978), and it is important that we consult this knowledge as we plan to use questions in our classrooms. In assessment, questions are generally regarded as

Reprinted from Afflerbach, P. (2007). Teacher questioning as assessment. In *Understanding and using reading assessment, K-12* (pp. 51-70). Newark, DE: International Reading Association.

a means to access student knowledge. Stevens (1912) found that roughly two thirds of the questions asked in observed classrooms focused on recitation and memory of facts. In this case, students who were expected to memorize text information often proved up to the task and accurately answered low-level comprehension questions. Durkin (1978) examined fourth-grade classrooms and interviewed teachers about their reading comprehension instruction. She found that many teachers equated comprehension instruction with asking questions about text, as if posing the question somehow taught students how to answer it. In fact, this study signified the need for rethinking how reading is taught and making clearer the relationships between reading, teaching, and answering questions. The study also concluded that since questions are not an adequate means for teaching, then there is the need for the explicit instruction of reading strategies.

Questioning is prominent in present-day classrooms, but it occurs most often in the initiate–respond–evaluate (IRE) discourse form. The IRE model describes classroom practice in which teachers Initiate classroom talk by asking questions, students Respond to the questions, and then the teacher Evaluates students' responses (Cazden, 1986; Mehan, 1979). Following is an example of the IRE form:

Initiate (teacher): What is a compass rose?

Respond (student): It's the part of a map that shows directions.

Evaluate (teacher): Yes, that's correct.

IRE discourse often focuses on "known answer" questions, in which the students' task is, in part, to figure out what the teacher wants to know. In reading lessons, IRE questions often focus on literal and simple inferential comprehension of text. It is not that such comprehension is not important—it is critical. It is that failure to move beyond such understanding of student understanding with our questions is a missed opportunity to both promote and evaluate students' more complex thinking.

Categorizing and Classifying Questions

A history of good question asking is informed by theories of learning. These theories help us conceptualize how our questions may tap particular types of knowledge that students gain from reading. As learning theories are generated and our understanding of learning and how to assess it evolve, different approaches to asking questions also evolve. For example, Bloom's taxonomy of learning (1956) proposes that learning can range from relatively simple understanding (assessed with a literal comprehension question) to complex evaluative understanding (assessed with questions that focus on students' critical appraisal of what is learned).

Bloom's taxonomy of learning defines six levels of increasingly sophisticated human learning and performance that relate to our reading. If we believe that our reading instruction should help students learn to generalize from what they read, to critically question the authors of the texts they read, and to apply what is learned from reading, Bloom's taxonomy offers a theoretical means to categorize our reading assessment questions in relation to these instructional goals. From relatively simple to increasingly complex, the taxonomy charts possible outcomes of students' reading and associated learning. The taxonomy can serve as an aid to our efforts to develop a rich and appropriate array of questions to ask students as they read. Table 6 focuses on the different types of learning in Bloom's taxonomy and suggests the focus of our questions that can help us understand the nature of students' learning in relation to each level of the taxonomy.

In spite of our knowledge of how to ask diverse and appropriate questions of students' reading, the increased prevalence of high-stakes tests (Afflerbach, 2005) is a major influence on questioning practice in classrooms. These tests are scored within the constraints of question response format, meaning that the cost of scoring students' responses to questions often dictates the type of questions that are asked. Machine-scored responses are relatively easy and cheap to score, compared with students' constructed responses

Table 6
Different Types of Questions Related to Different Categories in Bloom's Taxonomy of Thinking

Category of Bloom's Taxonomy	Questions can focus on
Knowledge	Recognizing, remembering
Comprehension	Understanding
Application	Using, applying
Analysis	Determining attributes, comparing and contrasting
Synthesis	Making hypotheses, planning, speculating
Evaluation	Rating, judging

to questions, and are favored over those items, including short and extended response items, which require human beings to score them. Further, these tests restrict the practice of having students regularly answer divergent thinking items or extensive constructed response items. Such items are useful when we are interested in students' understanding of text and when we acknowledge that there may be more than one correct answer to the question. A result is that to the degree that there is teaching to the test, there is teaching to low-level questions. The tests themselves thus act as a constraint on the types of questions and student assessment that may be conducted in classrooms. There is the tension of scientific research informing us about the depth and breadth of student learning that is possible in high-quality classrooms, the need for assessment questions that help us describe this learning, and the requirement that millions of students be assessed in reading with tests that are not capable of describing this breadth and depth.

To compound the issue of asking a limited range of questions (and knowing better), we are creatures of habit when it comes to current practice. Often, assessment practice is more a reflection of tradition than of principled decision making. Teachers not only ask questions but are also surrounded by questions. We receive a steady diet of questions: questions that follow reading selections and questions on quizzes, unit tests, and year-end examinations. This diet is often restricted, without providing examples of alternative questions. Unfortunately, as tests receive more and more attention, classroom practice that helps prepare students to take and succeed on high-stakes tests focuses on question types that appear on tests. Why would we ask middle school students to develop a theory of why poverty persists in East Africa when the high-stakes test question requires choosing, from alternatives, the capital of Tanzania? Teaching to the test is, in effect, teaching to an impoverished notion of what questions can tell us.

Pearson and Johnson (1978) characterize questions as textually explicit, textually implicit, and scriptally implicit. Each of the characterizations is important for us to understand, because they describe the types of reading, thinking, and answering that students must do to be successful. Consider the following paragraph:

> Emma smiled with satisfaction as Radar sailed over the last jump. She knew that the prize would be hers. After crossing the finish line, she did a celebratory gallop past the spectators. The judges awarded her the trophy for First Place, Steeplechase. The trophy

was silver with a young rider and horse jumping over a fence. As Emma got into the car with her parents, she thought of the place in her room where she would proudly display her award.

Textually explicit questions require students to locate answers that have exact wording in the texts they read. The answers are "right there" in the text. For example, the question, "What trophy did Emma win?" can be answered "First Place, Steeplechase." *Textually implicit* questions require that students gather information from at least two different parts of text to successfully answer the question. Here, a representative question is, "Why did Emma gallop past the spectators?" and an acceptable answer is, "She was celebrating winning the trophy." *Scriptally implicit* questions require that students integrate information from the text with information in their prior knowledge to successfully answer questions. A representative question is, "Do you think Emma's parents are proud of her? Why?"

The three distinctions of question type help us determine the type of comprehension and thinking that the student is capable of. They mark the growth of the reader from someone who can give back correct information from text to one who is manipulating knowledge contained in different parts of the text with his or her own prior knowledge. The question types may also provide information related to what and how much prior knowledge a student has (or needs) for a particular text. Each of the question types can reflect the ongoing development of how students read, think, and understand. The preceding examples also help illustrate how a student with little or no prior knowledge for the text content will be at a clear disadvantage in answering the same set of questions.

The work of Bloom, Pearson and Johnson, and others offers us frameworks for thinking about our questions. Categorization schemes for questions help us understand the type of thinking and learning that are reflected in students' answers to our questions. Thus, they help us understand what, exactly, we are asking students to do with our questions. The frameworks challenge us to consider what kinds of questions we ask and the frequency with which we ask them. Reading questions must focus on the content of what is read, but the different frameworks remind us that questions can ask for verbatim response, they can ask us to make generalizations from text, they can ask us to read between the lines as when we try to determine an author's purpose or intent, and they can ask us to evaluate the content and form of the texts we read. Each type of question plays a valuable role in helping us understand the important ways in which student readers develop.

Instructional Perspectives on Questioning

The past two decades have seen approaches to questioning that may serve the double duty of helping teachers gather assessment information about their students while helping students learn to ask important and appropriate questions themselves. These programs and models include the K-W-L strategy (Ogle, 1986), question–answer relationships (QARs; Raphael & Wonnacott, 1985), and questioning the author (Beck, McKeown, Hamilton, & Kucan, 1997). Ogle (1986), working with theories of cognition and metacognition, developed the K-W-L strategy that requires students to ask the following questions: What do I Know about the text? What do I Want to learn from the text? What did I Learn from the text? The strategy is popular not only as a questioning routine but as a means of helping students develop strategic approaches to reading. In fact, the strategy is a strong example of questioning that guides students' strategy use and reading, in addition to promoting text-based comprehension. The K-W-L strategy can help us assess both students' learning from text and their strategic approaches to reading. Our evolving understanding of how students think and learn should privilege particular types of questioning practice, especially as we consider the complex curricular goals and sophisticated student thinking that are hallmarks of high-quality instructional programs.

Question–answer relationship strategies (Raphael & Wonnacott, 1985) help students understand the connections between questions that are asked and the answers that students give in response. In effect, the QAR approach helps students become metacognitive about the relationship of the meaning that is constructed through reading with the comprehension questions we ask them. The approach is built on the assumption that it is important for student readers to know where their answers come from and the suitability of using different sources of information for answering different types of questions. The four categories of question–answer relationships are (1) right there, (2) think and search, (3) author and me, and (4) on my own. *Right there* means that students should be able to find the content for their answers to questions from one source in the text. *Think and search* means that student readers should find information from different sources. *Author and me* requires that students use prior knowledge related to the text in combination with inferences they make about the text. Finally, *on my own* means that while the question is related to the text, the student's answer may or may not be related, and answers emanate from students' prior experience and knowledge.

Questioning the author (Beck et al., 1997) is a means for teachers to help students learn good questions to ask of authors of the texts they read and for teachers to gauge the development of students' ability to read critically. Questioning the author helps the reader approach texts from a purpose-driven perspective. Students may ask, Why did the author write this? What is the author trying to tell me? How well does the author succeed at the task of writing well? What are the strong and weak points of the author's writing and argument? Are there alternative approaches to this? Knowledgeable students ask such questions. One result of questioning the author should be that students better appreciate talented authors' approaches to writing, which in turn may have influence on students' own writing. It may also help students make accurate attributions for their comprehension of text. Poor comprehension may be the result of poorly written text, and students who understand this (and who can identify such texts when they are reading them) are in a good position to make the correct attributions for their performance.

Many questions that are asked of students focus on literal and simple inferential comprehension. Such questions will always play an important role in reading assessment. However, they do not fully represent the types of questions that are important to ask of students, nor do they help us assess reading, learning, and thinking at more complex levels. Consider the critical and evaluative questions we may ask of students. Students and other citizens in democratic societies must be able to ask questions about the accuracy and trustworthiness of texts and the obvious and hidden agendas of the authors who create texts. Advertisements, editorials, political campaign documents, and other forms of persuasive text must be addressed with critical questions. Such questions help us determine if students understand the different purposes for authors writing particular types of texts, the apparent accuracy of accounts of factual information, the strength of an author's argument and claims, and the form and content of text (Muspratt, Luke, & Freebody, 1997).

Characteristics of Effective Questions

If we envision success for our students in and out of school, does this success revolve around answering literal comprehension questions? Does it involve a student's ability to read between the lines, to stand in critical judgment of authors and their works, and to use that which is read and understood in tasks and performances? The answers to these questions must influence how we conceptualize and use questions in our classrooms. And this conceptualization and use of questions must be informed by the most recent and compelling theory, research, and practice related to asking questions. We want our questions to help students demonstrate their present understanding of texts read in school, as well as anticipate their future success in life.

Questions are used to determine what a student has learned from reading a text. Questions are also used to help us best understand the thinking and reasoning that students do in relation to their reading. We must examine our curriculum and goals of instruction to help determine the types of questions we ask of our students. If we ask students to read so that they can give us back information from text, then factual questions are suitable. If we want students to demonstrate that they know facts and opinions and they know when an author is being persuasive, then we need to ask questions that reveal student knowledge related to persuasive writing and content learning.

Appropriate questions result from careful and often complex analyses of the important components of teaching and learning. First, good questions are tied to the text. They seek to identify student learning that occurs as a result of, and in relation to, reading. Good questions represent an inquiry into clearly defined areas of learning. We want our questions to focus on important points of learning and attainable goals. Questions should be aligned with our personal and districtwide learning goals and curriculum. They should reflect a clear understanding of how students learn and develop, of how knowledge is constructed in particular content areas, and how reading operates.

Slack (1998) developed a list of factors to consider when developing questions and determining a sequence for the question-asking process. Figure 4 presents a checklist based on these factors that we should consider as we seek to construct effective questions. Examination of the checklist demonstrates that we must focus on both the content and form of our questions so that they are appropriate, accessible, and answerable. As we develop assessment questions, we must remind ourselves that our questions model for students a specific manner of thinking about learning and knowing. Our questions teach students about particular stances they may take toward knowledge.

Consider the following five questions. Each could be asked as students complete a chapter on the American Revolution in their social studies textbook:

1. Where did colonial troops defeat General Cornwallis?

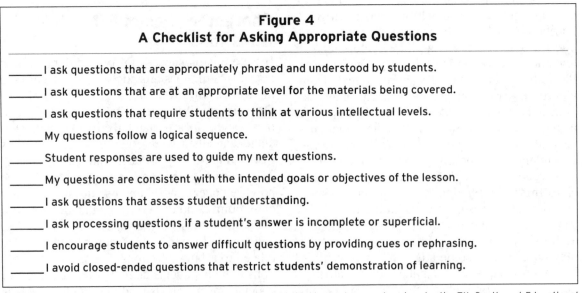

Figure 4
A Checklist for Asking Appropriate Questions

_____ I ask questions that are appropriately phrased and understood by students.

_____ I ask questions that are at an appropriate level for the materials being covered.

_____ I ask questions that require students to think at various intellectual levels.

_____ My questions follow a logical sequence.

_____ Student responses are used to guide my next questions.

_____ My questions are consistent with the intended goals or objectives of the lesson.

_____ I ask questions that assess student understanding.

_____ I ask processing questions if a student's answer is incomplete or superficial.

_____ I encourage students to answer difficult questions by providing cues or rephrasing.

_____ I avoid closed-ended questions that restrict students' demonstration of learning.

From Slack, J. (1998). *Questioning strategies to improve student thinking and comprehension.* Austin, TX: Southwest Educational Development Laboratory. Reprinted with permission.

2. What is the theme of this chapter?
3. Why did the author choose these examples to illustrate the main idea?
4. Was the author successful in his strategy?
5. How do you judge your performance on these questions?

The first question is informed by the perspective that students should learn and memorize historical facts. The information exists on the written page and is to be learned and remembered by the reader. The second question asks students to synthesize a theme based on their literal understanding. The perspective that readers should be inquisitive about the things they read and be aware of authors' strategies and intent informs the third question. The fourth question asks students to make critical judgment about the author's ability. Finally, the fifth question asks the student reader to look inward and provide an account of metacognitive processes. Each question is worth asking, and each yields responses that tell us much about a student's reading development. The challenge it to balance our question asking so that no type of question is ignored and no type of question predominates, in relation to our teaching goals.

The questions students encounter related to their reading can shape their stance toward reading and knowledge and their very beliefs about the authority of the text. As important, the questions we ask of students consistently communicate what we value. Low-level questions asked across an entire school year send students a consistent message that memorization and retrieval of information from text are important. More challenging questions invite students to problem solve, problem find, and partake in complex thinking. Across the school career, our questions help shape students' epistemologies, for they send consistent messages about the nature of knowledge, what is important in the texts we read, and what "correct" interpretations of texts should be.

Examining Different Types of Questions

In this section we will examine the types of questions we may ask related to students' reading. It is common to think of reading assessment questions as focused on comprehension, for this is a primary role of questions. However, the means by which we measure and describe students' comprehension of text should not be limited to series of literal and inferential comprehension questions. We should consider questions that help us understand if students are able to apply what they learn from reading, to generalize from what they read to their lives, and to adopt critical and evaluative stances toward texts and their contents.

Introduced earlier in this chapter, the initiate–respond–evaluate (IRE) approach to questioning and assessment can be a direct path to certain types of student learning. For example, we can ask students questions like, What is the capital of Kansas? and What is a tectonic plate? and effectively evaluate their responses. More complex IRE questions might ask students, How is the French Revolution like the American Revolution? As the question becomes more complex, so must our evaluation and assessment. In fact, IRE questions can be used to assess student learning and performance at diverse levels of thinking and understanding. In contrast to the promise of gearing our questions to increasingly difficult levels of thinking and learning, the IRE structure predominates and classroom questions related to reading are relegated to relatively low levels of thinking.

Several caveats are necessary for teachers considering the IRE structure in questioning routines or identifying it as an already prevalent mode of classroom discourse. First, IRE is teacher dominated: The teacher determines what questions will be asked and then asks them. In the extreme, the teacher can become the sole model of the types of questions asked and the placement of questions within lessons. If we ask an array of questions that revolve around what is understood from reading, using that which is understood, and reacting critically to texts that are read, it may well be that students are getting a healthy sampling of the important types of questions to ask. However, if we continually ask lower level questions (those that require students to only identify literal information and make simple inferences), this does not help students better understand how different question types encourage different types of thinking.

Second, the IRE pattern establishes the teacher as the sole determinant of the appropriateness of students' responses. The teacher is the single person with the "right" answer to the question. Over time, this classroom routine and the approach to knowledge that it represents can suggest to students that our knowledge and understanding of content is all that matters, that divergent thinking is not appropriate, and that there is a single arbiter of students' answers to reading questions. Third, the IRE pattern represents a teacher monopoly on assessment. When we do all the question asking and are in charge of all the answers, there may be missed opportunities for students to learn to do question asking, peer evaluation, and self-evaluation. If the teacher generates the questions and then evaluates student responses, there are missed opportunities for students to learn these important reading-related strategies.

Questions That Are Planned or Spontaneous, Divergent or Convergent

Classroom assessment questions can be spontaneous or planned, and divergent or convergent. Spontaneous questions follow the flow of reading lessons and are prompted by our careful observation and monitoring of the lesson. Spontaneous questions help teachers assess students' understanding as it is developing. These questions help us make determinations of the degree to which students have read, understood, and learned from text in relation to lesson goals. They provide information that helps the teacher decide to reteach, elaborate and enrich, and move ahead during the reading lesson. Spontaneous questions are well suited to helping us get useful information. We do not plan for students to encounter difficulties with our introduction and explanation of plate tectonics, but we should plan to have contingency questions that guide us to a detailed understanding of individual students' developing knowledge and current needs. The contingent and spontaneous questions fuel our ability to identify and capitalize on teachable moments.

Planned questions, on the other hand, can provide coverage of important school learning in relation to goals of the lesson, as determined a priori. We go into the questioning routine knowing what we want to check with our assessment questions—these must be targeted at important anticipated outcomes. Key vocabulary and the concepts they represent, main ideas, and supporting details are all examples of appropriate foci for planned questions. Students' responses to such questions help us determine their understanding of key concepts. When our students read an article about plate tectonics, we are interested in their understanding of earthquakes, the Richter scale, and the San Andreas Fault, as well as the tectonic plates themselves. As teachers we may develop familiarity with aspects of curriculum that pose challenges within particular lessons for particular students. For example, we may determine over time that the tectonic plate article is engaging but that students' understanding of how tectonic plate movement leads to earthquakes is elusive. Our attention to these challenges means that we can build a repertoire of planned questions, informed by our observations of student performance, that focuses on the relationship between tectonic plates and earthquakes. Student readers will benefit from a mixture of spontaneous and planned questions. The talented teacher approaches reading assessment with ideas for both.

We may ask students divergent or convergent questions. Convergent questions are made with the expectation that different students' responses, when accurate, will be similar or identical. There is often one "correct" response expected with convergent questions. For example, we can ask, Where is the San Andreas Fault? and be fairly confident that there is a single correct answer to the question. In contrast, divergent questions may encourage a classroom of students to each answer the same question in a different, suitable way. We can ask, Why would people build homes close to the San Andreas Fault? Determining the quality of the response may be more difficult with divergent questions, because the questions invite different paths to solutions, different explanations for phenomena, and different criteria for explanation. Thus, the means to evaluate responses to divergent questions should be developed with the understanding that answers may vary and still be correct.

Question Comprehensibility, Wait Time, and Passage Independence

When we ask questions we are often interested in how well students have comprehended text. Our questions are texts themselves, and we must query, What is the comprehensibility of the questions we ask? We typically think of difficulty in reading in relation to the match between the reader and the text, the degree to which a text contains new and difficult material, and the motivation that a reader may (or may not) have for reading. Assessment questions are a specific genre of text and we must scrutinize the questions we ask for how well students understand them. A difficult question can confuse students who, through more appropriate questions, might demonstrate comprehension of what they read. When we construct questions, we should consider the vocabulary of the question and the complexity of the prompt. If the vocabulary demands of our question exceed the vocabulary demands of what we want to learn about through questioning, then we need to revise our questions. (For more on making accommodations, see chapter 9, "Accommodation and Reading Assessment.") We should also anticipate the sense that a student might make out of a question that does (or does) not coincide with our intention.

Between a teacher's posing a question and a student's response to that question exists wait time. Every question that we ask may warrant wait time, from a seemingly simple literal comprehension question to a complex critical and evaluative question. We should not expect that comprehensive answers spring fully formed from students' minds. Thoughtful answers require thought and thought requires time. Wait time will vary from question to question and student to student. The amount of time needed to answer a question is influenced by several important factors, including focus of the question, students' comprehension of text, comprehensibility of the question, the complexity of the thinking required to give an adequate response, and students' individual differences. The wait time that is given to students' responses to questions should vary based on our best estimate of these factors. In effect, it is our responsibility to "get inside" the question and understand the demands that it creates for students, so we can develop legitimate estimates of how much time a student needs to adequately think about and answer a question. This estimate will be one with parameters so that we have a general sense of what a question demands and what our individual students require in terms of time to respond.

Sometimes students can answer our questions without comprehending the related text. Thus, questions should be vetted for text independence. Students may be able to provide correct answers when they have not comprehended the text addressed by the questions. This situation is prominent in multiple-choice question situations in which students with no idea of a correct answer in fact answer correctly, without any understanding of text: The lucky guess helps. Also, students may come to a correct answer by faulty reasoning or by using prior knowledge related to the text but not a product of comprehending the text. Asking students to provide reasons for their answers serves as a check on their answers, and it helps us best understand what a student was thinking when giving a particular answer.

A further consideration for our questioning is the demand that the response creates. Following our questions, students may be required to speak or write a response. This response format is one that must be considered as questions and sets of questions are created. Multiple-choice questions require that the reader choose the correct answer, often from among four or five possible answers. A well-developed multiple-choice question can provide valuable information about things students learn. As well, our questions may prompt students to provide constructed responses, responses that we may have labeled "fill in" in the not-so-distant past. Brief constructed responses require that students provide short answers, typically ranging from one to three sentences. Extended constructed responses can demand that students provide sentences, paragraphs, or sets of paragraphs. In each instance, our estimation of the item format that will best provide useful information is important. Like oral responses, written responses may have considerable wait time demands, not only for the students to find and retrieve information from their long-term memory but also to draft and revise the response to the question.

Good questions evolve over time because teachers who ask the questions pay attention to how students respond. A question and answer that seem excellent from our teaching perspective must be checked against students' performances and perspectives on the same, especially in culturally diverse classrooms. Before any question makes it into the classroom routine, we must ascertain that it works. We cannot be content with determining if a student's response to a question is "right" or "wrong." We must uncover the student thinking that led to the response to the question. Only the examination of this thinking will allow us to determine if what we imagined as a typical thought process and question response is what students actually do when responding to the question.

Assessing Responses to Questions in Retellings and Discussions

Earlier in this chapter we learned about the IRE discourse structure, which focuses on individual questions. Yet, in many classrooms there may be opportunities to assess students by listening to their retellings and discussions of the texts they read. We can get information related to students' understanding of text by examining the classroom context that surrounds reading. Do students discuss their understanding of stories and informational texts? Are they empowered to do so? Do students give retellings that help us fill in the gaps of our understanding of their comprehension? As a prelude to systematic questioning, what can a reader tell about what is read, unprompted? (Oral retellings of what students read are also examined in chapter 2, "Reading Inventories.") There are considerable benefits to student discussion of the things they read (Wells, 1989). As we become sensitive to the content and structure of students' discussions, we are able to find answers to our questions without asking them. Of course, done successfully, this demands that teachers are able to observe and analyze students' discussions in relation to a set of questions. Task analysis of the important things that students do when they read and practice with listening to students and matching discussion to questions can make this an important part of the classroom assessment routine.

Questions That Accompany Commercially Produced Curricula

Teachers who are knowledgeable about questioning and who have the time to do so can create series of questions for most of the texts their students read in class. More often, questions are part of commercially produced curricula, and it is important to scrutinize them. We must consider when and where the question we would ask was created. When questions are developed far from the here and now of reading in our classrooms, there may be reduced chance of a particular question being the best question. Questions can guide or follow thought. The questions that accompany textbooks in social studies, science, music, art, and literature are, hopefully, talented question writers' best estimation of what is needed to focus students on material and to elicit their responses. The questions tend to be knowledge-tracking questions, attending to how well students learn predetermined content. They are based on anticipated student work and outcomes, which may or may not be close to the work of particular students in our classrooms.

Approaches to questioning in commercially produced materials vary considerably. These questions anticipate an average level of understanding and insight, and they assume uniform progress among students. The questions, through their focus, predetermine the important information in the texts that students read. They also predetermine correct or acceptable answers. Teachers should always check the stated goals of the lesson and accompanying questions with their priorities. Will a set of questions tell us much about a student's learning and remembering key details and main ideas but little about how the reader can judge the trustworthiness of the author? Careful examination of the questions that accompany commercial reading materials can help teachers make decisions related to their suitability. A question (or set of questions) may be all that is needed by the teacher to determine that important learning is being assessed in an appropriate manner. In such cases, questions can be used as provided in teachers' manuals. In other cases, questions may focus on part of what the teacher considers to be important learning related to reading. Such questions should be augmented by the teacher's quest for more information. There may be questions that are directed toward eliciting important information, yet they do not present the best question for a particular student in a particular context. At different times in the school year and for different readers, the questions, What is the theme of this essay? Do you think the author makes a convincing argument? and Why? are entirely appropriate.

Questioning in Joan's Fourth-Grade Classroom

The students in Joan's classroom represent a diversity of reading achievement levels and reading interests. Throughout the school year, Joan is interested in making her questions count, and she sets as a personal professional development goal the ability to ask the right question. What is the right question? For Joan, the right question is determined by a complex set of factors: a student's developmental level as a reader, the content of the text that is read, the type of thinking that is important to model and then require of the student, and the testing landscape in the school and district. While these factors are at first burdensome for Joan as she formulates and chooses questions and determines when to ask them, she is confident that the questions in her classroom are worth students' while and that they reflect important teaching and learning. Joan's fourth-grade students are in their last year in a largely intact classroom. The classroom is self-contained, without any pullouts for particular content areas. One result is that Joan can approach her question-asking strategies across the school day and across content domains. Joan observes students reading and thinking in science, social studies, mathematics, and English, and this provides her with a continual source of information related to students' current state of development and corresponding instructional opportunities. She has the luxury of knowing her students across the school day and the responsibility of attending to the detail of their development so that her teaching and accompanying questioning are appropriate.

Joan is a strategic question asker, as she knows that good question-asking practice is not just a matter of having a range of questions that may evoke different types of student thinking and reveal different types of comprehension and learning. Joan knows that good questioning is also dependent on the interactive dynamics between teacher and student and question and answer. For example, in leading up to a relatively complex question that requires students to propose an explanation (i.e., How can global warming be slowed while students continue to use electricity and automobiles?), Joan knows that the student must demonstrate a literal understanding of the scientific findings related to global warming research. Assuming that this understanding exists without first questioning students to ascertain this could render the subsequent questions worthless.

To reach her goals for questioning, Joan relies on an "arc of questions" (Wolf, 1987) in which "simple factual inquiries give way to increasingly interpretive questions until new insights emerge" (p. 6). The questions help her address student learning and development related to learning about global warming, and the questions build on one another. While the set of questions is intended to help students demonstrate their knowledge and thinking at increasingly complex levels, it also has a diagnostic feature. More simple questions (e.g., What is one cause of global warming?) are asked prior to more complex questions (e.g., How can global warming be slowed or stopped?). This sequencing allows Joan to tailor questions to individual students. Joan finds it useful to think about an arc of questions in relation to students' current levels of reading ability and content area knowledge, along with Bloom's (1956) levels of thinking. Table 7 contains examples of questions that Joan includes in her arc of questions and indicates their increasing complexity and relationship to Bloom's taxonomy. This arc of questions represents Joan's comprehensive and hierarchical questioning routine, and it demonstrates her attention to using questions to help shape and assess her students' thinking.

Consequences and Usefulness of Questioning

Joan believes that it is important for students to apply what they learn from reading to

Table 7
Arc of Questions in Relation to Bloom's Taxonomy and Joan's Classroom

Scenario: Students are learning about global warming, reading from different texts.

1. Bloom's Taxonomy category: Knowledge, or recalling data or information.

   Joan's question to her students: What is one cause of global warming?

2. Bloom's Taxonomy category: Comprehension, or understanding the meaning, translation, interpolation, and interpretation of instructions and problems. Stating a problem in one's own words.

   Joan's question to her students: How does global warming occur?

3. Bloom's Taxonomy category: Application, or using a concept in a new situation or unprompted use of an abstraction. Applying what was learned in the classroom into novel situations in the work place.

   Joan's question to her students: What might happen with global warming as the number of automobiles increases?

4. Bloom's Taxonomy category: Analysis, or separating material or concepts into component parts so that its organizational structure may be understood. Distinguishing between facts and inferences.

   Joan's question to her students: What proof of global warming is offered by those people who claim it is a potentially deadly problem?

5. Bloom's Taxonomy category: Synthesis, building a structure or pattern from diverse elements. Putting parts together to form a whole, with emphasis on creating a new meaning or structure.

   Joan's question to her students: What would you include in a comprehensive plan to reduce global warming?

6. Bloom's Taxonomy category: Evaluation, or making judgments about the value of ideas or materials.

   Joan's question to her students: Are the alternative explanations for global warming that are given by those who are opposed to taking action against global warming credible? Why?

identify and solve problems, to engage in generative thought, and to be critical consumers of the information contained in the texts they read. She surveys questions and determines those that tap literal and simple inferential comprehension. As she categorizes her instructional goals in relation to Bloom's taxonomy, she can determine the degree to which the questions she asks of students focus on the different types of learning within the taxonomy. A result is robust questioning. Students need to establish accurate literal understandings of text, but they must also complement that understanding with the ability to answer questions about authors' motives, persuasive features of texts, and the degree to which claims in the text are supported with evidence. A more typical approach of using literal and inferential questions would not provide as rich assessment information.

There are several critical consequences and uses of the questions that Joan develops for her students. First, the questions help her understand how well students learn course content. The questions tap students' literal, inferential, and critical understandings of the texts they read. Second, the questions, having tapped students' literal and inferential comprehension, then require students to demonstrate diverse approaches to thinking and increased sophistication in their thinking. Questions help Joan understand how students use that which they comprehend. Importantly, questions serve to both provoke thinking and to assess it. For example, Joan asks how students might adopt different perspectives to comment on the portrayal of global warming in their science text. Without the question, it is not clear how many students would be moved to this type of thinking. And with the question, Joan also has a means for judging students' approaches to the thinking. Joan's questions provide process and product information about student reading development, information that can be used in both formative and summative assessment.

The consequences for Joan's students are substantial. They are continually asked to demonstrate their understanding of text through an array of questions that target literal and inferential understandings. These questions describe the extent to which students "get" the text. They also serve as practice for the high-stakes tests at year-end, which are heavily weighted to measure students' literal and inferential comprehension. Students in Joan's class get consistent models of how to think, provided by diverse types of questions, and they are learning to ask questions of themselves as they read. These questions fall into two broad categories—comprehension and metacomprehension—and help students independently determine the degree to which they understand texts that they read.

Over time, the varieties of questions that are asked in Joan's classroom (and in grades prior to and after fourth grade) have another serious consequence for students: They learn that what they read is often worthy of investigation and challenge. Questions model for students different ways of thinking and stances toward reading and knowledge. As fourth graders, these students are literally bombarded with advertisements and other types of propaganda that they encounter in newspapers, magazines, and on the Internet. Questions that uncover a hidden intent of text, an author's strategy for being persuasive, and the trustworthiness of text help students navigate their daily, personal lives and help us prepare students for critical reading throughout their lives.

Roles and Responsibilities Related to Questioning

Across a school career, the type and frequency of questions used in classrooms can have profound influence on students' thinking, their stances toward knowledge, and their epistemologies. Consider the student who receives an exclusive mix of literal and inferential comprehension questions across elementary school. The student may become adept at giving back text to answer literal comprehension questions and at combining literal information from text with prior knowledge to achieve inferential comprehension. The steady stream of questions focuses on knowledge checking, an important outcome of our reading. Unfortunately, this student may not have the opportunity to begin to question the authority of the text, to challenge an author's claims, or to determine the subtext that underlies an author's explicit and implicit arguments. In U.S. society where there is consistent initiative to convince people that they need to buy things and where truth is hard to find in political campaigns, our students must be able to ask questions of texts that put them in powerful (and not powerless) positions.

Joan is convinced that good teaching in fourth grade results not only in students learning in the content areas but also in further development of students' ability to think and reason. Future grades' curriculum in middle school and high school will demand that students master literal and inferential comprehension of texts so that they may critically evaluate them. Joan knows that application of knowledge learned from reading is not only demanded in the upper grades but also that such application of knowledge is central to much of the reading that students will do outside of school. She is responsible for certifying that students learn from text in each of the content areas and can apply the knowledge learned. She is responsible for helping her students prepare for high-stakes tests that will determine their futures. And she is responsible to the ideal that good questions beget more good questions: Students who are asked diverse and necessary questions learn new ways of thinking and can internalize and use these same types of questions in their future.

Joan's questions are informed by her ideas of good practice. She makes sure that she provides adequate wait time for all students to construct appropriate responses, and she makes sure her questions are comprehensible for her students. She conducts task analyses in relation to her questions, always double-checking to see that what she anticipates being involved in the process and product of student answers is actually there. Joan resists the idea of questioning becoming a comfortable habit in the classroom. She knows that questions can lead to the establishment and reinforcement of power relationships in classrooms. They can be used to acknowledge particular students' contributions or lack of contribution to the class. For Joan, asking, What's the right question? sets the parameters of her roles and responsibilities. She is focused on determining how and to what degree students are learning content from their reading. She regularly asks questions that focus on what students understand from the textbook chapter on earthquakes, the primary source texts in social studies, and the short story in English. She checks for her students' ability to understand math word problems.

Joan continually monitors her questions: She believes that most good questions need a tryout period. To refine and polish her questions, Joan pilots them, and this allows her to apply her knowledge from the task analysis to help troubleshoot those questions that Joan believes are important but that seem to be causing difficulty. She structures her question-asking routines so that they include opportunities for students to learn how to ask important questions of themselves. She models, explains, and discusses with her students why we ask questions, where questions come from, how they then connect to our learning goals and tasks, and how student responses to questions are evaluated. In addition, she amends the questioning routine that accompanies the commercially produced materials to include questions that direct students to the nature of questions, knowledge, and power.

Reliability of Questioning

As a teacher who creates many different types of questions for her students, Joan follows a detailed routine for ascertaining the reliability of the questions. At the heart of this routine is a task analysis of what, exactly, students must do to understand and respond to the questions. (For more information on task analysis, see Reading Assessment Snapshot: Task Analysis, p. 26.) The task analysis is conducted with the goal of creating questions that provide reliable information. It allows Joan to "go through the motions" that her questions will demand of her students and to experience, firsthand, what answering the question entails. She considers first the comprehensibility of the question. Will her students understand it? Is this literal question more challenging than the text students must read to answer the question? Next, she examines the fairness of the question. Does it privilege certain students who already know something of the content of assigned reading? Is the question straightforward and not confusing? Can the question be answered without reading the text? Next, Joan checks for confounds. (For more information on confounds, see Reading Assessment Snapshot: Confounds in Reading Assessment, p. 187.) Will a student's speaking or writing ability influence her interpretation of that student's reading achievement? She examines each question to determine the things a student must know and do to answer well. She considers the complexity of the question in relation to her students and estimates the wait time that is necessary for each to answer.

The reliability of her assessment also depends on her interactions with the students during questioning. When asking questions during a lesson, Joan can discuss, model, and suggest things that lead students to insights and correct answers. This is a regular part of Joan's question asking during class. In contrast, Joan is consistent in her treatment of students when asking summative assessment questions. She does not provide hints or clues when questions are related to unit tests, as she knows that students must be prepared to take consequential, high-stakes tests.

Validity of Questioning

Joan's questions must pass two stringent tests related to construct validity. The first test focuses on her conceptualization of reading comprehension as including literal, inferential, and critical or evaluative comprehension. Joan makes sure that her array of questions honors the construct of comprehension by asking questions that provide students with opportunities to demonstrate these different levels of thinking. The typical arc of questions in Joan's classroom reflects her knowledge of what it means to understand text. Students must construct literal and inferential meaning of the things they read, while understanding why texts are written, authors' acknowledged and unspoken agendas, and how the contexts in which we read can influence what we take from a text.

A second test relates to the thinking that is done by students as they answer questions. Bloom's taxonomy suggests increasingly complex and sophisticated thinking, and the array of questions in Joan's classroom reflects this construct. Thus, questions serve the dual role of providing detail on what students learn and providing a model of diverse and sophisticated thinking. They also reflect ecological validity, in that Joan strives to instill further inquisitiveness in her students by posing and modeling good question asking.

Summary

There are many types of questions we may ask when we assess our student readers. These questions should be informed by our knowledge of theories of thinking, our students, strategies, cognitive development, the role of the reader, and the curriculum. Across history, questions have been central to reading assessment. We ask questions because we want to know about student learning and progress. Questions are central to assessing and evaluating student reading, yet many questions do not reflect our detailed understanding of the suitability of particular types of questions for particular learning goals and reading curriculum.

Our questions should reflect the nature of learning and thinking we expect of our developing readers. Questions are influenced by diverse factors that include their structure, syntax, and vocabulary. As well, effective questioning practice reflects our attention to factors that include wait time, the questions' relation to retelling and discussion, and the development of series of questions that represent a range of comprehension levels and the range of content that we are interested in assessing.

References

Afflerbach, P. (2005). National Reading Conference policy brief: High stakes testing and reading assessment. *Journal of Literacy Research*, *37*, 151–162.

Beck, I.L., McKeown, M.G., Hamilton, R.L., & Kucan, L. (1997). *Questioning the author: An approach for enhancing student engagement with text.* Newark, DE: International Reading Association.

Bloom, B.S. (1956). *Taxonomy of educational objectives, Handbook I: The cognitive domain.* New York: David McKay.

Cazden, C.B. (1986). Classroom discourse. In M.C. Wittrock (Ed.), *Handbook of research on teaching* (3rd ed., pp. 432–462). New York: Macmillan.

Durkin, D. (1978). What classroom observations reveal about reading comprehension instruction. *Reading Research Quarterly, 14,* 481–533.

Guszak, F.J. (1967). Teacher questioning and reading. *The Reading Teacher, 21,* 227–234.

Huey, E.B. (1908). *The psychology and pedagogy of reading with a review of the history of reading and writing and of methods, texts, and hygiene in reading.* New York: Macmillan.

Mehan, H. (1979). *Learning lessons: Social organization in the classroom.* Cambridge, MA: Harvard University Press.

Muspratt, S., Luke, A., & Freebody, P. (1997). *Constructing critical literacies.* Creskill, NJ: Hampton Press.

Ogle, D. (1986). K-W-L: A teaching model that develops active reading of expository text. *The Reading Teacher, 39,* 564–570.

Pearson, P.D., & Johnson, D.D. (1978). *Teaching reading comprehension.* New York: Holt, Rinehart and Winston.

Pressley, M., & Afflerbach, P. (1995). *Verbal protocols of reading: The nature of constructively responsive reading.* Hillsdale, NJ: Erlbaum.

RAND Reading Study Group. (2002). *Reading for understanding: Toward an R&D program in reading comprehension.* Santa Monica, CA: RAND.

Raphael, T.E., & Wonnacott, C.A. (1985). Heightening fourth-grade students' sensitivity to sources of information for answering comprehension questions. *Reading Research Quarterly, 20,* 282–296.

Slack, J.B. (1998). *Questioning strategies to improve student thinking and comprehension.* Austin, TX: Southwest Educational Development Laboratory.

Stevens, R. (1912). *The question as a measure of efficiency in instruction: A critical study of class-room practice.* New York: Teachers College Press.

Thorndike, E.L. (1917). Reading as reasoning: A study of mistakes in paragraph reading. *Journal of Educational Research, 8,* 323–332.

Watson, J. (1913). Psychology as the behaviorist views it. *Psychology Review, 20,* 158–177.

Wells, G. (1989). Language in the classroom: Literacy and collaborative talk. *Language and Education, 3,* 251–273.

Wolf, D.P. (1987, Winter). The art of questioning. *Academic Connections,* pp. 1–7. Retrieved October 28, 2003, from http://www.exploratorium.edu/IFI/resources/workshops/artofquestioning.html

Questions for Reflection

- Videotape a reading lesson. Examine your questions: type of question, comprehensibility of the question, wait time, clarification, teacher dominance, and relation to different learning goals. Who asks questions, and who answers them? How much class time is involved? In relation to the information in this chapter, would you characterize the mix of types of questions you ask as optimal? Why?
- Can you provide an extended example of an arc of questions in a particular content area that helps you understand student achievement from the level of literal understanding through critical analysis and application of what is understood from reading?
- Think of a recent learning experience you had. How did you know how you were doing? How did you know how well you did upon completion of the task? What can this teach you about good questions to ask of students' reading, assessment, and self-assessment?

Focused Anecdotal Records Assessment: A Tool for Standards-Based, Authentic Assessment

Paul Boyd-Batstone

A tension exists between macrolevels and microlevels of assessment, according to Valencia and Wixson (2000), yet there is common ground. In the current U.S. educational environment, standards-based measures dominate assessment (Johnston & Rogers, 2002). Yet, over the past two decades, qualitative measures for assessment purposes, and observational records in particular, have expanded considerably (Bird, 1986; Fishman & McCarthy, 2000). On a macrolevel, content standards arguably supply systematic criteria for quantitative measures to report trends and establish policy. On a microlevel, qualitative measures such as rubrics, student profiles, and anecdotal records provide measures that fill in the gaps to give teachers immediate information to plan for instruction. The purpose of this article is to describe a technique for anecdotal records assessment that uses the lens of content standards for an initial focus. As a classroom teacher and as a teacher educator, I sought to develop a teacher-friendly, standards-based way to address recording, managing, and using anecdotal records for authentic assessment purposes. I call the system focused anecdotal records assessment (ARA).

Why Anecdotal Records Assessment?

Observational notes as a technique for recording a child's natural literacy experiences emerged from qualitative research (Emerson, Fretz, & Shaw, 1995; Guba & Lincoln, 1982; Lofland, 1971; Patton, 1990). Applying observational techniques for classroom-based, ongoing assessment has been called a variety of names such as alternative, informal, or authentic assessment (Cole, Ryan, & Kick, 1995; Reutzel & Cooter, 2004; Tierney, 1999). I prefer the term *authentic assessment*, as opposed to *alternative assessment*, because it is not defined by a juxtaposition to standardized assessment. Authentic assessment is defined by the active role the teacher plays in classroom-based assessment of actual literacy experiences. Taking observational notes allows the teacher to record a wide range of authentic experiences and even unintended outcomes of literacy development. These notes are used to record objective and subjective information as well as affective information, such as levels of engagement, curiosity, and motivational factors (Baker, Dreher, & Guthrie, 2000; Wigfield, 1997). With focused ARA, content standards initially frame the field of vision to guide observation; however, it is not designed to preclude the observation and recording of a full range of experiences related to reading and the language arts.

Being a teacher calls for skilled techniques in observing children, recording, and managing authentic assessment data. Recording observational data "explicitly depends on the human expert" (Johnston & Rogers, 2002, p. 381), the kid watcher (Goodman, 1978), and the sensitive

Reprinted from Boyd-Batstone, P. (2004). Focused anecdotal records assessment: A tool for standards-based, authentic assessment. *The Reading Teacher, 58*(3), 230–239.

observer (Clay, 1993). In other words, the one closest to the classroom experience is in a unique position to see and communicate a reliable and valid instructional perspective of the child. Rhodes and Nathenson-Mejia (1992) identified anecdotal records as a powerful tool for literacy assessment. Miller-Power (1996) argued that systematic, daily recording of children's actions was essential to generate focused instructional planning. Anecdotal records in particular have been used as one of multiple tools in authentic literacy assessment (Pils, 1991; Valencia, Au, Scheu, Kawakami, & Herman, 1990). Anecdotal records assessment is an essential component in the development and interpretation of student portfolios (Klenowski, 2002; Valencia, 1998). In addition, Rollins-Hurely and Villamil-Tinajero (2001) used observational records to assess the language proficiency of English learners.

A fundamental purpose of assessment is to communicate what the child knows and is able to do. Teacher-generated, anecdotal records provide an insider's perspective of the child's educational experience (Baumann & Duffy-Hester, 2002; Cochran-Smith & Lytle, 1990). This perspective is vital to communication with the child and the child's family about academic progress. Anecdotal records also facilitate assessment conversations (Johnston, 2003) as educational professionals describe their observations of student learning and consider ways to develop appropriate strategies to build on strengths and address academic needs. The more focused the observational records, the more helpful they can be in making daily decisions about instructional approaches.

A Collection of Techniques

Focused ARA employs content standards to initially focus observations. It uses several techniques for recording standards-based notes and a simple format for managing multiple records. It also supplies a way to analyze records and a place to address instructional recommendations. To more fully answer the question of what focused ARA is, I discuss each component of the process of standards-based, anecdotal records assessment in a problem-and-solution format. The five components to be addressed are as follows: observing children in instructional settings, maintaining a standards-based focus, making anecdotal records, managing anecdotal records, and using anecdotal records for assessment.

1. Observing Children in Instructional Settings

In attempts to record observations of children, two problems emerge: limited time and how to compose quality records. This two-fold challenge is illustrated by the following example. Each week, I observe teachers working with groups of students. They may be leading a discussion of a children's book. They are excited by the adrenaline rush they get when students authentically respond to reading. The students are making personal connections to the story and insightful comments, and they are asking probing questions. The lesson comes to a close just as the recess bell rings. The class files out the door to play. The student teacher desperately needs a bathroom break. Now what?

Observations must be recorded before the moment is lost to short-term memory. There is no time. The teacher draws a blank and is confronted with a host of perplexing questions: What should I write? How do I start? How did what I saw match up with content standards? What do I do with the information? How can I record information that will be readily accessible in the future? If I write one note about the students, how can I avoid rewriting the notes in each of their files? The observational data is at risk of being lost.

Observing children requires planning and preparation. In order to address the time constraints of the classroom, select which students to observe ahead of time. Avoid attempting to observe everybody all at once. I recommend dividing the students into four groups with five to seven in each group. Monday through Thursday of each week, observe a different group. On Fridays, observe the students who were absent or require further observation. In other words, the teacher focuses on only a handful of students to observe each day. This simple organizational technique can keep the teacher from drowning in anecdotal record taking. Another way to address time constraints is the use of adhesive computer address labels for writing the records (Rhodes & Nathenson-Mejia, 1992). Prior to observing, write the current date and the student's initials on each label. All that the teacher carries, then, are five to seven dated and initialed blank labels. I also recommend carrying a few extra labels just in case it becomes necessary to write further observations. Selecting students and preparing the labels for recording observations will save valuable time, but having tools in place is only part of the solution. Prior to observation, one needs to establish a focus.

2. Maintaining a Standards-Based Focus

Reality is complex. When confronted with myriad situations that take place during instruction, it is easy for the teacher to become distracted and neglect to observe actions directly related to the subject of instruction. Think of how experienced photographers approach taking pictures. They are experts at drawing the eye to a subject and, prior to entering the studio, will sketch a series of poses to establish a dominant focus for the pictures. In contrast, inexperienced photographers often take pictures without realizing that the foreground or background images create significant distractions.

In much the same way with anecdotal record taking, teachers require a dominant focus to avoid being distracted by disruptive or unusual behaviors, personality differences, and so forth. This is not to exclude important information about a student that a teacher should note. There are a number of tools for inventory and survey of developmental levels, interests, unique qualities, and affective aspects of the reading process (for a comprehensive listing, see Reutzel & Cooter, 2004). But, in order to train the eye for observing instructional experiences related to content standards, a dominant focus must be established. Teachers already do this with lesson planning; therefore, it follows to use the selected content standard for observational purposes.

Establishing a content standard focus has several advantages. First, it directs the attention of the teacher to persistently observe what students know and do with regard to specific instructional content. (Consequently, the teacher resists distraction in a given moment of instruction.) Second, the verbs in well-written content standards facilitate composing observational data. The verbs initiate the focus for observation.

The field of vision for observation is set by the verbs found in each standard. Are the students, for example, *identifying* vocabulary or *matching* words to pictures? Are they *asking* clarifying questions or *retelling* the story? Borrowing the key verbs from the content standard saves time with on-the-spot composing of anecdotal records. The teacher is not wasting time trying to think of what to record because, prior to instruction, the content standard was selected and the key verbs noted. The verbs in Table 1 were extracted from the California Reading/Language Arts Framework for California Public Schools (1999) Content Standards and organized according to various facets of reading and language arts. (This is not an exhaustive list.)

The focus, initially established by the content standards, guides observation for assessment. This is not to advocate a rigid and narrow field of vision. Experienced teachers observe and record multiple features of student performance at a glance. However, using a selected content standard as a point of reference ensures that an instructional focus is maintained during an observation period.

3. Making Anecdotal Records

Following instruction, write specific anecdotal records on adhesive address labels that have been dated for reference. Once records are taken, the labels are peeled off and then pasted to a specially designed form—one per child. Maintaining a key with a listing of the selected standards is highly recommended. The standards key provides a place to record and collect selected

Table 1
Meaningful Verbs for Writing Anecdotal Records

Strategies	Listening	Writing	Reading	Speaking
Uses (strategies)	Distinguishes	Writes	Blends	States
Organizes	Determines	Prints (legibly)	Reads	Describes
Generates	Recognizes	Spells	Tracks	Shares (information)
Classifies	Identifies	Illustrates	Decodes	Recites
Compares	Responds	Capitalizes	Follows words	Represents
Contrasts	Asks	Defines	Rereads	Relates
Matches	Questions	Indents	Uses references	Recounts
Plans	Clarifies	Describes	Studies	Retells
Provides	Discerns	Summarizes	Highlights	Reports
Connects (ideas)	Analyzes	Organizes		Concludes
Arranges	Follows directions			Quotes
Supports	Reacts			Delivers
Confirms	Points out			Requests
Selects	Points to			Asks
Chooses	Gestures			Indicates
Demonstrates				Confirms
Presents				
Clarifies				

Table 2
Anecdotal Records Standards Key

1	Date: Standard:	2	Date: Standard:
3	Date: Standard:	4	Date: Standard:
5	Date: Standard:	6	Date: Standard:
7	Date: Standard:	8	Date: Standard:

standards for future analysis of the anecdotal records (see Table 2).

Writing quality anecdotal records is facilitated by keeping in mind the following considerations: Write observable data, use significant abbreviations, write records in the past tense, support records with examples as evidence, don't use the C-word (*can't*), and avoid redundancy.

Write Observable Data. In order to ensure writing quality records, there are several questions that clarify the word choice for observable data. First, close your eyes and ask yourself these questions: Does the wording tell me what the student is doing? Do I see the child matching words to pictures? Is that an observable action? Conversely, a favorite phrase from the lexicon of expressions commonly used by educators is "on task." If you close your eyes and try to imagine what "on task" looks like, you draw a blank.

Two more questions deal with quantitative data: How many and how much? What you can count can be observed. How many words were spelled correctly? How many times did the student self-correct? How much time did the student read independently? Conversely, avoid using phrases that imply an embedded interpretation, such as "a lot," "a few," or "many times."

Some words are very tricky, such as *know* and *understand*, and yet they are essential to instruction. The reality is that one cannot directly observe the inner process of acquiring knowledge or understanding. These words are conclusions drawn from a composite of a student's demonstration of a skill or expression of summarizing or synthesizing concepts. We realize that a student has gained understanding by observing related actions. Children demonstrate their knowledge or understanding by responding to questions or performing a task. Note the difference in these kinds of records:

> Observable: "Wrote 3 sentences," "Read for 5 minutes," "Misspelled 6 words," "Defined vocabulary," or "Answered 2 comprehension questions."
>
> Not observable: "Wrote a few sentences," "Read a lot," "Misspelled words many times," "Knew vocabulary," or "Understood the story."

Use Significant Abbreviations. Table 3 provides some helpful abbreviations to speed the writing of records.

Write Records in the Past Tense. Remember that the moment after an event takes place, it moves into the past. Knowing to write records in the past tense streamlines the composing process. There is less need to consider how to conjugate verbs. Maintaining the past tense makes for consistent and more accurate records.

Support Records With Examples as Evidence. Include an example of what the student did. Any time the observer can cite a specific example, the record will more accurately

Table 3
Helpful Abbreviations

Abbreviation	Meaning	Example
ID	Identified	ID main idea
X	Times	Misspelled *tried* 3×s
→	To or in relation to	Matched picture → words (see next example)
T	Teacher	Retold story → T
S(s)	Student(s)	Read to 4 Ss for 5 minutes
RA	Read alone	RA → 2 minutes
RT	Read with teacher	RT → 2 paragraphs
RS	Read with another student	RS entire book
SC	Self-corrected	Wrote *unitid* SC → *united*
WA	Wrote alone	WA 3 sentences
WT	Wrote with teacher	WT 4 paragraphs
WS	Wrote with another student	WS 7 sentences
def	Defined	def 6 terms correctly
Δ (delta sign)	Changed	Δ initial focus in writing
N or ø (null sign)	Did not observe	ø clarifying questions

generate a clear recommendation for instruction (e.g., "WA *picture* 3 different ways—*pitur, pictr, piture*"). Examining the record triggers a recommendation for *r*-controlled word lessons.

Don't Use the "C-Word." There is a temptation to use the word *can't* when attempting to record an observation about what the student did *not* do. It is much more accurate to simply state that the student did not do a particular task than to imply that the student is unable to perform the task by writing *can't*. Note the difference in the following statements: "Can't write a five-line poem" versus "Did not write a five-line poem." The first statement is not an observation but an indictment against the student, whereas the latter expresses what did not happen, without implying a lack of ability on the student's part.

Use the null sign ø for a negative. Attempting to quickly report what was not observed proves cumbersome. It takes too many words to explain what was expected versus what was observed. A rapid way to state what was not seen is to preface the record with a null sign or the capital letter *N*. Then write the observational statement so that it reads like this: "ø—asked observational questions" or "N—identified past tense irregular verb." The record states what was expected to be seen; only the sign places it in the negative.

Avoid Redundancy. A frequent problem in writing anecdotal records is including needless repetition when the implication is obvious, such as "the student retold the story" or "the student identified the main character." There is no need to repeat the subject. The ARA form clarifies who is being observed. The same cautionary note applies to rewriting the student's name multiple times. We have all been taught to write complete sentences with a subject and a predicate; however, for the sake of time, it is not necessary. With focused ARA, the subject is already identified on the label by initials. There is no need to write his or her name again, and the fact that the subject is a student is implied in the process. Rather than initiating writing with a subject, begin with a key verb: "Matched picture to vocabulary."

4. Managing Anecdotal Records

Using adhesive computer address labels to record observations has several advantages (Rhodes & Nathenson-Mejia, 1992). The size forces the writer to economize. I repeat the following mantra each time I attempt to write anecdotal records: "Lean is clean; wordy is dirty." The value of an assessment can easily be lost in a deluge of words. Succinct writing clarifies the entire process. Another advantage of using these labels is that, unlike sticky notes, the adhesive holds the labels firmly in place on ARA student forms for access later.

A single-page ARA student form is shown in Table 4. The form has several design features to facilitate managing records. There is room for up to eight observational records, and then there is a section for sorting observations into strengths or needs. After that, there is space for instructional recommendations based upon the child's identified strengths and needs. The final section is a boxed area for noting any special needs accommodations. The teacher prepares a binder with an ARA student form for each child in the class. After anecdotal records are taken and at a convenient time during the day, the teacher simply sticks a computer address label in the appropriate box for each child. Once a child's form is filled, it is ready for an analysis of strengths and needs and instructional recommendations.

5. Analysis of Anecdotal Records

Anecdotal records assessment is informed by comparing the standards to the child's performance. The standards also inform the selection of strategies and activities for instructional recommendations. Periodically, analyze the compiled records for each student. The time between analyses may vary according to your own academic calendar. Consider analyzing the records every six to eight weeks. This is when the anecdotal records standards key (see Table 5) becomes useful. It is difficult to remember the

Table 4
Anecdotal Records Assessment Form

Student's name ______________________	Evaluator's name ______________________
1	2
3	4
5	6
7	8

Assessment statement

Summary of records: ______________________

Recommendation of next steps: ______________________

Accommodation for special needs:

various standards that were selected to guide observation over a period of weeks. Therefore, the anecdotal records standards key reminds the teacher of specific standards.

Reference each standard as you comb through the anecdotal records. Decide whether or not the student met the standard. Code the records as follows: Mark the records with an *S* to indicate an area of strength in comparison with the appropriate standard; mark the records with an *N* to indicate an area of need in relation to the standards. The records occasionally note a point of information that is neither a strength nor a need, such as the student's home language. Points of information are coded with an *I* (see Table 6). In addition, you may want to expand the range of coding to include anomalies or unique features with a *U*, or affective components of reading with an *A*. ARA is adaptable to the needs of the teacher.

Table 5
Anecdotal Records Standards Key

1	Date: 9/26 Standard: Concepts about print. Identify author, illustrator, and book features.	2	Date: 9/30 Standard: Comprehension. Ask for clarification and explanation of stories and ideas. Organization and delivery of oral communication: Retell stories, including characters, setting, and plots.
3	Date: 10/3 Standard: Vocabulary and concept development. Identify simple multiple-meaning words.	4	Date: 10/10 Standard: Written and oral English-language conventions. Grammar: Identify and correctly use various parts of speech, including nouns and verbs, in writing and speaking.
5	Date: 10/17 Standard: Writing applications. Write a brief narrative based on their experiences.	6	Date: 10/21 Standard: Writing applications. Write a brief narrative based on their experiences. Spelling: Spell frequently used, irregular words correctly.
7	Date: 10/28 Standard: Vocabulary and concept development. Use knowledge of individual words in unknown compound words to predict their meaning. Vocabulary and concept development: Identify simple, multiple-meaning words.	8	Date: 11/5 Standard: Writing applications. Write a brief narrative based on their experiences. Punctuation: Use appropriate ending punctuation marks.

Once the records are coded for strengths, needs, or information, simply list an abbreviated summary of the strengths and the needs in the space provided below the records. Separating the records into strengths and needs allows the teacher to summarize what patterns are being exhibited by the student. The summary also helps clarify and generate appropriate instructional recommendations.

Recommendations

Once the anecdotal records are summarized in terms of strengths and needs, student-specific recommendations can be made. In essence, the teacher is customizing instruction and support for the individual. To be effective and practical, the recommendations should be task oriented. New teachers have the most difficulty with this part of the process. It is not uncommon to see recommendations written as teacher strategies rather than student activities. A common trap these teachers fall into is to recommend a word wall to address any number of needs related to literacy development without specifying what the child is to do. To me, it sounds like something akin to "Take two word walls and see me in the morning." Without a task associated to the strategy, the recommendation can be meaningless.

Remember to write recommendations with the children's parents in mind. What would you say to parents? They would need specific tasks to do with their children, like sorting words into families of *-ar*, *-er*, *-ir*, -or, *-ur*. Providing task-oriented recommendations based upon the content standards clarifies the recommendations and ensures the practicality of the activity.

Table 6
Anecdotal Records

Student's name: Julia V. (pseudonym)	Evaluator's name: (Teacher)
1 9/26 J.V. S ID book's author, illustrator, title S ID copyright, year, publisher I Eng. learner = Spanish	2 9/30 J.V. S Asked clarifying questions S Retold beginning of story N MisID main character
3 10/3 J.V. S Classified vocab. words in self-generated categories	4 10/10 J.V. N Did not distinguish adjectives from verbs S Provided descriptive words to chart poem
5 10/17 J.V. Absent	6 10/21 J.V. N Wrote 2 paragraphs S Used cluster diagram as a prewriting organizer S SC 3 words writing *libary, troubel,* and *litle*
7 10/28 J.V. S Used *aerodynamic* in sentence N Matched 2 out of 5 vocab. words to definition	8 11/5 J.V. N Wrote 1 paragraph narrative w/assistance N No ending punctuation in 2 sentences

Assessment statement

Summary of records (Strengths): Asks clarifying questions; retells story beginnings; generates categories to classify words; uses descriptive words; uses prewrite organizers, self-corrects writing

(Needs): Misidentifies characters; parts of speech; writes 1 or 2 paragraphs with assistance; matching words to definitions; ending punctuation

Recommendation of next steps (Strengths): Continue to read books with her; encourage "who, what, why, how" questions; develop primary/secondary categories for words; use tree diagrams as a prewrite tool for more complex organization

(Needs): Character study and story mapping; compose cinquain poems to learn parts of speech; encourage 3 to 5 paragraph writing; match key vocab. to pictures; review ending punctuation rules

Accommodation for special needs:

N/A

A quality assessment is like a well-woven fabric. Components are all interrelated. Looking at the assessment, one can see (a) how the observations are standards based, accurately coded, and summarized in terms of strengths and needs and (b) how the selection of specific recommendations is the outcome. The relationships between components are strong. In other words, with focused ARA the recommendations are the direct result of the observation and analysis. The technique represents a complete process in observation and assessment.

Applications

There are three primary applications of focused ARA: formative assessment for determining instruction that matches the strengths and needs of the students, summative assessment for conferring with families about a child's progress, and a combination of both formative and summative assessment for consultation with a support staff.

Using and maintaining focused ARA generate substantive teacher observations as formative assessment for instructional planning. In contrast to standardized testing, which is far removed from the classroom setting, focused ARA utilizes the insights of an observant teacher to provide quality instruction. The process is based upon classroom experience, performance, and content standards. It allows the teacher to design instruction built upon individual strengths and needs. Focused ARA underlines the fact that standards-based performance assessment requires a relationship with the student to match strategies and activities to strengths and needs. The recommendations are tailored to the student.

The focused ARA is a useful tool for summative assessment. It outlines teacher comments to cite observations, summarize strengths and needs, and provide well-thought-out recommendations. When reporting a child's progress in a parent conference, focused ARA can be used to cite how a child performed to meet content standards on specific dates and how the teacher planned to address strengths and needs. Summarizing strengths establishes a positive note. Parents see from the outset that the teacher is advocating on behalf of their child. Summarizing needs follows naturally and provides the foundation for individualized recommendations. In the case of special needs, the focused ARA allows for addressing accommodations.

Prior to developing an alternative plan for instruction, support staff such as administrators, specialists, counselors, and school psychologists often ask to see a record of six weeks of interventions. Focused ARA meets that requirement in an organized fashion, providing evidence of student performance and teacher recommendations. This kind of information organized on a single sheet of paper can be invaluable to collaboration with the entire support system at a school site.

In Sum

In an educational environment that attributes significant weight to standardized measures for assessment, focused anecdotal records assessment provides teachers with an authentic tool to record observations in light of content standards. As part of a regular observational rhythm in the classroom, the teacher can manage records, analyze observational data, and provide standards-based recommendations. The system facilitates communication between the children, their families, and educational professionals participating in the assessment process. Focused ARA is a tool to work common ground across authentic and standardized assessment.

References

Baker, L., Dreher, M.J., & Guthrie, J.T. (2000). *Engaging young readers: Promoting achievement and motivation*. New York: Guilford.

Baumann, J., & Duffy-Hester, A. (2002). Making sense of classroom worlds: Methodology in teacher research. In M. Kamil, P. Mosenthal, P.D. Pearson, & R. Barr (Eds.), *Methods of literacy research* (pp. 77–98). Mahwah, NJ: Erlbaum.

Bird, L. (1986). The art of teaching: Evaluation and revision. In K. Goodman, Y. Goodman, & W. Wood (Eds.), *The whole language evaluation book* (pp. 15–24). Portsmouth, NH: Heinemann.

California Reading/Language Arts Framework for California Public Schools. (1999). Sacramento, CA: State Department of Education.

Clay, M. (1993). *An observation survey of early literacy achievement.* Auckland, New Zealand: Heinemann.

Cochran-Smith, M., & Lytle, S.L. (1990). *Insider/outsider: Teacher research and knowledge.* New York: Teachers College Press.

Cole, D., Ryan, C.W., & Kick, F. (1995). *Portfolios across the curriculum and beyond.* Thousand Oaks, CA: Corwin Press.

Emerson, M., Fretz, R., & Shaw, L. (1995). *Writing ethnographic fieldnotes.* Chicago: University of Chicago Press.

Fishman, S., & McCarthy, L. (2000). *Unplayed tapes: A personal history of collaborative teacher research.* Urbana, IL: National Council of Teachers of English.

Goodman, Y. (1978). Kidwatching: Observing children in the classroom. In A. Jagger & M.T. Smith-Burke (Eds.), *Observing the language learner* (pp. 9–18). Newark, DE: International Reading Association.

Guba, E., & Lincoln, Y. (1982). *Effective evaluation.* San Francisco: Jossey-Bass.

Johnston, P. (2003). Assessment conversations. *The Reading Teacher, 57,* 90–92.

Johnston, P., & Rogers, R. (2002). Early literacy development: The case for "informed assessment." In S.B. Neuman & D.K. Dickinson (Eds.), *Handbook of early literacy research* (pp. 377–389). New York: Guilford.

Klenowski, V. (2002). *Developing portfolios for learning assessment.* London: Routledge/Falmer.

Lofland, J. (1971). *Analyzing social settings.* Belmont, CA: Wadsworth.

Miller-Power, B. (1996). *Taking note: Improving your observational note taking.* York, ME: Stenhouse.

Patton, M.Q. (1990). *Qualitative evaluation and research methods.* Newbury Park, CA: Sage.

Pils, L. (1991). Soon anofe you tout me: Evaluation in a first-grade whole language classroom. *The Reading Teacher, 45,* 46–50.

Reutzel, D.R., & Cooter, R. (2004). *Teaching children to read: From basals to books.* Columbus, OH: Merrill/Prentice Hall.

Rhodes, L., & Nathenson-Mejia, S. (1992). Anecdotal records: A powerful tool for ongoing literacy assessment. *The Reading Teacher, 45,* 502–509.

Rollins-Hurely, S., & Villamil-Tinajero, J. (2001). *Literacy assessment of second language learners.* Boston: Allyn & Bacon.

Tierney, R. (1999). Literacy assessment reform: Shifting beliefs, principled possibilities, and emerging practices. In S. Barrentine (Ed.), *Reading assessment: Principles and practices for elementary school teachers* (pp. 10–29). Newark, DE: International Reading Association.

Valencia, S. (1998). *Literacy portfolios in action.* Fort Worth, TX: Harcourt College.

Valencia, S., Au, K.H., Scheu, J.A., Kawakami, A.J., & Herman P.A. (1990). Assessment of students' own literacy. *The Reading Teacher, 44,* 154–156.

Valencia, S., & Wixson, K. (2000). Policy-oriented research on literacy standards and assessment. In M.L. Kamil, P.B. Mosenthal, P.D. Pearson, & R. Barr (Eds.), *Handbook of reading research* (Vol. 3, pp. 909–935). Mahwah, NJ: Erlbaum.

Wigfield, A. (1997). Motivations, beliefs, and self-efficiency in literacy development. In J.T. Guthrie & A. Wigfield (Eds.), *Reading engagement: Motivating readers through integrated instruction* (pp. 14–33). Newark, DE: International Reading Association.

Questions for Reflection

- The author notes that two common difficulties in observing children in instructional settings and recording those observations are (1) working within a limited time and (2) organizing data to compose quality records. Have you experienced these difficulties in your own classrooms? What techniques do you use to focus your observations if you encounter these difficulties? What are the advantages of using the techniques mentioned in the article?
- What are your ideas on how to make focused anecdotal records assessment (ARA) a "part of a regular observational rhythm in the classroom"? What recommendations can you make for combining both the formative and summative assessment that result from ARA for consultation with support staff?

"I'm Not Stupid": How Assessment Drives (In)Appropriate Reading Instruction

Danielle V. Dennis

"Hey, Dr. Dennis, you know what I think? Just because I don't always understand what I read doesn't mean I'm stupid."

—Javaar, sixth-grade student

Javaar (all student names are pseudonyms) made this statement after I introduced the new instructional program my school district purchased for struggling middle school readers. Phonics and decoding strategies were the focus of the program in which my sixth-grade students were expected to spend most of each lesson practicing how to chunk phonemes. Then they read about cats that sat on mats and answered literal comprehension questions about what the cat sat on. Like many teachers, I felt a tension between what I was supposed to teach and what I knew my students needed. Javaar's comment, and the ensuing nods of agreement from other students, opened my eyes. My students forced me to look at what they knew about literacy, to find their strengths, and to use instructional strategies that were appropriate for them—striving young adolescent readers.

State of Accountability

In response to the requirements of the No Child Left Behind Act of 2001 (NCLB), the State of Tennessee revised the Tennessee Comprehensive Assessment Program (TCAP), a criterion-referenced standardized assessment that monitors students' proficiency on the state content standards in grades 3–8 (see www.state.tn.us/education/assessment/achievement.shtml). The content standards follow the criteria set by the Tennessee Reading Policy, which calls for "uninterrupted, direct, and explicit reading instruction using a comprehensive SBRR [scientifically based reading research] program that systematically and effectively includes the five essential elements of reading (phonemic awareness, phonics, fluency, vocabulary, and comprehension), taught appropriately per grade level" (Tennessee State Board of Education, 2005, p. 4). According to the same policy, schools must use TCAP results to make instructional decisions about individual students.

TCAP scores are reported across three levels: advanced, proficient, or below proficient. Students scoring below proficient do not answer enough questions correctly to satisfy the minimum state requirements at that grade level. When scores are reported by the state, teachers and schools do not receive information that demonstrates which content standards students complete successfully and which require additional instruction. Score reports provide only the level at which students scored on each overarching section of the TCAP.

What do criterion-based test reports tell middle-level educators about struggling readers? Essentially, score reports reflect students' abilities to master grade-level content standards as measured by state-mandated assessments, such as

Reprinted from Dennis, D.V. (2009). "I'm not stupid": How assessment drives (in)appropriate reading instruction. *Journal of Adolescent & Adult Literacy, 53*(4), 283-290.

TCAP. Students either score above, at, or below grade level on the standards measured by a particular test. Although this information is helpful for schools in determining whether students have successfully mastered the reading standards, these scores do not reveal why struggling readers are testing below grade level. In other words, the data we have from standardized reading assessments force us to ask the question, What abilities do struggling middle school readers possess?

If instructional decisions for young adolescent readers are made based on TCAP results, then are these decisions made on the assumption that all students who score below proficient are missing the same basic skills? Research on the instruction offered to struggling elementary school readers demonstrates that this is often the case, and that ensuing instruction promotes skills required for emergent readers (Buly & Valencia, 2002; Pressley & Allington, 1999; Rupp & Lesaux, 2006). Linn (2000) asserted that using scores from standardized assessments in this way has "undesirable effects on teaching and learning because they [lead] to a narrowing of the curriculum and an over-emphasis on basic skills" (p. 8). Although no "scientific evidence" exists revealing a connection between testing and increased achievement (Afflerbach, 2005; Allington, 2002a), many school districts use data from these assessments to make indiscriminate decisions about individual students (Afflerbach, 2005; Allington, 2002a; Buly & Valencia, 2002). According to Afflerbach (2005), using results from standardized reading assessments as estimates of individual growth are "at best an approximation of the students' actual achievement level" (p. 158). Students scoring below proficient on state assessments are identified and placed in supplemental or remedial reading classes, which often focus on phonemic awareness and decoding skills regardless of the grade or reading level of the students in the class (Allington, 2001; Buly & Valencia, 2002; Franzak, 2006).

Consider the school day of a student who earns below-proficient scores on the state reading assessment. The student spends part of the day practicing phonemic awareness and decoding strategies while spending the majority of the day with difficult subject-area texts he or she is expected to comprehend independently. At no point during the day is the student exposed to "just right" text (Allington, 2007; Hall, 2007). Allington (2007) considered placement of adolescents in supplemental reading courses that focus on early reading skills an "unintended effect" of federal education policy and explained that "most struggling readers find themselves spending much of the school day in learning environments where no theory or empirical evidence would predict any substantial learning" (p. 7). Hall (2007) noted the discrepancy between the literacy expectations of struggling readers and the behaviors they demonstrate and suggested that struggling adolescents attempt to comprehend content area texts that are much too difficult. To appear successful with the task, struggling readers are forced to focus on specific facts within the text (Franzak, 2006; Hall, 2007), but this surface-level approach to reading does not teach students how to engage or interact with text.

Study Context

I knew students were assigned to my class because they failed the state reading assessment, but what did that really tell me as their teacher? My first step was to look at all of the assessment information I collected on my students. Did the state reading assessment tell me they were missing the skills required of early readers, such as phonics or decoding? No. Informal reading inventories demonstrated that most of my students were able to read the words on the page and were able to comprehend text, but they did so at levels below the grade in which they were enrolled. In general, the assessment data I gathered suggested that problems with fluency, limited vocabulary, and use of comprehension strategies were hindering their reading success. I developed a plan that built on and supported their strengths, which meant explaining to the administrative team why the new remedial reading program was not the best instructional tool for my students. With data in hand, and a formulated plan, I took the team step-by-step through what I learned by first looking at what the students knew and then developing a framework for literacy instruction.

Method

What I found when I moved beyond standardized tests and a prescribed curriculum were patterns in assessment data that allowed me to more accurately address my students' literacy needs. I individually administered ($N = 94$) five assessments that measured phonemic awareness, phonics, fluency, vocabulary, and comprehension skills (see Table 1). Preliminary data analysis suggested that most of the students in the study earned below-grade-level scores in the categories of meaning (comprehension and vocabulary), word identification, and reading rate. However, cluster analysis, a statistical procedure used to link students with similar abilities and needs, revealed that many students were strong in one or more of these categories (see Table 2). Notably, four distinct groups emerged from the

Table 1
Assessments Administered to Students

Assessment administered	Skills measured: Phonemic awareness	Phonics	Fluency	Vocabulary	Comprehension
Woodcock-Johnson Diagnostic Reading Battery	X	X			
Test of Word Reading Efficiency (TOWRE)	X	X	X		
Spelling Inventory	X	X			
Peabody Picture Vocabulary Test (PPVT)				X	
Qualitative Reading Inventory-4 (QRI-4)			X	X	X

Table 2
Cluster Analysis

Group	Meaning	Word identification	Rate
1 Ron	++	-	-
2 Latoya	+	++	--
3 Enrique	--	++	+
4 Jacob	-	--	++

Note. ++ scores > .5 SD above sample mean; + scores < .5 SD above sample mean; - scores < .5 SD below sample mean; -- scores > .5 SD below sample mean.

cluster analysis, each representing both the abilities and needs of young adolescent readers, and none representing students missing phonics and decoding skills.

I highlight the characteristics of each group by describing a prototypical profile of one student to represent the linked abilities of all of the students in each group. Then, I offer suggestions, linked to the characteristics of the group, for the instruction needed to build upon each group's strengths.

Group 1: Ron—The Strategic Reader

According to his Qualitative Reading Inventory–4 (QRI–4) results, Ron's independent reading level on both narrative and expository text is grade 5, and he demonstrates the ability to negotiate appropriately matched text with deep understanding. Ron enters text with high levels of prior knowledge, as measured by the QRI–4 background knowledge questions. Ron's scores on the spelling inventory are in line with grade-level peers, and his vocabulary knowledge is strong. At first glance, Ron's word identification scores are of concern, but further analysis reveals that his ability to decode real words is only slightly below grade-level peers (grade equivalent [GE] = 5). It is his inability to decode nonsense words (GE = 3) that decreases his overall word identification scores. For example, Ron easily identified the word *chromosome*, but was unable to identify the nonsense word *blighten* (though he was able to identify the words *light* and *eaten* on the real word assessment). Finally, Ron's reading rate was slower than about half of the students assessed (words correct per minute [WCPM] = 93).

Focusing instruction on decoding would be much like a doctor treating the wrong symptom of an illness, because data reveal Ron's word identification abilities are appropriate for his grade. Further, Cunningham et al. (1999) concluded that assessment and instruction of nonwords may not be effective because those words are "harder and less valid decoding items because they require a task-specific kind of self regulation" (p. 411). Providing Ron with time to read appropriately matched text—text written at his independent reading level—will let Ron increase his volume of reading, which encourages development toward reading text at his grade level (Allington 2002b, 2007; Krashen, 1989). Though Ron's reading rate was lower than his peers, Spear-Swerling (2004) noted that students in the Strategic Reading phase often reread text when it does not make sense and referred to this as an appropriate fix-up strategy to aid comprehension. By increasing Ron's access to appropriately matched text, teachers offer the opportunity for Ron to use appropriate fix-up strategies on a more regular basis.

Group 2: Latoya—The Slow Word Caller

Latoya revealed the highest level of spelling knowledge of any student in the study, which displays her ability to apply experiences with the association of word spellings and pronunciations that lead to word memory (Ehri & Rosenthal, 2007). Latoya was able to spell words such as *resident* and *discovery*, indicating familiarity with harder prefixes and suffixes and unaccented final syllables (Bear, Invernizzi, Templeton, & Johnston, 2008). She earned higher overall decoding scores than Ron, but unlike Ron her scores were driven by her ability to decode nonsense words (GE = 6; real words GE = 5). Further, Latoya's reading rate was slower than any of her peers (WCPM = 81). Nathan and Stanovich (1991) proposed that students who successfully focus attention on decoding skills and reveal a slow reading rate often demonstrate a deficit in known word meanings. This assertion is further evidenced by Latoya's meaning scores, which were largely influenced by low scores on the vocabulary assessment and the background knowledge questions on the QRI–4. Latoya's independent reading level on both narrative and expository text is at the fourth-grade level.

Latoya demonstrated her ability to apply knowledge of words on the spelling inventory and decoding skills on the assessment of nonsense words, indicating that, like Ron, additional instruction in decoding is redundant for Latoya. Providing Latoya with opportunities to read books at her independent level, engaging her in vocabulary instruction using words from the text, and building her background knowledge will increase her understanding of the text as she reads. With increased knowledge of words in context, Latoya will also increase her reading rate (Nathan & Stanovich, 1991). Though Latoya possesses some of the skills required by readers in the Strategic Reading phase, her abilities place her within the Automatic Word Recognition phase of reading (Spear-Swerling, 2004), because she does not demonstrate the ability to consistently use vocabulary and comprehension strategies. Thus, explicit instruction in these areas will benefit Latoya, particularly when matched with independent text.

Group 3: Enrique—The Automatic Word Caller

Like most of the English-language learners in the study, Enrique exhibited the ability to decode words quickly and accurately (WCPM = 108) but earned lower scores on measures of comprehension and vocabulary than both Ron and Latoya. Enrique's independent reading level on narrative text is mid-third grade, while his independent reading level on expository text is mid-second grade. The discrepancy between the two types of text is highlighted by Enrique's scores on the vocabulary assessment and QRI–4 content questions, which suggest a lack of background knowledge and are lower than those of any other group in the study.

Much like Latoya, Enrique requires intensive instruction in vocabulary and comprehension strategies using narrative and expository text at his independent reading level. Unlike Latoya, Enrique demonstrates his knowledge of words with rapid decoding skills, which will necessarily slow once Enrique learns the meaning of words in context (Nathan & Stanovich, 1991; Spear-Swerling, 2004). Particular attention must be paid to vocabulary instruction in expository, or content area, text because these texts require students to continually build upon their prior knowledge to learn new material. Reader behaviors, such as questioning strategies, will also encourage Enrique to slow his reading to consider if the text makes sense as he reads (Caldwell, 2008).

Group 4: Jacob—The Rapid "Reader"

Jacob displays the ability to read quickly, scoring significantly higher than his peers on measures of reading rate (WCPM = 113). Similar to Enrique, Jacob's speed inhibits his ability to make meaning from the text, as evidenced by his third-grade independent reading level score on narrative text and his low-second-grade level on expository text. Like his scores on all of the assessments administered, Jacob's word identification scores are considerably lower than those of his peers. Much like Ron, however, once his scores in that category are separated, it is apparent that he earned significantly lower scores on nonsense word decoding (GE = 2) than on decoding of real words (GE = 3). On the spelling inventory, Jacob was able to spell words such as *scrape* and *nurse*, indicating an ability to recognize vowel patterns, but was unable to spell words such as *squirt* or *smudge*, suggesting that words with complex consonants are difficult for him (Bear et al., 2008).

Based on his low spelling scores, Jacob requires intensive word study with instruction offered at his developmental level rather than at the level required of early readers. Jacob needs opportunities to read appropriately matched text, with a particular focus on building background knowledge. Saenz and Fuchs (2002) asserted that students who earn lower scores on assessments of expository text comprehension than on narrative text comprehension are less able to draw on their prior knowledge to make inferences from expository text. Spear-Swerling (2004) acknowledged that building students' background knowledge and explicitly teaching inferencing strategies is essential for students, like Jacob, who do not yet use the text as a tool for gathering information.

Tiered Instruction for Striving Readers

I now worry that too many school districts are making the same sort of decision that my district made for struggling young adolescent readers: purchasing a single commercial reading program for instructional intervention (Allington, 2001; Buly & Valencia, 2002; Ivey & Baker, 2004; Shanahan, 2005). With increased pressure on schools to raise the scores of struggling readers on state-mandated high-stakes assessments, middle school leadership teams are using these data when placing struggling students in remedial reading classes, without accompanying information designed to reveal the abilities these students display (Dennis, 2008).

Under current reading policies, Ron, Latoya, Enrique, and Jacob will all receive intensive intervention in an instructional program that likely focuses on phonemic awareness and decoding skills, because they earned below-proficient scores on the TCAP. As Franzak (2006) noted, "If 'reading' is defined and treated as a set of hierarchically listed tasks, some readers will continue to occupy the bottom rung of the literacy ladder" (p. 231). When students are not taught according to their individual abilities and needs, but instead are taught based on the premise of a one-size-fits-all instructional program, we are not providing them with opportunities to climb the literacy ladder. Tiered intervention plans, such as Response to Intervention, offer educators a step-by-step process for individually evaluating students' instructional needs. Gersten et al. (2009) offered a five-step process for implementing a multitiered intervention plan in the primary grades. I revised their recommendations to match adolescents' unique literacy needs and involve the entire school community.

Step 1

Use state reading assessment data (e.g., TCAP) to identify students who score below proficient. Using state reading assessment results as an approximation, or screening tool, for determining students' ability levels is appropriate (Afflerbach, 2005; Linn, 2000). However, teachers and administrators must continue through the steps of the tiered plan to match adolescent readers to suitable instructional models, based on readers' individual needs.

Step 2

Conduct a series of reading assessments, including an Individual Reading Inventory, to determine the varying needs of individual students. Keep in mind that not all students who earn below-proficient scores on the state reading assessment require intervention. As Klenk and Kibby (2002) asserted, most struggling readers are not in need of dramatically different instruction from their peers, but do need more intensive instruction of various skills. This is highlighted within and across the four profiles presented. Each group demonstrates specific abilities and needs that must be addressed through appropriate instruction and then differentiated based on the unique reading abilities of each student.

Continually assess students throughout the year and alter instruction to match demonstrated growth and abilities. Revise groups purposefully and often. To monitor growth over time, formally assess students at the middle and the end of the year. (Students who do not demonstrate marked progress should be referred to a student study team for evaluation of need for special services.)

Step 3

Next, group students according to results from Step 2 (see Figure 1). Students in all four groups benefit from opportunities to read text at their independent level, as well as the chance to engage in instructional level text with teacher support and guidance. This requires teachers to use dynamic teaching strategies to accommodate the varying needs of this heterogeneous population (Fountas & Pinnell, 2001). Dynamic grouping allows teachers to provide instruction to changing groups of students based on text type, interest level, level of background knowledge, and reading level, all factors that influence successful negotiation of text.

Ron, Latoya, Enrique, and Jacob all need word study instruction, with a particular focus on building content knowledge. Though the method of instruction may look similar, the words chosen for each student are necessarily different, based on each student's independent reading level and word knowledge. Enrique and Jacob, in

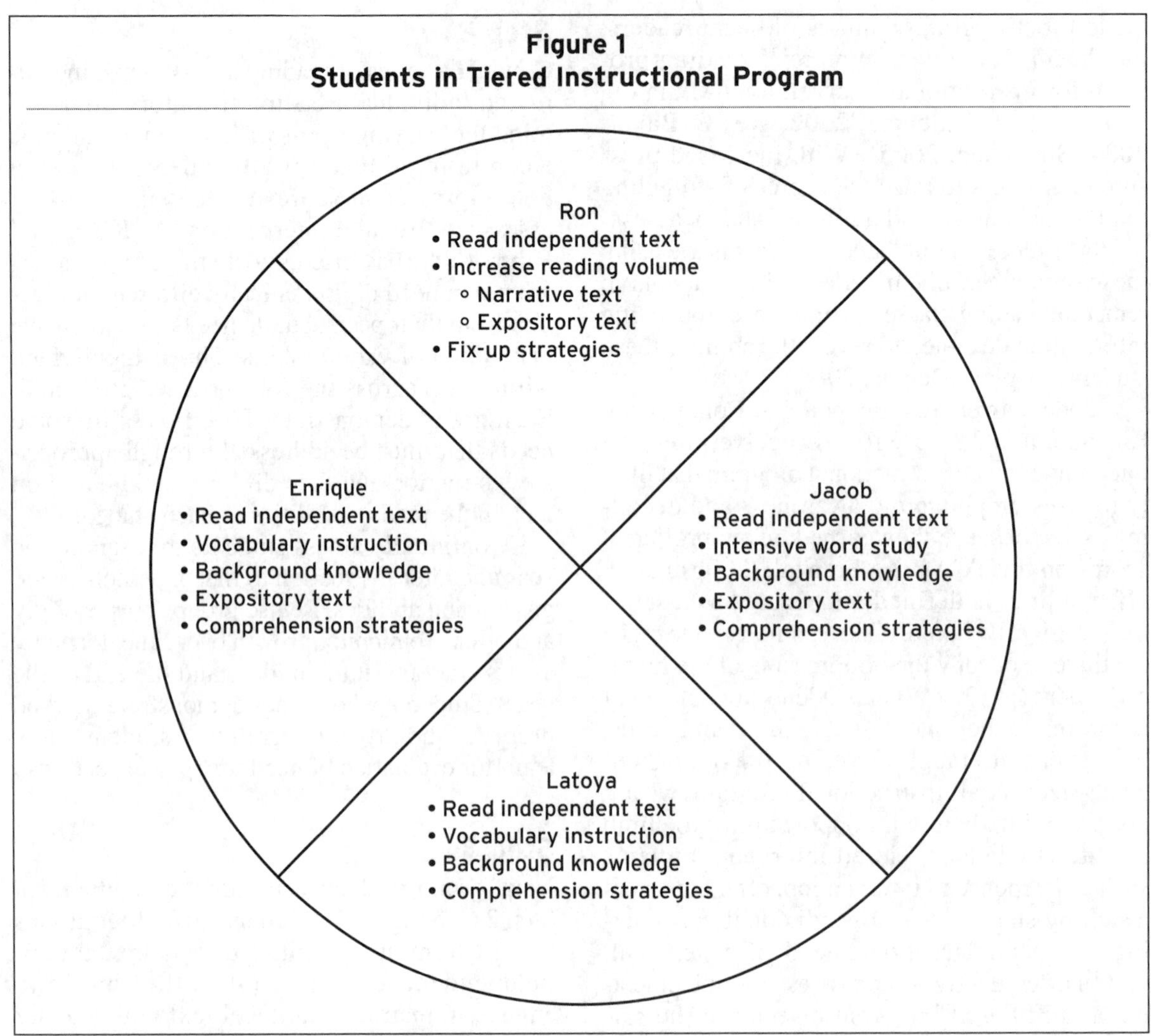

particular, require substantial vocabulary work in the context of expository text.

Each of these students will benefit from explicit comprehension instruction, based on texts at their independent reading level. In a meta-analysis of instructional interventions designed to promote students' comprehension, Mastropieri, Scruggs, Bakken, and Whedon (1996) found that interventions with a focus on self-questioning and self-monitoring of strategy use were most effective. Thus, it is not enough to teach students comprehension strategies; they must also learn to monitor their use of the strategies learned and to question their understanding of the text as they read. These are reader behaviors that students must have modeled for them (Caldwell, 2008).

Step 4

Include students in setting literacy goals, and ask them to offer ideas for monitoring their growth (Hall, 2007). Then, involve them in self-evaluations of meaningful literacy tasks. Struggling adolescent readers participate in a variety of reading behaviors both in and out of school (Franzak, 2006; Hall, 2007). To provide reading instruction that focuses on students' strengths rather than their weaknesses, Hall (2006) recognized that "it becomes critical to reconsider how we conceptualize the ways teachers might think about reading instruction, struggling readers, and the multitude of influences that can affect student learning and growth" (pp. 425–426). Such an approach requires educators to include adolescents in the decision-making and goal-setting activities necessary to improve their literacy abilities (Hall, 2007).

Step 5

Involve all teachers in Steps 2–4. Provide professional development on appropriate instructional methods to personnel working with struggling adolescent readers. In order for students to reach their established literacy goals, all school personnel must be involved in the instructional process. Students will need opportunities to read independent-level text in science and social studies, as well as in reading/language arts. We cannot expect to increase student achievement in one class period devoted to reading instruction but instead must involve all members of the instructional team (Allington, 2007).

Addressing Varying Needs and Abilities

With the deeper working knowledge of the abilities of struggling young adolescents provided through these data, policies and instructional decisions may begin to accurately address the varying needs and abilities of these students. Certainly, what was learned through this research is that struggling young adolescents demonstrate complex, heterogeneous reading abilities requiring significantly different instructional interventions. In order for those interventions to be successful, we must consider the abilities with which our students enter the classroom, based on substantial data, and turn our focus to how best to build upon those abilities to provide meaningful instruction to our striving readers.

References

Afflerbach, P. (2005). National reading conference policy brief: High stakes testing and reading assessment. *Journal of Literacy Research*, *37*(2), 151–162. doi:10.1207/s15548430jlr3702_2

Allington, R.L. (2001). Research on reading/learning disability interventions. In A.E. Farstrup & S.J. Samuels (Eds.), *What research has to say about reading instruction* (3rd ed., pp. 261–290). Newark, DE: International Reading Association.

Allington, R.L. (Ed.). (2002a). *Big brother and the national reading curriculum: How ideology trumped evidence*. Portsmouth, NH: Heinemann.

Allington, R.L. (2002b). You can't learn much from books you can't read. *Educational Leadership*, *60*(3), 16–19.

Allington, R.L. (2007). Intervention all day long: New hope for struggling readers. *Voices From the Middle*, *14*(4), 7–14.

Bear, D.R., Invernizzi, M., Templeton, S., & Johnston, F. (2008). *Words their way: Word study for phonics, vocabulary, and spelling instruction* (4th ed.). Upper Saddle River, NJ: Pearson.

Buly, M.R., & Valencia, S.W. (2002). Below the bar: Profiles of students who fail state reading assessments. *Educational Evaluation and Policy Analysis*, *24*(3), 219–239. doi:10.3102/01623737024003219

Caldwell, J.S. (2008). *Reading assessment: A primer for teachers and coaches* (2nd ed.). New York: Guilford.

Cunningham, J.W., Erickson, K.A., Spadorica, S.A., Koppenhaver, D.A., Cunningham, P.M., Yoder, D.E., et al. (1999). Assessing decoding from an onset–rime perspective. *Journal of Literacy Research*, *31*(4), 391–414.

Dennis, D.V. (2008). Are assessment data really driving middle school reading instruction? What we can learn from one student's experience. *Journal of Adolescent & Adult Literacy*, *51*(7), 578–587. doi:10.1598/JAAL.51.7.5

Ehri, L.C., & Rosenthal, J. (2007). Spellings of words: A neglected facilitator of vocabulary learning. *Journal of Literacy Research*, *39*(4), 389–409. doi:10.1080/10862960701675341

Fountas, I.C., & Pinnell, G.S. (2001). *Guiding readers and writers: Grades 3–6*. Portsmouth, NH: Heinemann.

Franzak, J.K. (2006). *Zoom*: A review of the literature on marginalized adolescent readers, literacy theory, and policy implications. *Review of Educational Research*, *76*(2), 209–248. doi:10.3102/00346543076002209

Gersten, R., Compton, D., Connor, C.M., Dimino, J., Santoro, L., Linan-Thompson, S., et al. (2009). *Assisting students struggling with reading: Response to Intervention and multi-tier intervention for reading in the primary grades. A practice guide*. (NCEE 2009-4045). Washington, DC: National Center for Educational Evaluation and Regional Assistance, Institute of Education Sciences, U.S. Department of Education. Retrieved from ies.ed.gov/ncee/wwc/publications/practiceguides/

Hall, L.A. (2006). Anything but lazy: New understandings about struggling readers, teaching, and text. *Reading*

Research Quarterly, 41(4), 424–426. doi:10.1598/RRQ.41.4.1

Hall, L.A. (2007). Bringing television back to the bedroom: Transactions between a seventh grade struggling reader and her mathematics teacher. *Reading Research and Instruction, 46*(4), 287–314.

Ivey, G., & Baker, M. (2004). Phonics instruction for older students? Just say no. *Educational Leadership, 61*(6), 35–39.

Klenk, L., & Kibby, M.W. (2002). Re-mediating reading difficulties: Appraising the past, reconciling the present, constructing the future. In M. Kamil, P. Mosenthal, P.D. Pearson, & R. Barr (Eds.), *Handbook of reading research* (Vol. 3, pp. 667–690). Mahwah, NJ: Erlbaum.

Krashen, S. (1989). We acquire vocabulary and spelling by reading: Additional evidence for the input hypothesis. *Modern Language Journal, 73*(4), 440–464. doi:10.2307/326879

Linn, R.L. (2000). Assessments and accountability. *Educational Researcher, 29*(2), 4–16.

Mastropieri, M.A., Scruggs, T.E., Bakken, J.P., & Whedon, C. (1996). Reading comprehension: A synthesis of research in learning disabilities. In T.E. Scruggs & M.A. Mastropieri (Eds.), *Advances in learning and behavioral disabilities* (Vol. 10, Part B, pp. 201–227). Greenwich, CT: JAI.

Nathan, R.G., & Stanovich, K.E. (1991). The causes and consequences of differences in reading fluency. *Theory Into Practice, 30*(3), 177–184.

Pressley, M., & Allington, R.L. (1999). What should educational research be the research of? *Issues in Education: Contributions From Educational Psychology, 5*(1), 1–35.

Rupp, A.A., & Lesaux, N.K. (2006). Meeting expectations? An empirical investigation of a standards-based assessment of reading comprehension. *Educational Evaluation and Policy Analysis, 28*(4), 315–333. doi:10.3102/01623737028004315

Saenz, L.M., & Fuchs, L.S. (2002). Examining the reading difficulty of secondary students with learning disabilities: Expository versus narrative text. *Remedial and Special Education, 23*(1), 31–41. doi:10.1177/07419325020230010 5

Shanahan, C. (2005). *Adolescent literacy intervention programs: Chart and program review guide.* Naperville, IL: Learning Point Associates.

Spear-Swerling, L. (2004). A road map for understanding reading disability and other reading problems: Origins, prevention, and intervention. In R.B. Ruddell & N.J. Unrau (Eds.), *Theoretical models and processes of reading* (5th ed., pp. 517–573). Newark, DE: International Reading Association.

Tennessee State Board of Education. (2005). *Tennessee reading policy.* Nashville: Author. Retrieved September 17, 2009, from www.state.tn.us/sbe/Policies/3.104%20Reading.pdf

Questions for Reflection

- Consider Javaar's statement from the beginning of the article. Has a student ever expressed to you something similar to this? Have you ever felt a tension between what you were supposed to teach and what you knew your students needed? How can the techniques in this article help you reconcile this?
- Can you think of your students who share similar characteristics with Ron, Latoya, Enrique, and Jacob? Have you noticed patterns in your assessment data? How would you go about developing a plan that builds on and supports their strengths as readers?

Parents and Children Reading and Reflecting Together: The Possibilities of Family Retrospective Miscue Analysis

Bobbie Kabuto

Carol (all names are pseudonyms), a single working mother, expressed frustration at watching her daughter Christie's unwillingness to read *Buzz Said the Bee* (Lewison, 1992):

> You are making me so uncomfortable. You are acting so reluctant. This is such a waste of good energy. I have to run away when she acts like this and when I'm bombarded with this horrible energy. She can't possibly be learning. I know what she needs to accomplish and this is not it.

Christie is a third grader who reads at a preprimer level, based on results from the Qualitative Reading Inventory–4 (QRI–4; 2006). She struggles with reading both in and out of school. Christie's struggles also become her family's struggles. Taylor (1993) discussed the burden placed on families when she wrote, "When we evaluate children we get lost in our own abstractions and children fail. When children fail, families are placed in jeopardy. Sometimes families fail" (p. 26).

Carol and Christie were participants in a Family Retrospective Miscue Analysis (Family RMA) study that combined Retrospective Miscue Analysis (RMA) with family literacy. The purpose of the study was to investigate how RMA could be used to help parents and children navigate the reading process, with the goal of helping parents better understand their children's reading strengths. In this article, I present the study and argue that RMA provided a space for Carol to identify with Christie as a reader, which in turn allowed Carol to better support Christie. I conclude with the implications of this study for reading specialists and classroom teachers.

Reading and Reflecting Through RMA

Family RMA brings parents and children together to discuss reading by requiring parents and their children to participate together in oral readings and RMA discussions. RMA, which is a retro-reflective discussion about a reader's miscues, is based on the work of miscue analysis (K. Goodman, 2003a).

Miscues are produced responses that differ from expected responses in texts. For example, a reader reads "I went into her house" for the expected sentence "I went into her home." Miscue analysis views miscues as windows into the reading process (K. Goodman, 2003a). That is, miscues can help us infer what readers are thinking when they read (albeit never perfectly). Miscue analysis has been the cornerstone procedure for helping teachers understand the strategies used by readers as they construct meaning from texts (Brown, Goodman, & Marek, 1996).

Research has suggested that readers employ a combination of reading cueing systems in the process of making sense of texts (K. Goodman, 1996; Smith, 1997). In particular, readers will

Reprinted from Kabuto, B. (2009). Parents and children reading and reflecting together: The possibilities of family retrospective miscue analysis. *The Reading Teacher, 63*(3), 212–221.

integrate the graphophonic (letter/sound), syntactic (grammar), and semantic (meaning) cueing systems. Research has also suggested that an imbalanced use of these cueing systems can cause readers to struggle with texts (Smith, 1997). For instance, Smith (1997) contended that readers who focus too much on letters and sounds in pronouncing unknown words acquire tunnel vision. According to Smith, this causes readers to overload from processing large amounts of visual information, which distracts them from reading comprehension.

Although there is a strong research base that demonstrates the effectiveness of RMA as an instructional tool with readers in elementary (Moore & Gilles, 2005) and secondary schools (Moore & Aspegren, 2001) as well as adult learners (Paulson, 2001), this study takes a new approach to the study of RMA by using it with families. More specifically, RMA offers a context in which parents and their children can become more aware of their strengths as readers through the process of revaluing (K. Goodman, 2003b). Revaluing readers involves shifting the focus from reading as accurate, oral production to reading as comprehension (Y. Goodman, 1996). With this shift in focus, we help readers to recognize and concentrate on their strengths by valuing what they *can* do (K. Goodman, 2003b). Therefore, RMA discussions address the merit of high-quality miscues, which are miscues that do not change the meaning of the sentence or story (e.g., substituting *sofa* for *couch*). Ultimately, this study aspired to help parents and children to view miscues as part of common reading behaviors.

Family RMA Inquiry Questions

Recognizing that little research has been conducted on RMA with family units, I saw the possibilities that Family RMA could offer parents and their children. The questions that framed the investigation of Family RMA with Carol and Christie were as follows:

- How did Family RMA provide Carol and Christie with a space for exploring reading strategies and processes?
- What reading strategies did Carol adopt in working with Christie as a result of their Family RMA sessions?
- How did Carol's and Christie's perceptions about themselves and each other as readers evolve as a result of their Family RMA experience?

A Case Study in Family RMA

Christie is 8 years old. She is a third grader who has been labeled with a speech and language disability and she receives special services in school. She lives with her mother, Carol, in a middle class suburban area. Carol is a college-educated professional who works from home, and Christie is her only child.

Christie told me that she enjoys participating in extracurricular activities, such as skating, swimming, and dance. However, she was not as positive about school, or about reading in particular. Although Christie said that she likes to read, her other comments created a different picture. When Christie was asked to read during the Family RMA sessions, she provided excuses such as "it makes me tired." There were other times when I attempted to probe into Christie's perceptions about reading and she supplied the response, "I don't want to talk about it."

As described in the beginning of this article, Carol was frustrated by Christie's reluctance toward reading. In addition, Carol expressed disappointment with the types of support that Christie was receiving in school, which did not provide Christie with enough reading services despite the fact that she was reading at a preprimer level. Carol felt that the most important thing about reading was comprehension, and she did not feel that Christie was able to understand what she was reading. This compelled Carol to advocate for Christie to receive more instruction that addressed comprehension and less instruction that emphasized letter–sound relationships.

Consequently, Carol volunteered for the Family RMA study with the hope of learning different ways to work with Christie that would focus on comprehension rather than oral production. Initial reading data on Christie painted a picture of a reader with tunnel vision. Not only did Christie say that she sounded out words when she had difficulty, but also she used this strategy consistently when reading orally, causing her to stretch out words until they were unrecognizable. However, it is interesting that although Christie's oral reading was laborious, she was nevertheless able to retell the story. Her retellings always consisted of the major characters, details of the setting and plot, and the story problem. Overall, initial reading data suggested that Christie did not have flexible use of cueing systems or other types of word-solving strategies when orally reading.

Family RMA Sessions

Family RMA consisted of at least one parent, his or her child, and the researcher (Kabuto, the author), and it took place in the local public library. The 10 total sessions alternated between miscue analyses and RMA discussions for the child and miscue analyses and RMA discussions for the parent (see Table 1). During each RMA session, parents and children participated together in observing the oral readings and discussing high-quality miscues for a twofold reason. First, children had the opportunity to listen to and reflect upon their parents' miscues. When Christie was asked who was a good reader, for instance, she replied that her mother was. In order for Christie to realize that miscues are the result of her efforts in constructing meaning, the discussion of how her mother (who Christie feels is a good reader) makes miscues became critical if Christie was to transform her perceptions about what readers do when they read. Christie was therefore able to make connections between her high-quality miscues and those of her mother.

Second, by asking parents to orally read and then discuss their miscues, parents have the opportunity to reflect critically upon their understandings of reading and upon themselves as readers. Therefore, allowing parents to participate in RMA sessions makes their experiences and their definitions of reading transparent.

Table 1
Family RMA Session Outline

Session	Description
1	Reading interviews for the child and parent
2	Conduct miscue analysis with the child
3	Conduct RMA session with the child Conduct miscue analysis with the parent
4	Conduct RMA session with the parent
5	Conduct miscue analysis with the child
6	Conduct RMA session with the child Conduct miscue analysis with the parent
7	Conduct RMA session with the parent
8	Conduct miscue analysis with the child
9	Conduct RMA session with the child
10	Closing reading interview

In this way, parents are also able to view their strengths and use them as a means of interpreting their children's strengths.

Family RMA Data

The data collected during the course of the study consisted of the following categories: parent interviews, child interviews, observational and reflective notes, oral readings, and RMA discussions.

Parent Interviews. At the beginning of the study, I interviewed Carol using the Burke Reading Inventory (Y. Goodman, Watson, & Burke, 1987) about her definition of reading, how she learned to read, her perceptions of the important aspects of reading, and how she felt about herself as a reader. In addition, I gathered information about Carol's perceptions of Christie's reading abilities, Christie's progress in school, how Carol saw the school's role in providing services to support Christie's reading and writing, and Carol's goals for Christie's literacy progress. Carol was also interviewed using the Burke Reading Inventory at the end of the 10 weekly sessions. Finally, each session included interviews regarding daily home literacy practices and school activities.

Child Interviews. I interviewed Christie at the beginning and the end of the study with the Burke Reading Inventory (Y. Goodman et al., 1987). The reading interview contained the same questions as those given to her mother. I also interviewed Christie regarding daily home literacy practices and school activities.

Observational and Reflective Notes From Participant Observation. This study involved participant observation, which is an ethnographic research design in which a researcher becomes actively involved in the research process (Agar, 1996). Consequently, documenting how my role and ideologies of reading coconstructed the research is of critical importance. My theoretical framework is important to acknowledge, as it influenced the ways in which I approached this research. It situates reading as a constructive process with meaning at the core. Following the ethnographic tradition, I wrote observational notes at every session. The sessions were also audiotaped and later transcribed. The observational notes provided contextual information and captured spontaneous dialogue that evolved out of our sessions. After I transcribed each session's audio data, the transcriptions and observational notes were examined together to write reflective notes that discussed my role in the research and the overall themes evolving out of each session.

Oral Readings and Selection of Miscues. At the beginning of the study, I assessed Christie using QRI–4 (2006). The initial QRI–4 data provided a benchmark range for selecting books on Christie's instructional reading level. In order for her to produce high-quality miscues, Christie read books that were one level above her instructional level, which would challenge but not frustrate her. Carol was asked to read articles out of magazines such as *Time* or *Newsweek.* (Table 2 outlines the miscue analysis texts that were used for Carol and Christie.) Although these magazines are generally written on a middle school level, the articles tend to have unconventional grammatical structures and unfamiliar vocabulary, which can cause readers to miscue. In fact, Carol averaged 5 miscues per 100 words over the course of the study when reading this type of material.

I administered the miscue analysis through standard reading miscue procedures (Y. Goodman et al., 1987). The oral readings lasted approximately 15 minutes, and story retellings were elicited after the oral readings. Once the session was over, I listened to the audiotape and marked Christie's and Carol's miscues on a prepared typescript using conventional miscue codings (Y. Goodman et al., 1987). I analyzed the retellings using procedures developed by Y. Goodman and Marek (1996).

Retrospective Miscue Analysis. Once the miscue procedures were completed, the typescript was analyzed for high-quality miscues, which were determined on the basis of the following two main criteria: (1) Does it make sense in the sentence? (2) Is it grammatically acceptable in the sentence? Graphic similarity was not an immediate criterion for two reasons. First, readers can substitute words that are not visually similar but still make sense and are grammatically acceptable, such as reading *couch* for *sofa*. Second, readers may omit words that do not affect either the meaning or the grammar of the sentence, which obviates any discussion of visual similarity. Although high-quality miscues were selected with regard to meaning and syntax, discussions of graphic cues were undertaken when relevant. For instance, when Carol substituted *stockholders* for *shareholders*, discussion of how Carol's miscue was graphically similar to the expected word was important.

Once the sentences with high-quality miscues were outlined, I selected two for the RMA discussions. When there were more than two sentences with high-quality miscues, miscues that focused on high-quality word substitutions

Table 2
Text With Corresponding High-Quality Miscues

Reader	Text	High-quality miscues	
		Sentence	**Miscue**
Christie	*Buzz Said the Bee* (Lewison, 1992)	"And sat on a pig" (p. 9). "And the pig said, 'Oink'" (p. 20).	"And sat on the pig." "The...and the pig said, 'Oink.'"
	Goodnight Moon (Brown, 1947)	"And there were three little bears sitting on chairs" (p. 4).	"And there three little bears who took a seat."
		"Goodnight kittens and goodnight mittens" (pp. 15–16).	"Goodnight kittens. Goodnight mittens."
	Monkey See, Monkey Do (Gave, 1993)	"Monkey out of sight" (p. 6).	"Monkey under the table."
		"Monkeys go fast" (p. 13).	"Monkeys go free."
Carol	"Corporate Activism: Out of Control" (Davidson, 2007)	"Corporate leaders are pouring their shareholders' money into activist social causes like never before—over $10 billion worth in 2005" (p. 28).	Corporate leaders are pouring their stockholders' money into activist social causes like never before–over $10 billion worth in 2005.
		"I think Ben & Jerry's demonstrated that it is possible for a corporation to be quite profitable and to use its power to solve some societal problems at the same time" (p. 28).	"I think Ben & Jerry's demonstrated that it is possible for a corporation to be quite profitable and use its power to solve some social problems at the same time."
	"Conspicuous Consumption" (Stein, 2007)	"'The clients tell us we can raise our prices even more,' he says" (p. 118).	"'The clients tell us we can raise our prices even more,' he said."
		"At the BLT Restaurant in New York City and Washington, chef Laurent Tournel is serving a $92 rib-eye steak, and he's pretty sure he's holding back" (p. 118).	"But the BLT Restaurant in New York City and Washington, chef 'something French' is serving a $92 rib-eye steak, and he's pretty sure he's holding back."

or grammatical rearrangements were primarily selected. Table 2 lists the high-quality miscues that were discussed. The high-quality miscues were transferred to the RMA session organizer (see Figure 1).

During each RMA session, Carol and Christie were asked to orally reread the text to prepare for the discussion. Once they read the text, I played the section of audiotape with the preselected high-quality miscue. The discussion began with me asking Carol or Christie the interpretive question, "Can you tell me what you did here?" This question was followed up with those outlined in Figure 1.

Each RMA session was transcribed and triangulated with observational notes and initial and closing interviews to uncover themes and transformations of behaviors over the course of the sessions. Themes that emerged suggested that Carol and Christie became more empowered in discussing their reading as they began to challenge their misconceptions about reading and themselves as readers. Here I will contend that Family RMA provided a space for exploring

Figure 1
RMA Session Organizer

RMA Guiding Questions

Title of book or text read: ____________________

Miscue Number ________ Line Number ________ Counter Number ________

Miscue ____________________

____

1. Can you tell me what you did here?

2. Why do you think you made the miscue?

3. Does the miscue make sense?

4. Does the miscue sound like language?

5. Does the miscue look/sound like the text?

6. Was the miscue corrected? Should it have been? Why?

7. Did the miscue affect your understanding of the text?

Note. Adapted from Goodman & Marek (1996).

reading, encouraged Carol to adopt a variety of reading strategies for Christie, and allowed for Carol's and Christie's perceptions about themselves and each other as readers to evolve.

A Space for Exploration

In our first RMA session, Carol talked about her experiences with reading. Carol remembered having difficulty with reading as a fourth grader and receiving reading services outside of school. She reminisced about reading Margaret Mitchell's *Gone With the Wind* and suddenly realizing that she was "getting it" and that she could "understand." Particularly striking was when she said, "And I know that I was not reading every word but I could understand." Over the course of our Family RMA sessions, there was some conflict in how Carol talked about her own reading and what she thought reading should be like. Although Carol said that she knew that she did not read every word, she expected Christie to read every word and read accurately.

Although Carol did not argue that the most important thing about reading was comprehension, she was not sure how people reached the point of good comprehension. Initially, Carol felt that Christie needed to read accurately to understand the text. However, after listening to Christie's oral readings and retellings, Carol was surprised at how much Christie actually comprehended. During the eighth session, Carol commented,

> I didn't realize that there was comprehension. You remember that wonderful time when she [Christie] commented that the mice wouldn't share the apple cider or whatever it was because they didn't help. I didn't even get that to be honest with you. I was so concentrated on her [oral] reading. I didn't comprehend.

These conversational asides, or what I call RMA outtakes, were moments that highlighted revelations about reading. RMA outtakes were always related to our RMA sessions but never embedded within them. They were critical spaces where transformed knowledge about reading surfaced. Within these spaces, Carol began to realize that there is a difference between making sense as you read, what K. Goodman (1996) called *comprehending*, and overall story *comprehension*. While focusing on Christie's oral reading, Carol was paying attention to Christie's performance in the act of comprehending. However, Carol assumed that because Christie made miscues, she must not understand what she was reading. The RMA session encouraged Carol to appreciate that there are different qualities of miscues. Although low-quality miscues can negatively affect Christie's comprehension, high-quality miscues are the result of her successful attempts to construct meaning.

In the end, this shift in focus allowed Carol to take a deeper look into the types of miscues that Christie made. In the final interview, Carol talked about this shift in focus. She said,

> There has been so much focus on words. What we are doing here is reminding me that it's a balancing act. It [learning with RMA] is showing how things fall into place. I see that there is comprehension that occurs in that effort of filling in those words.

For Christie, participating in Carol's RMA sessions created a safe space for exploring reading. In essence, Christie could talk about her reading beliefs outside of the context of her reading performance. Although there were times when she openly avoided reading, as the pressure to perform was emotionally taxing on her, Christie enjoyed listening to and talking about Carol's oral readings. The Family RMA sessions capitalized on this desire.

During an RMA session with the text "Conspicuous Consumption" (Stein, 2007), we discussed the sentence "At the BLT Restaurant in New York City and Washington, chef Laurent Tournel is serving a $92 rib-eye steak, and he's pretty sure he's holding back" (p. 118). Carol substituted *but* for *at* and said "something French" for Laurent Tournel. In discussing Carol's first substitution miscue (*but* for *at*), I asked Christie whether Carol's miscue sounded like language, and she replied, "No." I asked why, to which Christie replied, "Because it is wrong." Christie also felt that Carol should have self-corrected because she "did not read what was in the book." Christie's view of reading was not based on making sense but was instead based on reading accuracy. Christie allowed herself to believe that the substitution of *but* for *at* did not sound like language, when in fact it did.

Although accuracy plays its role in reading, my goal was to encourage Christie to realize that she should not sacrifice making sense for accurate oral production of text. Carol's miscues and RMA discussions provided a safe space for Christie to focus on meaning rather than accuracy, away from her sometimes laborious oral readings. At the closing interview, I again asked Christie if she would like to be a better reader. This time, she quickly replied, "Yes. Because I want to be a teacher." Her comment proposed there was a seismic shift in her thoughts about reading.

Reading Interactions and Strategies

As mentioned earlier, one of Carol's goals was to find ways to work with Christie that would concentrate on comprehension. By making her own comprehension strategies transparent through RMA discussions, Carol was better able to recognize that the strategies she already possessed also could be used with Christie. The previously described miscue, where Carol said "something French" for Laurent Tournel, is a good example. Christie enjoyed Carol's use of this strategy. When I asked Christie what Carol did, Christie immediately replied, "She's good." Carol added, "Because it kept the flow instead of me stammering and losing the continuity of the meaning of the sentence. It was just something French. Would it matter? Do we know him?" Carol talked extensively about how this strategy compensated for not knowing the pronunciation:

> In other words, I know that's an area that I would stumble that would break my concentration and make me focus on something that would take me totally away from the story and the information given. So I don't waste my time with it. Sometimes when I am not reading out loud, I just use the first letter and that's it. There's G and F and that's it and maybe I'll get Mr. G. I don't bother wasting my mental powers on that. I'm not wasting my mental strengths on something that I'm not strong at.

In fact, Christie recognized many of Carol's word-solving strategies that did not disrupt her reading flow or comprehension. After Carol read the passage from "Conspicuous Consumption," Christie noticed that Carol deliberately substituted a phrase as a placeholder for difficult words. Christie said, "She put in a word when the word is not working."

Over time, these types of patterns emerged within Christie's oral reading. At our final RMA session, we discussed the phrase "Monkey out of sight" (Gave, 1993, p. 13). Christie initially read *our* for *out*, but changed the sentence to read "Monkey under the table." During the RMA session, I asked Christie what she did. She replied, "I didn't know that word so I looked at the picture." Instead of producing a grammatically unconventional phrase that would not make sense, Christie produced a phrase that showed how she used the story pattern to make a sensible prediction. Her prediction, in turn, reflected her knowledge of grammatical cues, as her produced phrase lacked a verb, as does the sentence on the page. Rather than overly attending to graphic cues that would cause her to struggle, Christie placed greater importance on creating a parallel text that matched the picture and the grammatical structure of the sentence and made sense (K. Goodman, 1996).

Over the course of the Family RMA sessions, Carol regularly commented on how she changed the ways in which she worked with Christie at home. During the closing interview, Carol articulated the importance of what she learned through participating in RMA:

> It [Family RMA] is showing me how to work with Christie more productively. Where to intervene; where not to intervene. To trust that she is learning, even though sometimes I'm afraid that she is not. She's making progress.

When I asked if there were things that Carol now did differently based on our RMA sessions, she replied, "Absolutely. Basically, if she's chosen a proper word even though it's not the exact word, I hold on! Who cares? I'm more patient."

Carol learned to be a strategic partner in reading with Christie, while Christie learned to be a strategic reader. Returning to Carol's words, reading and working with struggling readers is a "balancing act." To attend to every detail can cut away at the self-esteem (sometimes little self-esteem) that struggling readers hold. Carol's developing patience was due, at least in part, to a transformation of her perceptions about Christie and herself as readers.

Transforming Perceptions

By critically reexamining her assumptions about reading, Carol was better able to take an essential look at herself as a reader. This process occurred over the course of the RMA sessions. Throughout the study, I have suggested that Carol's participation encouraged her to see both her own reading and her responses to Christie's reading differently. Carol was able to challenge her initial perceptions about the nature of miscues as negative behaviors that need to be corrected. Instead, Carol began to consider miscues as windows into Christie's working models of reading and language development (Owocki & Goodman, 2002). Carol articulated this point at the closing interview when she said, "Her abilities are actually better than I had hoped."

Just as important, Carol needed to view Christie through her own experiences with reading. At the conclusion of the study, Carol remarked,

> I'm a better reader since we started. First of all, I had experiences that discouraged me from reading. I have realized that all of these things I thought were odd were actually very, very good.

The transformation of self-perception was intrinsically linked to the way that Carol and Christie transformed their perceptions of each other. In other words, if Carol had not transformed the way that she viewed herself as a reader, she would not have been able to acknowledge Christie's reading strengths, and vice versa. Carol highlighted this theme when she said,

> I give her more credit. And I have found that she can read much more sophisticated books instead of *Run Jane Run*. I remember in my reading program reading *Run Jane Run* and thinking that I'm a little bit more sophisticated than that and my comprehension was beyond. My empathy is with her.

Carol viewed Christie's experiences through the window of her own experiences, both past and current. Christie's transformations helped her adopt new reading strategies that focused on meaning. She began producing what Moore and Brantingham (2003) called "smart miscues." With this substitution strategy, Christie made deliberate, purposeful miscues that did not change the meaning of the text and that acted as placeholders for the unknown word or set of words. With the use of smart miscues, Christie was able to rebalance her focus on meaning, placing more effort in areas that built on her strengths (such as in the example of "Monkey under the table"). The result was an increase in reading flow and agency in implementing reading strategies that worked for her.

The Implications of Family RMA for Schools

This article has taken preliminary steps toward acknowledging the possibilities that RMA has to offer parents, children, teachers, and reading specialists. Although more research is needed to assess the benefits of modifying Family RMA to fewer sessions, as teachers and reading specialists within schools cannot necessarily implement Family RMA on the scale to which it was presented here due to time constraints and the responsibility of working with a large number of students, this work has implications for the teaching of reading.

The findings from this case study of Carol and Christie suggest that we should expand the ways in which we develop and implement parental involvement in the teaching of reading. Owocki and Goodman (2002) wrote, "It is important to help children and families understand that errors are really not mistakes" (p. 7). Family RMA, as described in this article, is a way of helping children and families to reconsider the nature of miscues through positioning parents and their children as coparticipants, or coresearchers, in studying the reading process.

Researchers do not dispute the importance of integrating families into the curriculum and creating fruitful partnerships that can enhance learning in the home (Gregory, Long, & Volk, 2004; Owocki & Goodman, 2002; Taylor, 1993). The field of family literacy has highlighted how families are mediators of literacy (Gadsden, 1994; Moll, Amanti, Neff, & Gonzalez, 1992; Taylor, 1983). Families engage their children in different types of literacy practices and events both inside and outside of the home. Although some parents read bedtime stories to their children, other parents take their children to language and religious schools, such as Greek, Japanese, or Hebrew schools.

This Family RMA work adds to the literature on family literacy to emphasize how parents' beliefs and perceptions of literacy frame the ways in which they interact with their children in the home. The intergenerational nature of literacy learning means that family members relate to one another through recollections of their past experiences around reading with the desire of creating goals for themselves as readers (Gregory, Long, & Volk, 2004).

Because parents, children, teachers, and reading specialists have different definitions of reading and what it means to be a reader, conflicts and tensions can occur. Parents do not always have the same knowledge as teachers and reading specialists. There is no guarantee that the discourses of school personnel will match those of parents. Family RMA provides a venue where teachers and reading specialists can bridge the divide caused by parents' misconceptions and discourses about reading and encourage parents to see reading as meaning construction. By doing so, teachers can position parents as researchers into the strengths and struggles of their children. In this manner, we create common discourses with family members. Instead of providing decontextualized practice such as flash cards or worksheets, which can be devoid of meaning, Family RMA allows teachers and reading specialists to make learning meaningful and purposeful for parents.

Consequently, Family RMA also creates an emotionally safe space for struggling children. Readers like Christie have the opportunity to talk about reading, away from their own struggles, through their parents' experiences. Family RMA generates distance but creates a forum through reader responses where readers can make experiential connections to other participants. In their Family RMA process, Carol and Christie were better able to create quality relationships with each other and with reading.

Family RMA encourages readers to make personal connections and to build on their strengths. Readers start to challenge the author's text to learn that "right" and "wrong" answers do not exist in terms of reading (Rosenblatt, 1992). These important concepts are learned within a community of parents, children, teachers, and reading specialists, who come together to read and reflect as members of that community. Family RMA is another way to develop caring and emotionally supportive partnerships between homes and schools.

References

Agar, M. (1996). *The professional stranger: An informal introduction to ethnography.* New York: Academic.

Brown, J., Goodman, K.S., & Marek, A.M. (Eds.). (1996). *Studies in miscue analysis: An annotated bibliography.* Newark, DE: International Reading Association.

Gadsden, V. (1994). Understanding family literacy: Conceptual issues facing the field. *Teachers College Record, 96*(1), 58–86.

Goodman, K.S. (1996). *On reading: A common-sense look at the nature of language and the science of reading.* Portsmouth, NH: Heinemann.

Goodman, K.S. (2003a). Miscues: Windows on the reading process. In A. Flurkey & J. Xu (Eds.), *On the revolution of reading: The selected writings of Kenneth S. Goodman* (pp. 107–116). Portsmouth, NH: Heinemann.

Goodman, K.S. (2003b). Revaluing readers and reading. In A. Flurkey & J. Xu (Eds.), *On the revolution of reading: The selected writings of Kenneth S. Goodman* (pp. 421–429). Portsmouth, NH: Heinemann.

Goodman, Y.M. (1996). Revaluing readers while readers revalue themselves: Retrospective Miscue Analysis. *The Reading Teacher, 49*(8), 600–609.

Goodman, Y.M., & Marek, A.M. (Eds.). (1996). *Retrospective miscue analysis: Revaluing readers and reading.* Katonah, NY: Richard C. Owen.

Goodman, Y.M., Watson, D., & Burke, C.L. (1987). *Reading miscue inventory: Alternative procedures.* New York: Richard C. Owen.

Gregory, E., Long, S., & Volk, D. (2004). Syncretic literacy studies: Starting points. In E. Gregory, S. Long, & D. Volk (Eds.), *Many pathways to literacy: Young children learning with siblings, grandparents, peers and communities* (pp. 1–5). New York: Routledge-Falmer.

Moll, L.C., Amanti, C., Neff, D., & Gonzalez, N. (1992). Funds of knowledge for teaching: Using a qualitative approach to connect homes and classrooms. *Theory Into Practice, 31*(2), 132–141.

Moore, R.A., & Aspegren, C.M. (2001). Reflective conversations between two learners: Retrospective Miscue Analysis. *Journal of Adolescent & Adult Literacy, 44*(6), 492–503.

Moore, R.A., & Brantingham, K.L. (2003). Nathan: A case study in reader response and Retrospective Miscue Analysis. *The Reading Teacher, 56*(5), 466–474.

Moore, R.A., & Gilles, C.J. (2005). *Reading conversations: Retrospective Miscue Analysis with struggling readers, grades 4–12.* Portsmouth, NH: Heinemann.

Owocki, G., & Goodman, Y.M. (2002). *Kidwatching: Documenting children's literacy development*. Portsmouth, NH: Heinemann.

Paulson, E. (2001). The discourse of Retrospective Miscue Analysis: Links with adult learning theory. *Journal of College Reading and Learning, 32*(1), 112–127.

Rosenblatt, L.M. (1992). *The reader, the text, the poem: The transactional theory of the literary work*. Carbondale: Southern Illinois University Press.

Smith, F. (1997). *Reading without nonsense* (3rd ed.). New York: Teachers College Press.

Taylor, D. (1983). *Family literacy: Young children learning to read and write*. Portsmouth, NH: Heinemann.

Taylor, D. (1993). *From the child's point of view*. Portsmouth, NH: Heinemann.

Literature Cited

Brown, M.W. (1947). *Goodnight moon*. New York: Harper & Row.

Davidson, P. (2007, May). *Corporate activism: Out of control*. NewsMax, pp. 28–29.

Gave, M. (1993). *Monkey see, monkey do*. New York: Scholastic.

Lewison, W.C. (1992). *Buzz said the bee*. New York: Scholastic.

Stein, J. (2007, November 12). *Conspicuous consumption*. Time, 170, p. 118.

Questions for Reflection

- This study combined Retrospective Miscue Analysis (RMA) with family literacy in order to investigate how RMA could be used to help parents and children navigate the reading process, and to help parents better understand their children's reading strengths. What other ways can schools involve families in assessment practices? What other possibilities exist for combining assessment with family literacy?
- The author suggests that more research is needed to assess the benefits of modifying Family RMA to fewer sessions, because teachers and reading specialists within many schools cannot necessarily implement Family RMA on the scale to which it was presented here due to time constraints and the responsibility of working with a large number of students. What ideas do you have for modifying Family RMA to work with larger numbers of students? What steps could you take to get started with using Family RMA in your school?

Assessing English-Language Learners in Mainstream Classrooms

Susan Davis Lenski, Fabiola Ehlers-Zavala, Mayra C. Daniel, and Xiaoqin Sun-Irminger

A great many classroom teachers in the United States find themselves teaching English-language learners (ELLs). The total number of ELLs in the public schools is more than 4.5 million students, or 9.6% of the total school population (National Center for Education Statistics, 2002). This number continues to rise because more than a million new U.S. immigrants arrive annually (Martin & Midgely, 1999). Not all communities have large populations of ELLs, but many do, and others will experience changes in the diversity of their populations, especially schools in the inner suburbs of metropolitan centers (Hodgkinson, 2000/2001).

Because assessment is a critical part of effective literacy instruction, it is important for classroom teachers to know how to evaluate ELLs' literacy development. Nevertheless, many teachers are unprepared for the special needs and complexities of fairly and appropriately assessing ELLs. To complicate the matter further, the U.S. federal No Child Left Behind Act (NCLB) of 2001 has established assessment mandates that all teachers must follow. Title I of NCLB requires that ELLs attending public schools at levels K–12 should be assessed in the various language domains (i.e., listening, speaking, reading, and writing). According to NCLB, ELLs must be included in statewide standardized testing. The results of the tests are reported in a segregated data format that highlights the achievement of each subgroup of students. As with all subgroups under NCLB, ELLs must make Adequate Yearly Progress (AYP) for the schools to meet state requirements (Abedi, 2004).

Over the years, ELLs have historically lagged behind their native–English-speaking counterparts, and this achievement gap is not likely to close in the near future (Strickland & Alvermann, 2004). ELLs come to public schools in large numbers, and they have unique learning and assessment needs. ELLs bring a wide range of educational experiences and academic backgrounds to school. They represent a variety of socioeconomic, cultural, linguistic, and ethnic backgrounds. In school, ELLs need to simultaneously develop English competence and acquire content knowledge. An overwhelming majority of assessment tools are in English only, presenting a potential threat to the usefulness of assessments when ELLs' lack of English prevents them from understanding test items.

Whether ELLs are newcomers to the United States or from generations of heritage language speakers, they are disadvantaged if assessment, evaluation, and the curriculum do not make allowances for their distinctive differences (Gay, 2001; Gitlin, Buendía, Crossland, & Doumbia, 2003; Greenfield, 1997). This article provides recommendations for literacy assessment practices for teachers of ELLs that will inform their instruction.

Toward Appropriate Assessment of ELLs

The assessment of ELLs is a "process of collecting and documenting evidence of student learning and progress to make informed instructional, placement, programmatic, and/or evaluative

Reprinted from Lenski, S.D., Ehlers-Zavala, F., Daniel, M.C., & Sun-Irminger, X. (2006). Assessing English-language learners in mainstream classrooms. *The Reading Teacher*, 60(1), 24–34.

decisions to enhance student learning, as is the case of assessment of the monolingual or mainstream learner" (Ehlers-Zavala, 2002, pp. 8–9). Assessments of ELLs, however, are more critical. Many teachers have little experience with ELLs and may not understand the challenges faced by students in the process of acquiring English. Because assessment practices pave the way to making instructional and evaluative decisions, teachers need to consider all educational stakeholders (i.e., the students themselves, parents, administrators, and other teachers) as they plan to assess students from different cultural backgrounds.

Hurley and Blake (2000) provided guiding principles that teachers should consider when assessing ELLs:

- Assessment activities should help teachers make instructional decisions.
- Assessment strategies should help teachers find out what students know and can do... not what they cannot do.
- The holistic context for learning should be considered and assessed.
- Assessment activities should grow out of authentic learning activities.
- Best assessments of student learning are longitudinal...they take place over time.
- Each assessment activity should have a specific objective-linked purpose. (pp. 91–92)

Furthermore, because the NCLB legislation drives state standards, teachers should consider those standards as they assess ELLs. Standards can assist teachers in planning effectively linked instruction and assessment practices for ELLs at all levels of instruction and across the curriculum. In the absence of district or state standards, teachers can consult the standards that professional organizations, such as Teachers of English to Speakers of Other Languages (TESOL; 1997) have prepared (see www.tesol.org/s_tesol/seccss.asp?CUD=95&DID=1565). They may also consult the work other professionals have developed (Lenski & Ehlers-Zavala, 2004).

Assessing English-Language Learners

Teachers who assess ELLs must ask themselves a number of basic questions such as these: Who am I going to assess? How am I going to assess them? Why am I going to assess them? What specific aspects of literacy am I going to assess? When am I going to administer the assessment? Can I evaluate my students in my own classroom? In order to answer these questions, teachers should investigate their students' prior schooling before assessment.

Learn About ELLs' Literacy Backgrounds

English-language learners come to public schools with vastly different backgrounds. Teachers should never assume that students who share the same language will observe the same cultural practices or understand the same types of texts. Even speakers of the same language exhibit differences in their lexicon, in the grammar that they use, and in the formality and informality of expression that is acceptable in their everyday lives (Chern, 2002). ELL teachers should, therefore, become aware of their students' backgrounds before assessment takes place.

According to Freeman and Freeman (2004), ELLs fall into four categories that help teachers understand their background: newly arrived students with adequate formal schooling, newly arrived students with limited formal schooling, students exposed to two languages simultaneously, and long-term English-language learners. (See Table 1 for a complete description of these categories.) Knowing which category best describes an ELL can help teachers begin to learn about their students.

Understanding that ELLs come from different types of literacy backgrounds can help teachers as they develop appropriate assessments. Students' needs are mediated by who the students are, which includes their type of literacy background. Oftentimes, an understanding of students is fogged by the use of acronyms such

Table 1
Categories of English-Language Learners

Newly arrived students with adequate formal schooling • Have been in the country for fewer than five years, • Have had an adequate degree of schooling in their native country, • Perform in reading and writing at grade level, • Find it relatively easy to catch up with their native-English-speaking peers, • Have difficulty with standardized tests, • Have parents who are educated speakers of their L1 (native language), • Developed a strong foundation in their L1, • Demonstrate the potential to make fast progress in English, and • Have found it easy to acquire a second or third language.	**Students exposed to two languages simultaneously** • Were born in the United States but have grown up in households where a language other than English is spoken, • Live in communities of speakers who primarily communicate in their L1 or go back and forth between languages, • Have grown up being exposed to two languages simultaneously, • May have not developed academic literacy in either L1 or L2 (second language), • Often engage in extensive code-switching, thus making use of both linguistic systems to communicate, and • Have acquired oral proficiency in a language other than English first but may not have learned to read or write in that language.
Newly arrived students with limited formal schooling • Have recently arrived in an English-speaking school (fewer than five years), • Have experienced interrupted schooling, • Have limited native-language and literacy skills, • Perform poorly on achievement tasks, • May not have had previous schooling, • May experience feelings of loss of emotional and social networks, • Have parents who have low literacy levels, and • Could have difficulty learning English.	**Long-term English-language learners** • Have already spent more than five years in an English-speaking school, • Have literacy skills that are below grade level, • Have had some English as a second language classes or bilingual support, and • Require substantial and ongoing language and literacy support.

Note. Adapted from Freeman and Freeman (2003).

as "ELLs," which, on the surface, seem to point at group homogeneity rather than heterogeneity. Differences are blurred in the use of such acronyms; consequently, there is always the potential to forget how diverse ELLs truly are. Understanding each ELL's background will help a teacher to choose the most appropriate assessment and instruction.

Predictability Log. An ELL's knowledge base might include traditional and nontraditional literacies. Teachers can understand the types of literacies ELLs bring to the classroom by completing a predictability log (PL). A PL helps teachers understand their students' prior literacy experiences and the factors that helped shape them. (See Table 2 for an example.) According to Snyder (2003), assessing students' abilities to predict can assist teachers in creating a learning environment that is rich in predictable printed language. To use a PL, teachers should target the questions that are most relevant for the students' situations. Teachers can gather data for a PL from a variety of sources: by interviewing the students, talking with the students' parents, observing the students in a classroom context, and talking with others who know the students (e.g., family members, other teachers, community members). A bilingual specialist or someone who is fluent in the students' native language can also be of assistance in completion of the log. Whether the teacher or another adult gathers the data, the information can provide the teacher with a deeper grasp of the students' literacy backgrounds.

Using Predictability Logs. Information from PLs can help teachers understand that students who have been exposed to effective literacy practices in other contexts, such as their countries of origin, may be further along in their literacy development. Furthermore, in understanding that ELLs differ in the literacy practices of their native language (L1), teachers may be in a better position to determine whether those literacy practices are facilitating or interfering with the development of literacy in English—the learners' second language. This situation is contingent upon the degree of similarity or difference between English and the native language of the students. An example of this would be the knowledge students bring to the learning process regarding concepts of print. An ELL who is a native speaker of Spanish may benefit from having been exposed to concepts about print in Spanish because they are similar to those a native speaker of English would know (i.e., reading from left to right). Conversely, an ELL who is a native speaker of Arabic may display a different understanding of concepts about print learned in Arabic (i.e., reading from right to left).

Decide on the Purposes for Assessment

Once teachers know about a student's literacy background and knowledge base, they need to think about the reasons for further assessment. The purposes for assessment can be quite diverse; they can range from student placement to instructional decisions and from program development to program evaluation. It is critical that teachers identify the purposes for assessing their students before choosing the assessment instrument to be used.

As teachers consider the purposes for assessment, they should ask, "Does my assessment connect to the language and content standards

Table 2
Predictability Log Questions

Language use

- What languages does the student know and use?
- What types of alphabets does the student know?
- What language and literacy experiences interest the student?

Knowledge

- What is the student's cultural background?
- What does the student enjoy doing out of school?
- In what areas or ways has the student helped classmates?
- What has the student said or what stories has the student told?

Events or experiences that matter to the student

- What has happened to the student recently that has been important?
- Have any major events occurred, especially recently, that have been of great interest to the student?

Narrative

- What kinds of stories does the student enjoy?
- What specific stories does the student know well?
- Can the student tell a story about a relative or a good friend?
- What activities is the student involved in?

Relationship

- What is the student's family situation?
- Who are the key family members in the student's life?
- Has the student left anyone behind in his or her home country?
- Who are the student's best friends?
- Is there anyone whom the student talks about frequently?
- Whom might you contact to follow up on one of the student's interests or needs?

Aesthetics and ethics

- What personal belongings does the student bring to class or wear?
- What objects or ideas appeal to the student?
- What values has the student expressed through actions or stories?

Note. Adapted from Snyder (2003).

and goals?" Teachers should also think about whether their assessment practices are consistent with their own instructional objectives and goals. When teachers think about the purposes for assessment beforehand, they can make better decisions about what information they should gather about their students.

Teachers can use language and content standards as the basis for what ELLs ought to know, and these standards then provide the purposes for assessment. For example, one of the TESOL standards is "Students will use learning strategies to extend their communicative competence" (TESOL, 1997, p. 39). Teachers can use this statement to develop an instrument to assess how well students are satisfying the standard. Figure 1 provides an example of an assessment that Ehlers-Zavala (second author) developed based on the standard.

Decide How to Assess Students

Teachers of ELLs should conduct multiple forms of evaluation, using a variety of authentic assessment tools (e.g., anecdotal records, checklists, rating scales, portfolios) to fairly assess the placement and progress of their students and to plan instruction. Authentic assessment tools will provide direct insights on the students' literacy development and showcase students' progress and accomplishments. Assessments also serve as mechanisms that reveal what instruction needs to be modified to help the students reach the necessary standards and goals.

Adopt a Multidimensional Approach Including Alternative Assessments (AAs). Reading is a complex interactive process. According to O'Malley and Valdez Pierce

Figure 1
Sample Checklist for Reading (Grades Pre-K–3)

Student:

Date:

ESL Goal, ESL Standard: Goal 1, Standard 3
"To use English to communicate in social settings: Students will use learning strategies to extend their communicative competence" (TESOL, 1997, p. 39).

Progress indicator	Student performed task independently (✓)	Student performed task with help (✓)	Student was unable to perform the task (✓)
Understands new vocabulary			
Recites poems			
Retells stories			
Uses new vocabulary in story retelling			
Formulates hypotheses about events in a story			

(1996), the term *interaction* refers not only to the interactions between the reader, the text, and a given context but also to the interactions among the mental processes involved in comprehension. These range from the decoding of words on the printed page to making use of prior knowledge and "making inferences and evaluating what is read" (p. 94). Indeed,

> the assessment of reading ability does not end with the measurement of comprehension. Strategic pathways to full understanding are often important factors to include in assessing students, especially in the case of most classroom assessments that are formative in nature. (Brown, 2004, p. 185)

For this reason, it is important that teachers consider AAs to document ELLs' performance and growth in reading.

Alternative assessments provide teachers with a more complete picture of what students can or cannot do as they encounter reading materials. Through the use of AAs, teachers gain a direct view of the students' reading development in a variety of contexts and under different circumstances. AAs go beyond traditional testing, which provides a very narrow and discrete view of the students' capabilities when confronted with a reading task. They also evolve naturally from regular classroom activities and allow students the opportunity to show growth in literacy as they learn and practice.

Alternative assessment tasks are a more appropriate and fair way to measure ELLs' progress (Gottlieb, 1995; O'Malley & Valdez Pierce, 1996; Smolen, Newman, Wathen, & Lee, 1995). They provide teachers with the opportunity to identify what students need regarding reading instruction and literacy support. From information gathered as a result of AAs, teachers can devise a plan to instruct students in more meaningful ways because they have direct insights on the needs of each one. Finally, through AAs teachers can assess ELLs' literacy in more naturally occurring situations and thus document students' progress more thoroughly and progressively (Ehlers-Zavala, 2002).

As teachers attempt to put into practice multiple AAs, they may want to approach this task incrementally and consider the following practical suggestions:

- Learn what constitutes alternative or authentic assessment of ELLs. Examples of AAs generally include observations (i.e., anecdotal records, rating scales, checklists), journals (i.e., buddy journals, dialogue journals, reader response), conferring, questionnaires, portfolios, and self-assessments.
- Develop a philosophy of second-language acquisition that will assist you in the evaluation of ELLs.
- Know your district's curriculum of the program before planning assessments. The curriculum (specifically the reading curriculum) in any given school program must be sensitive to the students' needs, the institutional expectations, and the availability of resources. Because these will vary from setting to setting, it is nearly impossible to attempt to prescribe any guidelines or universal curriculum for all instructional settings (Grabe, 2004); thus, teachers must know the reality of their own localities.
- Implement the assessments once you have understood the features of the tools available and have determined the appropriateness of implementation at any given time.
- Plan assessments that yield data that can be used for evaluative and instructional purposes.
- Ensure that students understand how to use self-assessments (i.e., logs, journals).
- Use the results of your assessments to modify instruction.
- Communicate assessment results to the respective stakeholders (i.e., students, parents, administrators, community) in clear and meaningful ways.

The key to successful alternative assessment is thorough planning and organization (O'Malley & Valdez Pierce, 1996). As teachers plan, they should identify the purpose of the assessment, plan the assessment itself, involve students in self- and peer assessment, develop rubrics or scoring procedures, set standards, select assessment activities, and record teacher observations. For a helpful reminder of effective assessment practices, Figure 2 offers a teacher's bookmark on alternative assessment practices that Ehlers-Zavala developed.

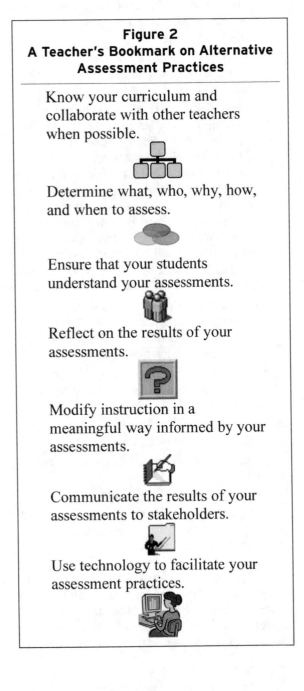

Figure 2
A Teacher's Bookmark on Alternative Assessment Practices

Know your curriculum and collaborate with other teachers when possible.

Determine what, who, why, how, and when to assess.

Ensure that your students understand your assessments.

Reflect on the results of your assessments.

Modify instruction in a meaningful way informed by your assessments.

Communicate the results of your assessments to stakeholders.

Use technology to facilitate your assessment practices.

Assess in Nontraditional Ways. Teachers should keep in mind that all assessments in English are also assessments of English. Because ELLs are in the process of acquiring language as they acquire content, teachers need to ensure that their assessment addresses the linguistic component of the learning continuum. Therefore, teachers should provide ELLs with opportunities to demonstrate knowledge in nontraditional ways (O'Malley & Valdez Pierce, 1996). Specifically, teachers might consider some of the following suggestions when assessing ELLs:

- Involve students in performance assessment tasks.
- Offer students opportunities to show and practice knowledge in nonlanguage-dependent ways through Venn diagrams, charts, drawings, mind maps, or PowerPoint slides.
- Promote participation in nonthreatening situations that encourage experimentation with the target language of study. Assess language learning in the participation activities.
- Before assessing students, teachers can help ELLs develop reading strategies that in themselves could constitute alternative forms of literacy assessment (Lenski, Daniel, Ehlers-Zavala, & Alvayero, 2004).
- Use the Language Experience Approach as assessment rather than just for instructional purposes (Lenski & Nierstheimer, 2004). As students read their language-experience stories, informally assess their oral reading fluency.

Modify Traditional Assessments. There will be times when teachers have to give ELLs traditional assessments. Some tests should not be modified because their results are based on standardized procedures. If in doubt, teachers should contact an administrator or bilingual teacher about which tests should or should not be modified. A rule of thumb, however, is that teacher-written tests can be modified for ELLs, but achievement tests should not be modified. When teachers modify traditional tests for ELLs, they learn what students know about the content without the barrier of language knowledge, and the assessment more accurately reflects what ELLs know and can do.

Teachers may consider the following assessment modifications appropriate for newcomers and ELLs who are in the process of acquiring English:

- Permit students to answer orally rather than in writing.
- Allow a qualified bilingual professional to assist with the assessment.
- Consider offering ELLs the possibility to demonstrate reading progress and growth through group assessments.
- Allow students to provide responses in multiple formats.
- Accept a response in the students' native language if translation support systems exist in the school or community.
- Allow ELLs to use a bilingual dictionary in the beginning stages of their language-learning experience in English (United States Department of Education, Office for Civil Rights, 2000).

Teachers who are developing ELLs' literacy but still need modifications for accurate assessment information might consider the following suggestions:

- Have an aide record students' answers.
- Divide assessment time into small chunks.
- Use visuals.
- Add glossaries in English or the first language.
- Simplify vocabulary.
- Begin the assessment with several examples.
- Simplify assessment directions.
- Write questions in the affirmative rather than the negative and also teach sentence structures so that students are familiar with the language of testing.
- Give students breaks during assessments.
- Give directions in students' native languages.

Assessment Materials, Activities, and Language Issues

Assessment should be conducted through the use of authentic reading materials that connect to the students' real-life experiences in their personal and academic contexts. "Literacy is intimately bound up with their lives outside the classroom in numerous and complex cultural, social, and personal ways that affect their L1 and L2 identities" (Burns, 2003, p. 22). For ELLs, literacy in English can be an extension of their identity both in school and at home.

Assessment materials should also be adjusted to the student's English proficiency level because a text that is not comprehensible will only measure the vocabulary that a student does not know. A valid look at an ELL's literacy can only be accomplished through pragmatic integrative assessment. When teachers use purposeful communication and authentic material, the results of the assessment are more useful.

Clearly, materials used to informally assess ELLs may be different from those that a teacher would choose to assess the literacy level of mainstream students.

A book that fosters an emotional link between the student and the written word is an authentic text for that particular reader, even if it is not what would ordinarily be appropriate for a grade level. Such a book may not be an academic text. Instead, for a young reader, it could be a comic book about Spider-Man or another superhero. For an adolescent female of Cuban American descent, it might be the chronicle of a young teenager's immigration, *Flight to Freedom* (Veciana-Suarez, 2002). When students determine whether a text is authentic, they use many important thinking processes. As teachers talk with students about why books are authentic to them, they can learn a great deal of information about students' literacy interests (Carrell & Eisterhold, 1983; Davidman & Davidman, 2001).

Engage Students in Collaborative Assessment Activities. Collaborative work helps ELLs feel safe, work comfortably at a level where incoming stimuli are kept at a minimum, and demonstrate literacy to teachers in informal ways (Kagan & Kagan, 1998; Krashen, 1993, 2003). Because conversations between students can scaffold learning (Vygotsky, 1934/1978), collaborative assessment activities provide a powerful lens through which to view ELLs' literacy.

Collaboration permits students to showcase their talents and work in a manner that is a good fit with their individual learning styles and intelligence (Kagan & Kagan, 1998). As students collaborate, they should be free to code-switch without being penalized. Code-switching is moving between the native language and English during an activity and helps ELLs keep conversations moving. It is a natural occurrence among bilinguals, and there are many purposes behind its practice; for example, to stress a point in communication, to express a concept for which there is no equivalent in the other language, to indicate friendship, to relate a conversation, or to substitute a word in another language (Baker, 2001). Teachers should bear in mind that when code-switching compensates for lack of knowledge (e.g., of a word or a grammatical structure), ELLs should be helped to acquire the linguistic knowledge they lack. This type of instructional support should be given in a friendly manner to ensure that students do not feel they are being punished for using their native languages (Freeman & Freeman, 2003).

Teachers can also add an important collaborative component to the instruction and assessment of ELLs when they invite families and community members to participate in literacy projects (Moll & Gonzalez, 1994; Young & Helvie, 1996). For example, parents who are fluent in the native language and also know English can assist teachers in some informal assessment measures. Parents can talk with students in both languages and can alert teachers to difficulties that students face. Parents can also help students record lists of books that they have read. If parents do not know how to write in English, they can keep tape-recorded logs, or simply speak to teachers in the native language. Teachers who are unable to find bilingual parents can seek assistance from bilingual paraprofessionals or from local and state resource centers.

Use the Students' Native Languages as an Assessment Resource. Students should be allowed to use their language abilities to complete literacy tasks (Brisk, 2002) and to express their knowledge in the language they know best when being assessed. Oftentimes, knowledge of the first language means that students possess linguistic skills that can assist them in mastering literacy tasks in the second language (Cummins, 1981). One of these tasks may relate to understanding the meaning of words. Sometimes students may think of what words mean in their first language and successfully guess the meaning of the equivalents in the second language. For example, a word like *compensation* may be understood by native speakers of Spanish if they know the Spanish term *compensación*. In this case, students may use a combination of letter–sound correspondence knowledge and pronunciation to figure out the meaning of the word. During assessment, ELLs may demonstrate their knowledge more accurately if teachers allow them to use their native languages to process their answers.

Encourage Self-Assessment

Self-assessments convey the message that students are in control of their own learning and the assessment of that learning. As students engage in self-assessment practices, they learn how their past learning is shaping their new learning. This type of assessment practice helps students understand that they can direct their learning, which paves the way to teaching students to become independent readers and learners.

As teachers use self-assessment with ELLs, they should keep in mind that ELLs vary in their linguistic ability and, by definition, are in the process of learning a language. Thus, teachers should be aware that ELLs might experience difficulties at first with self-assessments. In order to assist ELLs, teachers should provide them with support through substantial scaffolding activities. Teachers should model responses to self-assessment tasks and then provide students with group, peer, and finally independent practice. For example, a teacher might want to assess students' prior knowledge of a topic for a book students are going to read. Teachers might want to have students engage in self-assessment practices, but prior to asking students to do so, teachers need to model how to engage in a self-assessment activity. An example of a strategy that could be used for student self-assessment is a Connections chart (Lenski & Ehlers-Zavala, 2004). This strategy encourages students to read a story; stop at given points; and make connections to other books, past learning, and themselves. (See Figure 3 for an example of a Connections chart.) When students are engaged in this type of reflective activity, they learn how to use an important literacy strategy and provide teachers with information that could be used for making instructional decisions.

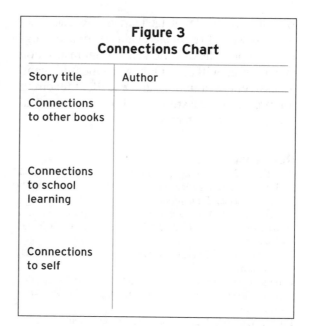

Figure 3
Connections Chart

Story title	Author
Connections to other books	
Connections to school learning	
Connections to self	

Effective Teaching Means Effective Assessments

English-language learners are not a homogeneous group; they can range from students who are emergent literacy learners in their first language to those who are proficient readers. Literacy in the first language mediates literacy in the second language (Odlin, 1989). Thus, literacy experiences that students may have had in their first language will influence their ability to acquire literacy in English. Because the range of literacy proficiencies may be quite vast in any classroom with ELLs, traditional testing formats are inadequate for the evaluation of the English literacy of the nonnative English speaker.

The most effective types of assessments teachers can use to make instructional decisions for ELLs are authentic performance-based assessments such as observations, journals, portfolios, and self-assessments. Performance assessment tasks allow teachers to simultaneously instruct and assess. When students undertake the process of completing an authentic performance assessment, the students plan, self-monitor, and evaluate progress continually, while creating a product. Throughout this process, the teacher is able to engage in ongoing informal assessment of the student's progress. No professionally prepared protocol will result in student learning if only a single test result is used to inform the development of the curricula. When authentic, performance-based assessments are administered throughout the year, they can provide not only a much more accurate picture of students' literacy development but also documented formative data that chart the students' literacy development.

Effective teaching, above all, is the key to the sustained achievement of all students, especially ELLs who struggle with reading. With effective teaching comes the teacher's ability to meet the needs of all students at all points in the educational continuum. Teachers must develop the ability to tailor instruction that helps all ELLs achieve English literacy. However, without a thorough understanding of students' background and current literacy levels, teachers will have difficulty providing effective instruction to meet the unique needs of ELL students.

Although instruction is the key to student learning, authentic assessment can help teachers understand the needs of their struggling readers who are English-language learners. Teachers can use assessment results to evaluate student progress and plan the direction classroom instruction and learning will take. Only when measurement, assessment, evaluation, and excellent teaching are present in classrooms will ELLs make real progress toward literacy.

References

Abedi, J. (2004). The No Child Left Behind Act and English language learners: Assessment and accountability issues. *Educational Researcher, 33*, 4–14.

Baker, C. (2001). *Foundations of bilingual education and bilingualism* (3rd ed.). Buffalo, NY: Multilingual Matters.

Brisk, M. (2002). *Literacy and bilingualism*. Mahwah, NJ: Erlbaum.

Brown, D.H. (2004). *Language assessment: Principles and classroom practices*. White Plains, NY: Pearson/Longman.

Burns, A. (2003). Reading practices: From outside to inside the classroom. *TESOL Journal, 12*(3), 18–23.

Carrell, P.L., & Eisterhold, J.C. (1983). Schema theory and ESL reading pedagogy. *TESOL Quarterly, 17*, 553–573.

Chern, C.-I. (2002, July). *Orthographic issues and multiple language literacies*. Paper presented at the IRA Multilingual Literacy Symposium, Edinburgh, Scotland. Retrieved February 16, 2006, from http://www.readingonline.org/international/inter_index.asp?HREF=Edinburgh/chern/index.html

Cummins, J. (1981). *Schooling and language minority students: A theoretical framework*. Los Angeles: California State University.

Davidman, L., & Davidman, P. (2001). *Teaching with a multicultural perspective: A practical guide* (3rd ed.). New York: Longman.

Ehlers-Zavala, F. (2002). *Assessment of the English-language learner: An ESL training module*. Chicago: Board of Education of the City of Chicago.

Freeman, D., & Freeman, Y. (2004). *Essential linguistics: What you need to know to teach reading, ESL, spelling, phonics, and grammar*. Portsmouth, NH: Heinemann.

Freeman, Y., & Freeman, D. (2003). Struggling English language learners: Keys for academic success. *TESOL Journal, 12*(3), 18–23.

Gay, G. (2001). Preparing for culturally responsive teaching. *Journal of Teacher Education, 53*, 106–115.

Gitlin, A., Buendía, E., Crossland, K., & Doumbia, F. (2003). The production of margin and center: Welcoming-unwelcoming of immigrant students. *American Educational Research Journal, 40*, 91–122.

Gottlieb, M. (1995). Nurturing students' learning through portfolios. *TESOL Journal, 5*(1), 12–14.

Grabe, W. (2004). Research on teaching reading. *Annual Review of Applied Linguistics, 24*, 44–69.

Greenfield, P.M. (1997). You can't take it with you: Why ability assessments don't cross cultures. *American Psychologist, 52*, 1115–1124.

Hodgkinson, H. (2000/2001). Education demographics: What teachers should know. *Educational Leadership, 57*, 6–11.

Hurley, S.R., & Blake, S. (2000). Assessment in the content areas for students acquiring English. In S.R. Hurley & J.V. Tinajero (Eds.), *Literacy assessment of second language learners* (pp. 84–103). Boston: Allyn & Bacon.

Kagan, S., & Kagan, M. (1998). *Multiple intelligences: The complete MI book*. San Clemente, CA: Kagan Cooperative Learning.

Krashen, S. (1993). *The power of reading*. Englewood, CO: Libraries Unlimited.

Krashen, S. (2003). *Explorations in language acquisition and use*. Portsmouth, NH: Heinemann.

Lenski, S.D., Daniel, M., Ehlers-Zavala, F., & Alvayero, M. (2004). Assessing struggling English-language learners. *Illinois Reading Council Journal, 32*(1), 21–30.

Lenski, S.D., & Ehlers-Zavala, F. (2004). *Reading strategies for Spanish speakers*. Dubuque, IA: Kendall/Hunt.

Lenski, S.D., & Nierstheimer, S.L. (2004). *Becoming a teacher of reading: A developmental approach*. Columbus, OH: Merrill Prentice Hall.

Martin, P., & Midgley, E. (1999). Immigration to the United States. *Population Bulletin, 54*, 1–44.

Moll, L.C., & Gonzalez, N. (1994). Critical issues: Lessons from research with language-minority children. *Journal of Reading Behavior, 26*, 439–456.

National Center for Education Statistics. (2002). *Public school student, staff, and graduate counts by state: School year 2000–01* (NCES Pub. 2003-348). Washington, DC: Author.

Odlin, T. (1989). *Language transfer: Cross-linguistic influence in language learning*. New York: Cambridge University Press.

O'Malley, J.M., & Valdez Pierce, L. (1996). *Authentic assessment for English language learners: Practical approaches for teachers*. Reading, MA: Addison-Wesley.

Smolen, L., Newman, C., Wathen, T., & Lee, D. (1995). Developing student self-assessment strategies. *TESOL Journal, 5*(1), 22–27.

Snyder, S.C. (2003). Foundations of predictability in L2 literacy learning. *TESOL Journal, 12*(3), 24–28.

Strickland, D.S., & Alvermann, D.E. (Eds). (2004). *Bridging the literacy achievement gap grades 4–12*. New York: Teachers College Press.

Teachers of English to Speakers of Other Languages. (1997). *ESL standards for Pre-K–12 students*. Alexandria, VA: Author.

United States Department of Education, Office for Civil Rights. (2000). *The use of tests as part of high-stakes decision-making for students*. Washington, DC: Author.

Veciana-Suarez, A. (2002). *Flight to freedom*. New York: Orchard.

Vygotsky, L.S. (1978). *Mind in society: The development of higher psychological processes* (M. Cole, V. John-Steiner, S. Scribner, & E. Souberman, Eds. & Trans.). Cambridge, MA: Harvard University Press. (Original work published 1934)

Young, M.W., & Helvie, S.R. (1996). Parent power: A positive link to school success. *Journal of Educational Issues of Language Minority Students, 16*, 68–74.

Questions for Reflection

- Examples of alternative assessments described in this article include observations (i.e., anecdotal records, rating scales, checklists), journals (i.e., buddy journals, dialogue journals, reader response), conferring, questionnaires, portfolios, and self-assessments. Which types of alternative assessments have you used with English-language learners? Which methods have you found to be the most effective? How do these assessments differ from the assessments administered to students whose first language is English?
- One practical suggestion offered in this article is for teachers to develop a philosophy of second-language acquisition that will assist in the evaluation of ELLs. What is your philosophy of second-language acquisition? How can this philosophy assist your assessment planning and your tailoring of instruction for the needs of your ELLs?
- The authors discuss the importance of using students' native languages as an assessment resource and give the example of how a student may use a combination of letter–sound correspondence knowledge and pronunciation to figure out the meaning of the word. What other ways can using students' native languages serve as an assessment resource? What ideas do you have for allowing students to use their existing first-language abilities to complete literacy tasks?

Show Me: Principles for Assessing Students' Visual Literacy

Jon Callow

"Have you ever learned something about looking up and down?" Jay asked me as we read a picture book together in his classroom. His third-grade teacher has recently been incorporating discussion of pictures and visual texts into her teaching. "The person what looks down is the strongest one" he informed me, referring to the concept of a low angle where the viewer is positioned looking up to a character in a picture, making them appear stronger and more powerful.

"That's really good information. And what about the person looking up?" I asked.

"She's terrified!" Jay responded, clearly imagining a weaker image, where the viewer is above a character that is looking up to them.

In this classroom in the western suburbs of Sydney, Australia, Jay (all student names are pseudonyms) and his classmates had been learning about visual literacy. Without using the term *low angle*, Jay was showing his developing knowledge about how visual texts make meaning, applying his knowledge to the picture book we were reading.

In Australia, visual literacy is integrated in all literacy syllabus documentation across states and territories. This inclusion recognizes that students need to develop new literacy skills, multiliteracies, in order for them to negotiate the growing number of texts that populate their home and school lives (Leu, Kinzer, Coiro, & Cammack, 2004; New London Group, 2000). These texts often use more than one mode, such as the visual and written modes on a cereal box; the audio mode for a podcast; or the audio, visual, written and gestural modes used with interactive multimedia or video games. The various combinations of these modalities are commonly referred to as multimodal texts (Anstey & Bull, 2006).

Although the need to address this evolving textual landscape is well founded at the theoretical level, there is an increasing call to develop the next level of implementation, that is the curriculum and assessment aspects that occur in varied school and learning environments (Ailwood et al., 2000; Kalantzis, Cope, & Harvey, 2003). Part of this development is the call for students to be able to interpret and create a variety of texts that can include a combination of writing, speech, visual images, and electronic and interactive media. A key aspect of the implementation is providing students with the concepts and language to be able to discuss what they see and view. Having a "language for talking about language, images, texts and meaning-making interactions" (New London Group, 2000, p. 24) is generally referred to in Australian educational terms as a metalanguage. Contemporary studies in sociocultural theory, building on Vygotsky's seminal work (1978), cite the importance of metalinguistic skills in developing conceptual and discursive understandings (Mercer, 2000).

The call for educators to teach these multiliteracies and associated metalanguage to students assumes that teachers know *why* these concepts and skills are so crucial as well as *what* aspects and features of multimodal texts to teach and assess and *how* to assess students' understandings and skills. To date, very little specific research has been done on the *what* of

Reprinted from Callow, J. (2008). Show me: Principles for assessing students' visual literacy. *The Reading Teacher, 61*(8), 616–626.

assessment with even less on the *how* of assessment within multimodal contexts, particularly when assessing the metalanguage students might have about visual images.

Returning to Jay and his classmates, for instance, it is evident that they are developing multiple "reading" skills or literacies as part of normal literacy instruction in the classroom. However, an important question that arises is how we then go about assessing what children know about visual images, in order to assist them and to better plan literacy experiences and instruction.

With this in mind, in this article I first present a theoretical overview of the concepts surrounding multiliteracies, with a focus on visual images. Having argued their importance and the need for a particular theoretical framing (that is, the *why* and the *what*), I then review broader assessment criteria in the realm of multiliteracies, investigating more specific studies of assessment techniques and tasks with particular focus on the investigation of a visual metalanguage (that is, the *how*). By integrating some of the practices from these studies with some key theoretical principles for understanding visual modalities, a Show Me framework is proposed and illustrated by a selection of assessment questions and tasks. The grade level focus for these tasks is flexible and could be applied to students from Kindergarten to grade 6 (called the primary school in Australia but equivalent to elementary in the United States).

Why Is Visual Literacy so Important, and *What* Key Concepts Do Educators Need to Understand?

In order to develop a solid assessment framework for visual literacy, a broader concept of reading is required when considering visual and multimodal texts. Written text unfolds in sequence, over sentences, paragraphs, and pages, while an image, with all its design and spatial elements, is received seemingly "all at once" when viewed (Kress, 1997; Walsh, 2006). Thus, a multiliterate individual will need to have a variety of skills to make meaning of all types of texts.

Kress and van Leeuwen (1996) have developed a visual grammar that provides a substantial description of how visual texts work. This visual grammar is based on linguistic studies as well as semiotics, which is the study of various sign systems, from painting and drawing to movement and sound (Berghoff, 1998). In the same way that reading theory provides educators with concepts and words to talk about written texts, this visual grammar or metalanguage provides a basis for analyzing and critiquing the visual aspects of texts in a multiliteracies context (Kress & van Leeuwen, 1996).

In the Kress and Van Leeuwen framework, images can be understood to be drawing on a variety of meaning-making resources, broadly grouped as representational meanings (where actions, events, or symbolic concepts are shown in an image); interpersonal meanings (where relationships are constructed between the viewer and what is viewed using resources such as high or low angles, use of color, and shot distances); and organizational meanings (where composition and layout choices influence an image) (Kress & van Leeuwen, 1996; Unsworth, 2001). There is an extensive literature providing analysis of published multimodal texts (Callow & Zammit, 2002; Howie, 2002; Zammit, 2000). This literature provides a substantial base for educators, informing how they might view, create, and teach about visual modalities.

The inclusion of a range of disciplines in this discussion is also important. Other authors such as Duncum (1999) and Sturken and Cartwright (2001) asserted that areas such as fine arts, film studies, or graphic design also offer useful descriptions of how visual texts can be understood. In terms of visual images, I have argued previously that a broader, interdisciplinary approach is needed, in order to move beyond the language-focused, print-driven philosophy that tends to dominate literacy education (Callow, 2005). This article presents the argument that, while maintaining the tools to consider the more compositional and structural aspects of images, as well as developing critical analysis, the affective and personal interpretation of viewing must also permeate our theory and assessment practices. For example, the enjoyment students show when reading and interpreting picture books is an affective response that is arguably just as valuable as developing their metalinguistic skills in interpreting and creating pictures. Alongside this would be opportunities to critique the choices picture book illustrators have made, considering what type of worldview is presented by the pictures. These three dimensions—the affective, the compositional, and the critical—go some way to reflecting a broader visuality (Callow, 2005). To illustrate this, consider the painting in Figure 1, done by a grade 6 student.

The compositional elements can provide a starting point. Some viewers might be drawn to the strangely box-shaped person, made salient by the use of black on the orange background, or perhaps to the large tree in the center. The colors suggest a dry landscape, with a mountain in the distance. Broad brush strokes create the background, and the figure is made of collaged black construction paper. The balance of the three trees is upset by the figure, shown with a long shot length, whose inky darkness has a sinister feel. Who is this curious person, eyes hidden, standing alone?

Figure 1
A Child's Painting of the Australian Outback

From an affective viewpoint, the child who painted the work may feel a sense of pride in her finished piece, and an Australian viewing the piece might immediately understand the image as referring to Ned Kelly, the most well-known Australian outlaw from the 19th century, with his signature armor and square metal helmet. The bold orange colors will remind others of the Australian landscape, and some may enjoy the child's style, which copies that of Sidney Nolan, a famous Australian artist. Personal interpretation and pleasure are woven with cultural knowledge.

A critical reader might question whether an outlaw should be honored in artworks and history books, while another may argue this outlaw championed the rights of the poor and is rightly regarded as part of Australian history and folklore. A critical literacy approach is being employed here, where some aspect of ideology is opened up. A broader visuality allows discussion, critique, and enjoyment around all types of visual texts.

Given this framework for understanding visual literacy, it follows that assessment should acknowledge the three dimensions of the affective, compositional, and critical. The specific aspects of these dimensions are summarized as follows.

Affective. Expressions of enjoyment when examining images or exploring pictures are signs of affective engagement. These may also be assessed by observation of facial features and gestures, the engaged discussions about a picture, and the evident pleasure taken as children participate in an activity. The affective also involves personal interpretation, where viewers bring their own experiences and aesthetic preferences to an image (Barnard, 2001).

Compositional. The use of specific metalanguage is key to this dimension. Concepts such as actions, symbols, shot length, angles, gaze, color, layout, salience, lines, and vectors reflect a metalinguistic knowledge about visual texts. These same concepts may also be present in longer, less linguistically succinct terms, where a child talks about looking at objects on a page because they are large or bright (salience). Teachers would need to know the concepts and related metalanguage when listening for such comments in an assessment context (Kress & van Leeuwen, 1996; Unsworth, 2001).

Critical. The assessment of sociocritical understandings will vary depending on the text and learning situation. For younger students, comments about how the illustrator didn't draw a scene clearly or effectively might be precursors to more complex critiques of choices made in illustrations. Older students may be using more specific comments, such as talking about how an image positions the viewer to think or feel a particular way. Although each aspect of visuality is important, ideological critique is perhaps the most challenging for students and teachers (Anstey & Bull, 2000).

From the previous discussion, we can posit some key principles for understanding the *what* of assessing visual literacy. All texts are part of changing global, local, and social contexts. Visual literacy, including students' viewing, creating and discussing of texts, should be considered from affective, compositional, and critical aspects. Multiliteracies should also include learning about how texts are constructed, and then this knowledge should be used to redesign new texts as part of applied practice (New London Group, 2000). Such pedagogical practice also needs to be part of a wider consideration of assessment and visual literacy. Based on these principles, the following section focuses on the *how* of assessment.

Developing the Show Me Framework

There are some common broad strands when presenting issues of the *how* of assessment in a multiliteracies environment. Kalantzis et al. (2003) have argued that "new learning" requires redefining *competence*, *ability*, *capacity*, and *intelligence*. Assessment techniques such as project assessment of in-depth learning tasks, performance assessment of completion of those tasks, quantification of the ability to work collaboratively in groups, and ongoing documentation of learning experiences through forms of portfolios should all be found in new learning environments (Kalantzis et al., 2003). This argument is consistent with current practices in general educational assessment principles (Cumming & Maxwell, 1999). For instance, the Australian state of Queensland's Education Department states that all assessment within multiliteracies environments needs to be embedded in authentic learning experiences, be continuous and formative, and be summative and systematic (Hayes, Mills, Christie, & Lingard, 2006).

Within this broader assessment context, a further set of principles has informed the development of the Show Me framework, emanating from studies that have a number of common themes. These themes include focused and purposeful student talk in assessment (Arizpe & Styles, 2007; Kiefer, 1993; Madura, 1998; Sipe, 2000); the importance of affective engagement with images (Arizpe & Styles, 2003; Carger, 2004; Pantaleo, 2005b; Walsh, 2003); the inclusion of students actively creating or manipulating visual texts (Arizpe & Styles, 2003; Callow, 2006; Johnson, 2003; Pantaleo, 2005a; Vincent, 2005) and the significance of explicit compositional concepts and metalanguage (Arizpe & Styles, 2007; Callow, 2003, 2006; Callow & Zammit, 2002; Walsh, Asha, & Sprainger, 2007). Arizpe and Styles's (2007) extensive review concludes that "providing or expanding the terms or metalanguage to discuss visual aspects is crucial to developing better understanding of the texts" (p. 371). The inclusion of a more critical dimension in visual literacy is also an important theme, with a call for ongoing research into how to best assess and teach students to be critical viewers (Callow, 2003; Unsworth, 2001; Walsh et al., 2007).

Combining guidance from these studies with the initial principles developed in the previous *what* and *how* sections, I propose a set of general principles as part of the development of the Show Me framework. Assessment techniques and tasks for this framework should do the following:

- Be part of authentic learning experiences
- Involve ongoing, formative, and summative assessment

- Provide students with varied means for showing their skills and conceptual knowledge, as well as the processes used in learning (this includes time to look and think deeply about visual and multimodal texts)
- Use authentic texts, such as picture books, information books, electronic texts, and texts that students create
- Value the affective, compositional, and critical dimensions of visual texts, as well as the interplay between the visual and written elements
- Include student-made visual responses (drawing, painting, multimedia) to the texts viewed and discussed
- Provide focused activities where student talk and understanding are focused on specific areas of visuality
- Involve students using a metalanguage as part of the assessment

These principles provide guidance to teachers and curriculum developers when designing assessment items as well as learning activities that could also be used as the basis for assessment.

Using the Show Me Framework

The final section of this article proposes some benchmarks, examples, and tasks that will develop the Show Me framework for use in classroom contexts. Based on the above principles and on some recent classroom-based action research (Callow, Hunter, & Walsh, 2006), the framework assumes developing visual literacy as part of purposeful and authentic literacy teaching and learning. As with assessment of reading and writing, visual literacy assessment should be part of a rich, integrated learning environment. The suggested questions and tasks can be modified as formative or summative assessment, as well as incorporated with learning experiences in themselves. Talk and active response to images form a central role in the tasks.

The Show Me benchmarks for this article are concerned with picture books and similar fiction-based images and multimedia. A similar framework for nonfiction and informational texts (including electronic texts) could be created from this framework. The framework is organized under the Affective, Compositional, and Critical dimensions, with the International Reading Association/National Council of Teachers of English Language Arts Standards 1, 6, and 11 matching each dimension accordingly (International Reading Association & National Council of Teachers of English, 1996).

The performance indicators described in Tables 1–3 are developed over three broad schooling stages, based on English syllabus levels for the Australian state of New South Wales (New South Wales Board of Studies, 1998). Similarly, the gradation and phrasing of indicators over these stages draws on the principles of the New South Wales English syllabus. As with any set of indicators, these are meant to be a guide for educators, who can develop their own indicators based on the context, class, and learning resources available.

Show Me in Grade 3

Let's consider how the Show Me framework might be used in a classroom setting. The classroom students described in our introductory vignette had been exploring visual literacy where visual texts from picture books to information text and video were not only used for content, but also specific visual aspects were explored. During one week, the picture books of Anthony Browne were used as part of the read-aloud and shared reading sessions. While reading the book *Gorilla* (Browne, 2000), the teacher pointed out how some pictures attract attention by their use of color, size, or angles. Working in pairs with their own copy of the book, the students were encouraged to find one picture they found curious or interesting, place a small sticky note on it, and then describe to each other what specific feature they thought made it interesting. The class also completed drawing and labeling activities and further extended discussion around the visual images in more of Browne's books. Later that week, after the story *Willy and Hugh*

Table 1
Show Me Framework: Affective Dimensions

Visual features to assess—metalanguage to use	Suggested assessment questions or statements	Grades K–2 performance indicators	Grades 3–4 performance indicators	Grades 5–6 performance indicators
Observe engagement (positive or negative) with the text. General indicators may include • Looks at images while reading • Comments on pictures • Uses positive or negative affective comments and expressions • Returns to look at particular pictures • Shows enjoyment in reading or viewing	*Before reading* Tell me what this book might be about from the pictures on the cover. *After reading* Can you find me a picture you really like? Why? Can you find me a picture you really dislike? Why?	Locates favorite pictures in book or multimedia narrative Discusses favorite character, using pictures to assist	Justifies favorite image from a book or website preference Gives reasons for disliking particular images or pictures	Identifies particular aspects of specific image that are appealing Explains why particular images appeal to him or her but may not appeal to others

Note. Affective Dimensions correlate to Standard 1 as described in Standards for the English Language Arts (IRA/NCTE, 1996)

Table 2
Show Me Framework: Compositional Dimensions

Visual features to assess—metalanguage to use	Suggested assessment questions or statements	Grades K–2 performance indicators	Grades 3–4 performance indicators	Grades 5–6 performance indicators
		What is happening?		
Choose a specific page to focus on during or after the reading. Have students determine whether images show actions, events, concepts, or a mix. General indicators and metalanguage may include the following: • Describes actions, events and settings, using evidence. • Explains symbolic images (e.g., handshake means friendship, uses terms like *symbol, theme, idea*)	Can you tell me what is happening or what actions are taking place? What story do the pictures tell? Tell me about the setting where this story is happening. Is this picture showing a theme, a felling, or an idea? How does this picture show this?	Points out and interprets actions in a picture or series of picture in a narrative Interprets an image as showing simple idea or concept (e.g., this is a happy, sad, angry, scary picture)	Explains actions in visual texts, using some metalanguage (e.g., explains how "scratch marks" in a comic denote movement) Interprets variety of concepts in a visual image (e.g., beauty, health, evil, wealth)	Notes use of more sophisticated symbolism and concepts (e.g., religious icons, environmental themes, cultural references) Explains how visual texts may have both actions and concepts represented

(continued)

Table 2 *(continued)*
Show Me Framework: Compositional Dimensions

Visual features to assess—metalanguage to use	Suggested assessment questions or statements	Grades K–2 performance indicators	Grades 3–4 performance indicators	Grades 5–6 performance indicators
How do we react to people or other participants in an image?				
Choose a page with a character that has a particular shot distance, use of angles, or use of color. General indicators and metalanguage may include the following: • Describes shot distance used, angle, and character gaze; explains the effect of each. • Describes colors and related moods or symbolism • Describes types of lines, shapes, or textures and how they create effects	Are we very close to the characters in the picture, midway from them, or a long way from them? Are we looking at eyelevel in this picture, down low, or high? Can you find a character whose gaze is looking at the viewer? How do these things make you feel about that character? Why do you think the illustrator used the particular elements on this page? Do they make you feel a certain way?	Uses simple terms to describe shot distance in illustrations or photos (e.g., close to use, far away from us) Describes if character is looking at the viewer and how he or she feels about the character Points out simple shapes in picture when asked Describes simple colors in pictures	Uses accurate terms to describe shot distance (e.g., close-up, midshot, long shot) and its effect on the image Notes if the character is looking down or up at the viewer, looking directly at the viewer or not Describes various colors, lines, or shapes in pictures and the emotional connotation of them	Uses accurate terms to describe shot distance, angles, and gaze and how this affects the viewer and the portrayed character. Describes complex images using color, line, shape, and texture Describes how specific colors may be associated with feelings or concepts in an image
How is the page designed?				
Choose a page with a variety of elements in the picture to assess page layout choices. General indicators and metalanguage may include the following: • Identifies salient part of image that initially takes his or her gaze and explains reasons • Identifies a possible reading path that the eyes might follow on the page • Identifies strong lines (vectors) that drew his or her gaze and points them out	Sometimes a part of a picture will really attract our attention. When you fir look at this picture, what part do you look at first?	Identifies an obvious salient feature in an image (largest creature, bright-colored object) With teacher direction, finds and traces strong lines in an image	Identifies salient feature in an image, citing reason why he or she thinks it stands out (e.g., he is bigger than the other monkeys on the page) Identifies simple reading path on more complex image, tracing path on the image and explaining why eyes might follow such a path	Uses terms like *salient*, shows examples in text, and discusses why illustrator may have accentuated specific elements Identifies more complex reading paths, discussing how reading path may vary, depending on the viewer

Note. Compositional Dimensions correlate to Standard 6 as described in Standards for the English Language Arts (IRA/NCTE, 1996)

Table 3
Show Me Framework: Critical Dimensions

Visual features to assess—metalanguage to use	Suggested assessment questions or statements	Grades K–2 performance indicators	Grades 3–4 performance indicators	Grades 5–6 performance indicators
Questions should be used sparingly and adapted for the text being read. Extended discussion on one question is more useful than brief discussion of too many questions. Key concepts and metalanguage may include • Inclusion and exclusion of racial, cultural, and social groups • Who is represented as being powerful or important and who is not • Discussion of what choices were made by the image maker and why they were made	What sort of people, family, or neighborhood does this book show? How is it different to your family or neighborhood? Are there any people "missing" from these pictures? Why do you think they weren't included? Who was the most important character in the book? Can you find me a picture that shows how important the character is? Can you show me a character who doesn't seem important? Why do you think the illustrator made the character look this way?	Can identify if his or her family or community is represented in books or media Uses visual evidence to justify how a character has been made to look friendly or unfriendly (e.g., large, angry giant with big eyes and nasty mouth) Notes how gender is often signified by color in a picture book	Discusses the ways different groups of people are visually represented in a story (e.g., the portrayal of slaves in *From Slave Ship to Freedom Road*; Lester, 1998) Suggests how a character could have been portrayed differently (e.g., the wolf in *The True Story of the 3 Little Pigs*; Scieszka, 1989) Explains why an illustrator may have chosen to create a story, represent genders, or use visual stereotypes to show good and bad characters	Discusses the ways different groups of people are visually represented in a story and how this might affect the interpretation of the story (e.g., all races are represented in pale blue in *Smoky Night*; Bunting, 1994) Explains how visual images can either support or stereotype minority groups, genders, or people in particular roles

Note. Critical Dimensions correlate to Standard 11 as described in Standards for the English Language Arts (IRA/NCTE, 1996)

(Browne, 1998) had been read, seven students were assessed individually using a selection of the Show Me framework's suggested questions.

In terms of the affective dimension, the teacher had noted all students enthusiastically talking about and discussing the picture books during the week. On an individual basis, each child was able to comment on a favorite page from *Willy and Hugh* (Browne, 1998), giving reasons why they each liked their chosen picture. Focusing on the compositional aspects of expression, size, and angle, Buster Nose (the bully of the story) was discussed with each child able to explain why he or she thought Buster looked powerful. Some said, "His face is really big" and "He takes up the whole room," while others commented on his expression and clothes—"His mouth is angry" and "His outfit has all spikes on it." Jay, from our opening quote, was the most articulate with his newfound knowledge about angles. He explained, "He's bigger and he's taking up more of the page and he's looking down. I can tell that because there's glasses on at an angle." When questioned about a symbolic picture of the two main characters shaking hands (with just the hands shown in close-up, suggesting friendship), no child interpreted this as showing care, friendship, or kindness. Rather, they all gave a literal description that they were just "shaking hands."

The critical dimension proved to be the weakest for these students, with most having limited responses about why they thought Browne may have written the book or what the theme might be. They gave short comments such as "being nice" or "be friendly to others," while some commented on a specific event in the book such as "if you accidentally knock someone over you can be nice to them," rather than a broader theme or idea.

To provide the students with a hands-on activity in assessment, they were asked to redraw a character, changing the angles or shot distance, and to sort a selection of 10 photos (a mix of high-angle, low-angle, and eye-level shots) into two groups—those that made the person look powerful or those that made the person look weak (see Table 4 for other activities). The students then commented on why they had made their choices. The teacher noted their use of metalanguage such

Table 4
Suggested Hands-On Activities to Support Assessment

Dimension	Suggested hands-on activities
Affective	Provide a selection of images from picture books, magazines, websites. Ask students to sort these into different categories. Say, for example, "Sort into the pictures you like and those you dislike." Depending on the images chosen, have students categorize those images that might appeal to different groups (adults, children, girls, boys, people who enjoy sports, animal lovers, etc.). Ask them why they chose to group particular images.
Compositional What is happening?	Ask students to draw a new scene from the story with different events. Have them change the facial expression on a character to represent different emotions. Ask them to re-create a picture using cut-out characters and various setting elements (buildings, trees, objects etc.). Have them retell the story after creating the picture.
How do we react to people or other participants in an image?	Sort a selection of images into —shot distances (close, mid, or long) —angles (low, eye-level, or high) Have students explain how they know what type of shot or angle it is and the effect it has on the viewer. Ask them to take digital photos of a classmate and experiment with angle, shot distance, and gaze. Have them redraw a character that attracts the viewer's attention with their eyes (gaze). Ask them to use different colors or media (pastel, collage, charcoal, pencil) and draw a character or setting from the book. Discuss whether the colour or media changes the feel of the story or character.
How is the page designed?	Give students a few small sticky notes and have them place them on pages that have a strong salient point. Discuss their choices. Have them redraw a scene from the book, making one thing salient, such as a person, place, or object. They could use colour, size, placement, or framing to achieve this.
Critical	Create and draw another type of character for the story who comes from a different family or neighbourhood. Ask "What do they look like?" Take a copy of a character from the book and ask children to add labels to show the choices the illustrator has made (e.g. the main female character is very slim, wears expensive clothes, is usually smiling). Ask them to explain their labels.

as *angle* (or words that showed that concept, such as *He's looking down at us*), *shot distance*, and *color*, as well as descriptions of actions, facial expressions, and feelings. This provided further information about the students' understandings of images and their use of metalanguage. Using the benchmarks, we could say that the data for this small group showed that most were developing toward grades 3–4 in their affective responses, with their understanding of compositional aspects also developing toward this level, except in their understanding of more symbolic images. The critical dimension showed students working toward the grades K–2 level. This assessment information would, of course, inform the next round of lesson planning and literacy activities.

This classroom example illustrates a majority of the Show Me principles, in that it is part of authentic, contextualixed learning in a class, involves formative assessment in this case, provides varied means for students to show their skills, uses authentic texts, and provides focused assessment activities involving specific metalanguage as part of the overall assessment process.

Planning for Assessment of Visual Literacy Skills

It has been argued in this article that if educators are to assist students in becoming multiliterate learners, specifically across multimodal and visual texts, then clear, rigorous, and equitable assessment must be part of that process. The introduction and development of the Show Me framework goes some way to provide an argument for assessment of visual literacy that is informed by sound theoretical underpinnings and supported by informed practical techniques and tasks. It is hoped that this article adds to a growing body of work supporting teachers and students in literacy education. The continuing work, then, is to apply and test a variety of assessment techniques in order to ascertain what concepts and metalanguage students already bring to visual images and, based on the findings, to plan for meaningful learning experiences to support their development as viewers, makers, and critics of visual and multimodal texts.

References

Ailwood, J., Chant, D., Gore, J., Hayes, D., Ladwig, J., Lingard, B., et al. (2000). *The four dimensions of productive pedagogies: Narratives and findings from the Queensland school reform longitudinal study.* Paper presented at the American Education Research Association Annual Conference, New Orleans, LA.

Anstey, M., & Bull, G. (2000). *Reading the visual: Written and illustrated children's literature.* Sydney, NSW, Australia: Harcourt.

Anstey, M., & Bull, G. (2006). *Teaching and learning multiliteracies: Changing times, changing literacies.* Newark, DE.: International Reading Association.

Arizpe, E., & Styles, M. (2003). *Children reading pictures: Interpreting visual texts.* London; New York: RoutledgeFalmer.

Arizpe, E., & Styles, M. (2007). A critical review of research into children's responses to multimodal texts. In J. Flood, , S.B. Heath, & D. Lapp (Eds.), *Handbook of research in teaching literacy through the visual and communicative arts* (Vol. 2, pp. 365–375). London: Routledge.

Barnard, M. (2001). *Approaches to understanding visual culture.* New York: Palgrave.

Berghoff, B. (1998). Multiple sign systems and reading. *The Reading Teacher, 51*(6), 520–523.

Callow, J. (2003). Talking about visual texts with students. *Reading Online, 6*(8). Retrieved July 1st, 2007, from www.readingonline.org/articles/art_index.asp?HREF=callow/index.html

Callow, J. (2005). Literacy and the visual: Broadening our vision. English Teaching: *Practice and Critique, 4*(1), 6–19.

Callow, J. (2006). Images, politics and multiliteracies: Using a visual metalanguage. *Australian Journal of Language & Literacy*, 29(1), 7–23.

Callow, J., Hunter, D., & Walsh, T. (2006). Visual literacy. In F.G. Team (Ed.), *School is for me: Pathways to student engagement* (pp. 33–38). Sydney: NSW Department of Education and Training.

Callow, J., & Zammit, K. (2002). Visual literacy: From picture books to electronic texts. In M. Monteith (Ed.), *Teaching primary literacy with ICT* (pp. 188–201). Buckingham, England: Open University Press.

Carger, C.L. (2004). Art and literacy with bilingual children: Literature becomes significant for children through engagements in art and talk about books. *Language Arts*, 81(4), 283–292.

Cumming, J.J., & Maxwell, G.S. (1999). Contextualizing authentic assessment. *Assessment in Education*, 6(2), 177–194.

Duncum, P. (1999). A case for an art education of everyday aesthetic experiences. *Studies in Art Education, 40*(4), 295–311.

Hayes, D., Mills, M., Christie, P., & Lingard, B. (2006). *Teachers & schooling making a difference: Productive pedagogies, assessment and performance.* Crows Nest, NSW, Australia: Allen & Unwin.

Howie, M. (2002, July). "Selling a drink with less sugar": Considering English curriculum and pedagogy as the shaping of a certain sort of person in teaching year 8. *English in Australia, 134*, 45–56.

International Reading Association & National Council of Teachers of English. (1996). *Standards for the English language arts.* Newark, DE; Urbana, IL: Authors.

Johnson, D. (2003). Activity theory, mediated action and literacy: Assessing how children make meaning in multiple modes. *Assessment in Education*, 10(1), 103–129.

Kalantzis, M., Cope, B., & Harvey, A. (2003). Assessing multiliteracies and the new basics. *Assessment in Education*, 10(1), 15–26.

Kiefer, B.Z. (1993). Children's responses to picture books: A developmental perspective. In K.E. Holland, R.A. Hungerford, & S.B. Ernst (Eds.), *Journeying: Children responding to literature* (pp. 267–283). Portsmouth, NH: Heinemann.

Kress, G. (1997). Visual and verbal modes of representation in electronically mediated communication: The potentials of new forms of text. In I. Snyder (Ed.), *Page to screen: Taking literacy into the electronic era* (pp. 53–79). St. Leonards, NSW, Australia: Allen & Unwin.

Kress, G., & van Leeuwen, T. (1996). *Reading images: The grammar of visual design.* London: Routledge.

Leu, D.J., Jr., Kinzer, C.K., Coiro, J., & Cammack, D.W. (2004). Toward a theory of new literacies emerging from the Internet and other information and communication technologies. In R.B. Ruddell & N. Unrau (Eds.), *Theoretical models and processes of reading* (5th ed., pp. 1570–1613). Newark, DE: International Reading Association. Retrieved July 1, 2007, from www.readingonline.org/newliteracies/lit_index.asp? HREF=leu/

Madura, S. (1998). An artistic element: Four transitional readers and writers respond to the picture books of Patricia Polacco and Gerald McDermott. In T. Shanahan & F.V. Rodriguez-Brown (Eds.), *47th yearbook of the National Reading Conference* (pp. 366–376). Chicago: National Reading Conference

Mercer, N. (2000). *Words and minds: How we use language to think together.* London: Routledge.

New London Group. (2000). Pedagogy of multiliteracies designing social futures. In B. Cope & M. Kalantzis (Eds.), *Multiliteracies: Literacy learning and the design of social futures* (pp. 9–37). London: Routledge.

New South Wales Board of Studies. (1998). *English K–6.* Sydney, NSW: Author.

Pantaleo, S. (2005a). "Reading" young children's visual texts. *Early Childhood Research & Practice, 7*(1). Retrieved July 1, 2007, from ecrp.uiuc.edu/v7n1/pantaleo.html

Pantaleo, S. (2005b). Young children engage with the metafictive in picture books. *Australian Journal of Language and Literacy, 28*(1), 19–37.

Sipe, L. (2000). The construction of literary understanding by first and second graders in oral response to picture storybook read-alouds. *Reading Research Quarterly, 35*(2), 252–275.

Sturken, M., & Cartwright, L. (2001). *Practices of looking: An introduction to visual culture.* Oxford, England: Oxford University Press.

Unsworth, L. (2001). *Teaching multiliteracies across the curriculum: Changing contexts of text and image in classroom practice.* Buckingham, England: Open University.

Vincent, J. (2005). Multimodal literacies in the school curriculum: An urgent matter of equity. In A. Méndez-Vilas, B. González-Pereira, J.M. González, & J.A.M. González (Eds.), *Recent research developments in learning technologies* (Vol. II, pp. 1–5). Badajoz, Spain: FORMATEX. Retrieved July 2, 2007, from www.formatex.org/micte2005/29.pdf

Vygotsky, L.S. (1978). *Mind in society: The development of higher psychological processes* (M. Cole, V. John-Steiner, S. Scribner, & E. Souberman, Eds. & Trans.). Cambridge, MA: Harvard University Press.

Walsh, M. (2003). "Reading" pictures: What do they reveal? Young children's reading of visual texts. *Literacy, 37*(3), 123–130.

Walsh, M. (2006). The "textual shift": Examining the reading process with print, visual and multimodal texts. *Australian Journal of Language & Literacy, 29*(1), 24–37.

Walsh, M., Asha, J., & Sprainger, N. (2007). Reading digital texts. *Australian Journal of Language & Literacy, 30*(1), 40–53.

Zammit, K. (2000). Computer icons: A picture says a thousand words, or does it? *Journal of Educational Computing Research, 23*(2), 217–231.

Literature Cited

Browne, A. (1998). *Willy and Hugh.* London: Red Fox.

Browne, A. (2000). *Gorilla.* London: Walker

Bunting, E., & Diaz, D. (1994). *Smoky night.* San Diego, CA: Harcourt Brace.

Lester, J., & Brown, R. (1998). *From slave ship to freedom road.* New York: Dial Books.

Scieska, J., & Smith, L. (1989). *The true story of the 3 little pigs.* New York: Viking.

Questions for Reflection

- Why do you think it is important for students to be able to interpret and create multiliteracies texts that include combinations of writing, speech, visual images, and electronic and interactive media? Why is it important for students to have a "metalanguage" for talking about images, texts, and meaning-making interactions? Why is it essential to assess these skills?
- Do your current assessments account for visual literacy? What ideas do you have for modifying your existing assessment practices to include the assessment of visual literacy?
- The Show Me framework establishes a foundation for the assessment of visual literacy and argues that if educators are to assist students in becoming multiliterate learners, specifically across multimodal and visual texts, then clear, rigorous, and equitable assessment must be part of that process. How can you extend this through your own work? What can you do to further apply and test a variety of assessment techniques and plan for meaningful learning experiences to support your students' development as viewers, makers, and critics of visual and multimodal texts?

Using Electronic Portfolios to Make Learning Public

Kevin Fahey, Joshua Lawrence, and Jeanne Paratore

In this article, we describe a plan for using electronic portfolios as a forum for establishing collaborative learning environments in which looking at and responding to student work assumes a place of centrality and importance. The purpose of this work was not to establish a system for collecting, organizing, and evaluating student work—a common purpose of electronic portfolios—but rather to change the ways teachers and students think about, talk about, and use data. Our work is based in two distinct contexts: urban middle school classrooms and undergraduate and graduate classrooms in a teacher education and educational leadership programs. Although outcome data from this work can be considered only preliminary, we believe sharing what we did, the early patterns in the data, and our current suppositions and understandings is consistent with the essential principle that underlies the work itself: the process of thinking about, talking about, and using data in a collaborative forum extends and deepens everyone's understanding about a problem or issue. It is our hope that sharing our work at this stage will trigger collaborative conversations and interactions that will guide and improve our own work and the work of others.

The efforts we recount began with a conversation between Kevin Fahey (first author), a professor at Salem State College in Salem, Massachusetts, and Joshua Lawrence (second author), a middle school teacher at the Timilty Middle School in Boston, Massachusetts. Although their teaching contexts are in many ways different, they shared a common interest and a common need: They each sought ways to create more collaborative learning environments, contexts in which everyone in the class, not just the teacher, cared about each student's learning. Their joint pursuit was based on the idea that the most powerful learning happens when it is supported by an entire community of learners (McLaughlin & Oberman, 1996; Newmann & Wehlage, 1995). It was grounded in now widely held theories that suggest that social interaction is an essential context for learning (Vygotsky, 1978) and that literacy practices, in particular, cannot be isolated from the social context (Gee, 1996).

Eventually, Fahey's and Lawrence's conversations and musings about how to change the learning context in their respective teaching settings led to a discussion of student work, and they talked about how looking at student work might provide a vehicle for changing the learning context in the classroom. The following was their reasoning: In many communities, looking at student work has become a central focus in the professional development of teachers. Researchers who have studied this process report that when student work creates the context for conversations about teaching and learning, participants' levels of engagement and interaction increase and there is evidence of positive change in classroom practices (e.g., Fisher, Lapp, & Flood, 2005; Langer, Colton, & Goff, 2003). In linking this work to their interest in creating a more collaborative learning environment in their respective classroom contexts, Fahey and Lawrence considered how they might create classroom contexts

Reprinted from Fahey, K., Lawrence, J., & Paratore, J. (2007). Using electronic portfolios to make learning public. *Journal of Adolescent & Adult Literacy, 50*(6), 460–471.

in which looking at and responding to student work assumed a similar place of centrality and importance. They envisioned a setting in which work was always public and responsibility for responding to and improving work was shared between and among teachers and students. They had a good idea of how they could take advantage of technology to create such a context, but they wondered how teachers who had never experienced such a classroom community might be able to create one. Was it reasonable to think that teachers who were only used to looking at student work with other teachers and who rarely made their work public either in their practice (Little & McLaughlin, 1993) or in their teacher preparation programs (McLaughlin & Oberman, 1996) could create such a public space in their classrooms? Was it reasonable to expect that adolescents who are so "peer-conscious" would be able to offer the type of honest and critical feedback that would lead to improved writing?

Fahey and Lawrence also wondered how school leaders who have had little experience with making their practice public and who often have worked in an isolated, competitive culture (Cuban, 1993; Evans, 1996; Fullan, 2001, 2005; Public Agenda, 2001, 2003; Sergiovanni, 2001) could support teachers' attempts to create a very different and more public, classroom community. They were troubled by research (Cuban; Dufour & Eaker, 1998; Little & McLaughlin, 1993; Louis & Kruse, 1995; McLaughlin & Talbert, 2001, 2002; Nelson & Sassi, 2005; Rosenholtz, 1989; Senge, 1990) that argued that when members of the school community—teachers, administrators, students—held very different understandings of fundamental issues of teaching and learning, schools and school systems tended to become "stuck," and little organizational learning or substantive change was possible. Simply put, how could teachers and school administrators who had never experienced collaborative school communities in which all work was made public create such places for their students? They hypothesized that the answer might reside in the use of electronic portfolios, and they derived a plan to test their ideas in both Fahey's undergraduate and graduate classrooms and in Lawrence's middle school classrooms. As they began to review and reflect on their outcomes, they invited a third author, Jeanne Paratore, a professor at Boston University, to think with them, and in particular, to consider this work within the context of both literacy and language learning and professional development. In the remainder of this article, we explain the plan, its implementation, and the lessons learned to date.

The Plan: An Electronic Portfolio Forum

Using open-source, bulletin-board technology, an electronic portfolio system was developed at the Timilty Middle School. This technology ensured that all student learning—papers, drafts, analyses, pictures, videos, and so forth—was made visible to the entire classroom community. Assigned work would no longer be done in isolation, passed into the teacher, and forgotten about. In addition, a virtual space was created where members of the community could look at one another's work, respond to it, reflect on it, and build on it. This space was intended to be thoughtful, respectful, and an essential part of any intellectual work done in the classroom. It was also designed to be visually engaging, with options for students to customize their user profile (Figures 1, 2, and 3).

On the forum, students self-register and create individualized usernames and passwords. The system tracks what students post and allows them to read and respond to one another's work. Users can post text directly to the forum, attach documents or image files, upload Web links, and edit their own work after getting feedback. Teachers control the forum areas in which students can view or work.

The same technology was introduced into a variety of classrooms in the undergraduate teacher preparation program at Salem State College, where teacher candidates share all of their lesson plan drafts, portfolios, rubrics, classroom material, and reflections. The undergraduates, in much the same way as the students at Timilty Middle School, are encouraged to give one another

Figure 1
Timilty Community Forum Front Page for School Year 2003-2004

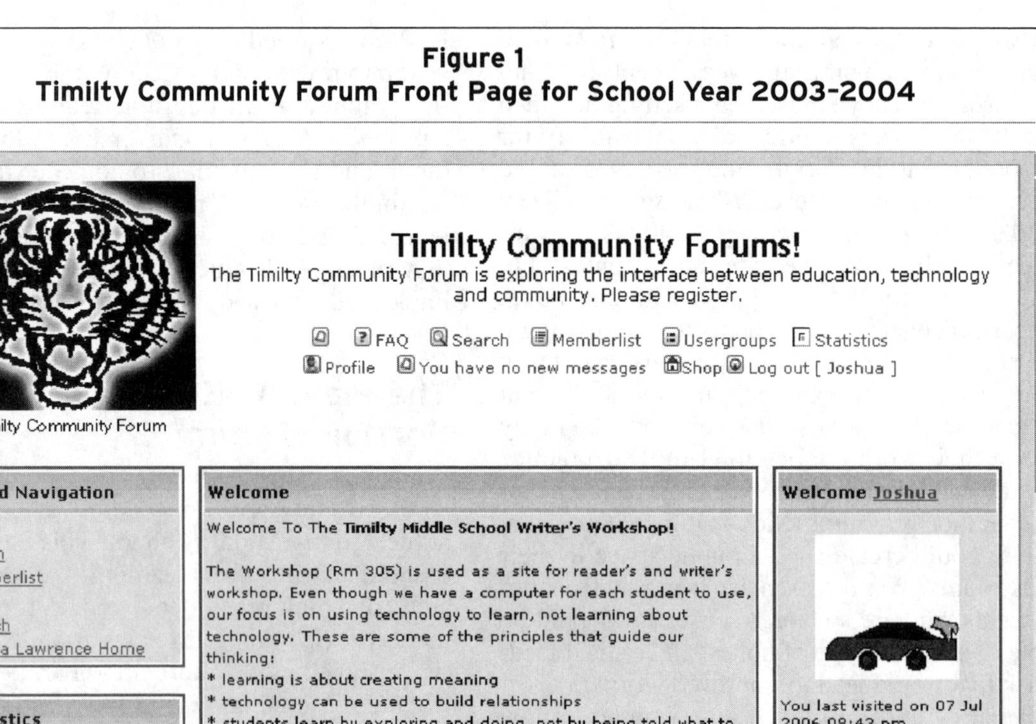

Timilty Community Forums!
The Timilty Community Forum is exploring the interface between education, technology and community. Please register.
FAQ Search Memberlist Usergroups Statistics
Profile You have no new messages Shop Log out [Joshua]
Timilty Community Forum
Board Navigation
Forum
Memberlist
FAQ
Search
Joshua Lawrence Home
Statistics
We have 319 registered users
Our users have posted a total of 4886 articles within
Welcome
Welcome To The Timilty Middle School Writer's Workshop!
The Workshop (Rm 305) is used as a site for reader's and writer's workshop. Even though we have a computer for each student to use, our focus is on using technology to learn, not learning about technology. These are some of the principles that guide our thinking:
* learning is about creating meaning
* technology can be used to build relationships
* students learn by exploring and doing, not by being told what to do
You can see these principles in work in our classroom through the following practices:
* mini-lessons to guide instruction and lots of time for student
Welcome Joshua
You last visited on 07 Jul 2006 08:43 pm
View posts since last visit (0)
The time now is 08 Jul 2006 01:19 pm

Figure 2
Student Response to Literature on Timilty Community Forum

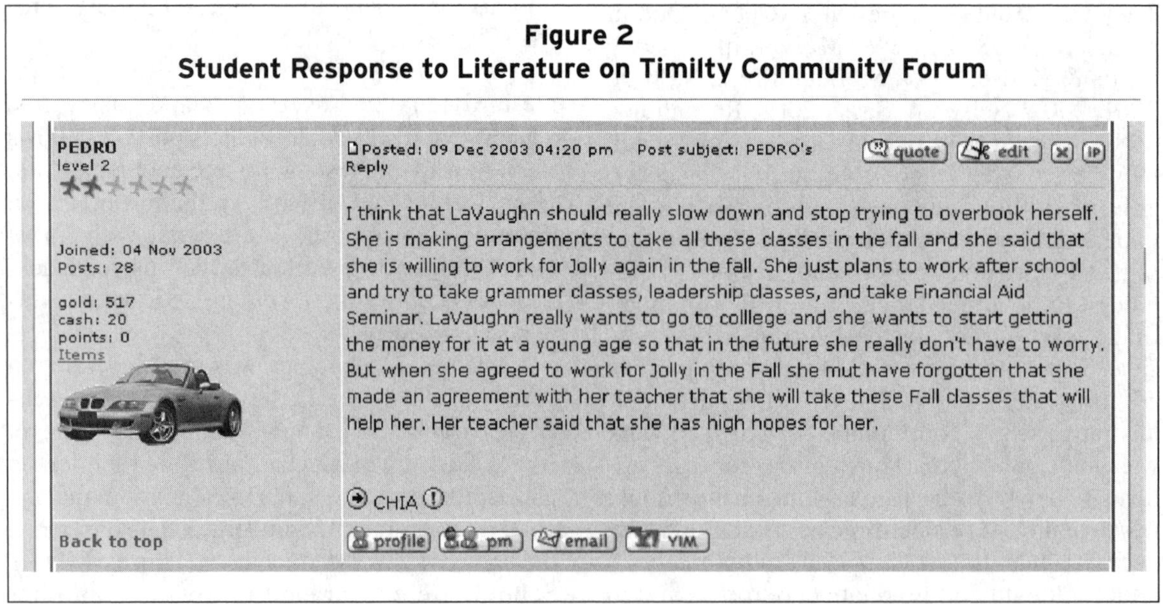

PEDRO
level 2
Joined: 04 Nov 2003
Posts: 28
gold: 517
cash: 20
points: 0
Items
Posted: 09 Dec 2003 04:20 pm Post subject: PEDRO's Reply
quote edit
I think that LaVaughn should really slow down and stop trying to overbook herself. She is making arrangements to take all these classes in the fall and she said that she is willing to work for Jolly again in the fall. She just plans to work after school and try to take grammer classes, leadership classes, and take Financial Aid Seminar. LaVaughn really wants to go to colllege and she wants to start getting the money for it at a young age so that in the future she really don't have to worry. But when she agreed to work for Jolly in the Fall she mut have forgotten that she made an agreement with her teacher that she will take these Fall classes that will help her. Her teacher said that she has high hopes for her.
CHIA
Back to top
profile pm email YIM

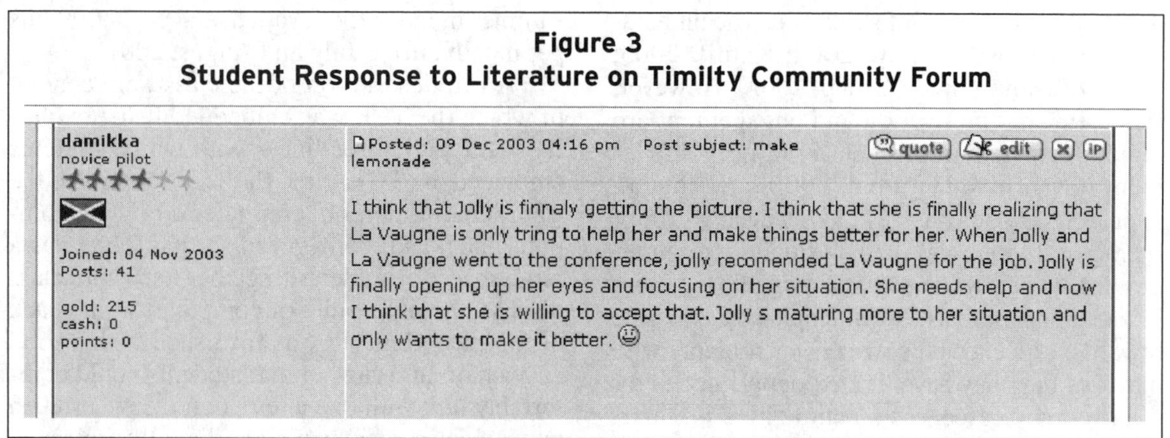

damikka
novice pilot
Joined: 04 Nov 2003
Posts: 41
gold: 215
cash: 0
points: 0
Posted: 09 Dec 2003 04:16 pm Post subject: make lemonade
quote
edit
IP
I think that Jolly is finnaly getting the picture. I think that she is finally realizing that La Vaugne is only tring to help her and make things better for her. When Jolly and La Vaugne went to the conference, jolly recomended La Vaugne for the job. Jolly is finally opening up her eyes and focusing on her situation. She needs help and now I think that she is willing to accept that. Jolly s maturing more to her situation and only wants to make it better.

Figure 3
Student Response to Literature on Timilty Community Forum

feedback, build upon one another's ideas, share experiences, and learn from one another.

The technology was also introduced into the graduate leadership preparation program at Salem State. Again, building upon the work of Timilty, aspiring school leaders share problems of practice, build upon each other's experience in curriculum design, give one another feedback, and challenge one another's ideas.

We begin our account by acknowledging that, to some extent, many teachers already use a range of practices that enable students to take responsibility for their own and one another's learning. For example, in classrooms in which teachers are using writers' workshop (Calkins, 1994) to frame writing instruction, students routinely share their written work and give one another feedback. Students might also peer edit, work in collaborative groups, design rubrics for the class's work, and even create exhibitions or demonstrations of what they have learned and share them with the entire community. In such classrooms, to some extent, teachers are asking students to make their work public and transparent. However, what is different about the classrooms described in this article is that students are required to make public all of their work all of the time. In these classrooms, all student work—homework assignments, drafts, feedback, questions, and final products—are always shared with every member of the classroom community. In addition, students understand that, with the teacher, they share the responsibility for one another's learning by reviewing this public work, giving feedback, and building upon it. The decision to make all of their assigned work public all of the time was a deliberate attempt to change the way students (and their teachers) think about writing and the nature of learning—to help them to acquire an understanding that literacy is a social act and good writers and good readers improve their comprehension and composition in collaboration with others.

Timilty Community Forum: Implementation

The demographic profile of the Timilty Middle School is typical of the other schools in Boston Public Schools (BPS) and other large urban public school systems (Lewis, Ceperich, & Jepson, 2002): 53.9% of students are African American and 39.9% are Hispanic. Many students speak English as a second language (37.3%) and most live in low-income homes (83%).

The academic struggles of students from low-income families who speak a language other than English or a nonstandard English dialect at home are well documented, particularly on measures of reading achievement (Snow, Burns, & Griffin, 1998). Understanding the cause of reading difficulties in adolescents is getting increased attention, but it is still poorly understood, due in part to the complexity of skilled adolescent reading (Biancarosa & Snow, 2004; Kamil, 2003; RAND Reading Study Group, 2004). However, it is clear that motivation and engagement are major factors in adolescent reading achievement (Guthrie & Wigfield, 2000) and that an approach that emphasizes the intrinsic worth of literacy activities and the building of a community that values those activities might have more impact than approaches that emphasize extrinsic rewards, especially for struggling students who may feel that they have limited opportunities for high-literacy careers in a competitive job market (Bandura & Locke, 2003; Csikszentmihalyi, 1990). The Timilty Community Forum (TCF) takes such an approach.

The Timilty Community Forum was established to create an online space for students to share their writing and reflections about what they were reading every day. The TCF's fundamental assumptions are (a) that adolescent students become increasingly sensitive to peer influence as they get older, and (b) that writing for peers would be highly engaging and intrinsically motivating to students (Eccles, 1999). The goal of the forum was to build a community where (1) everyone writes for everyone else and not just the teacher, and (2) everyone, not just the teacher, cares about everyone's writing.

In 2003, we implemented the TCF in six homerooms as a supplemental literacy block to their regular English language arts class. As we predicted, the middle school students were motivated by the use of technology. They enjoyed sharing their thoughts and reflections and discussing one another's ideas. One way to judge student enthusiasm and engagement is through the number of times they accessed the site (i.e., the number of "hits"). The TCF averaged 124,000 hits per month during the 2003–2004 school year. Nearly half (55) of the students we surveyed ($N = 112$) reported that they had logged onto the TCF during out-of-school time during the school year. The other students explained that they did not have access to the Internet at home. Nonetheless, many students continued to use the forum to stay connected with schoolwork during summer months: the forum averaged 14,000 hits per month during July and August 2004.

A full description of the classroom context in which the TCF was embedded helps to clarify the apparent readiness with which students embraced the TCF. First, the TCF reinvented the traditional notion of "computer lab." The computer lab was reconfigured so that there was a large space for students to gather for whole-class discussion with a suite of computers at the back of the class. The lab was furnished with a sofa, easy chair, and rug, so that students could comfortably talk with one another and view a screen upon which student work was digitally projected. Every attempt was made to turn the computer lab into a readers' workshop—that is, a place where students learned and practiced the craft of reading and writing (Calkins, 1994). In order to send the message that this was not a computer class, the computers were not used at all for the first month, so that the teacher and the class could develop a comfortable, social relationship that would allow shared writing and reflections to flourish in class and online.

As previously explained, making student work public is fundamental to the TCF classroom. Toward this end, each TCF class starts with the whole class gathered comfortably together at the front of the room. The teacher digitally projects selected portfolio entries from the previous day and leads a class minilesson on some aspect of reading or responding to literature for 10 to 15 minutes. Using student work as the basis for ongoing reading helps to clarify misconceptions that students might have, models aspects of effective student writing, and gives an opportunity for the teacher to demonstrate how to engage with students writing in a respectful manner.

An ongoing concern that we have about this approach is that some students may be reluctant to share their work with their class for fear that other students may mock them because of their writing ability or the content of their ideas. Besides providing a time for focused instruction, the minilesson also provides an opportunity at the start of every class to model how to respond respectfully to the work of others. Addressing the issue of respectful response to students' writing ability is relatively easy. In general, the teacher emphasizes the fact that in most cases students are being asked to provide their best thinking, but not necessarily their most polished writing. Although students are asked to refrain from using Internet slang, such as writing in all capitals or excessive use of emoticons, the teacher does not comment on misspelled or mistyped words during the minilesson and asks students to focus on the content of the writing in their discussion and online responses. Many students are familiar with online environments in which spelling and syntax conventions are lax, and they seem to easily accept and adopt the TCF emphasis on meaning over format.

A more difficult and persistent challenge is establishing a safe environment in which students can share personal connections and interpretations of literature in a public setting. In all urban middle schools, classroom management can be a critical component of good teaching practice. We create an effective classroom climate by establishing systematic classroom routines, beginning with the structure of each day's minilesson.

The minilesson at the start of every class has three distinct purposes. One is to define (or, later in the process, to remind students of) the boundaries of respectful discussion of student writing and to explain why these boundaries are essential for students to feel comfortable enough to share their thoughts and feelings. The second is to discuss earlier posts, abiding by the guidelines for respectful discussion. The third is to introduce (or review), model, and discuss a reading comprehension strategy and to apply it to a section of the focal text.

After the minilesson, students read individually or in small groups. Students' reading is guided by the comprehension strategy that was the focus of the minilesson and by the group's discussion of earlier posts. The last 20 minutes of class are reserved for students to respond to the reading on the TCF. Sometimes students, guided by the teacher, respond to specific questions that arise from the earlier discussion. For example, the teacher might ask students to make predictions, use connection strategies, post the meaning of words with which they struggled, or take a position on an issue that arose in the text (Beck & McKeown, 2001; Harvey & Goudvis, 2000; Pressley, 2006). When students finish their own writing, they read and respond to one another's work. Typically, students leave the class knowing that the conversation is unfinished and that it will begin again at the start of next class with a review of the just-completed work.

As one might expect, it is clear that student learning style and personalities influence how and what they share online. Many students strongly prefer writing online, even when talking about personal topics. When we asked students to describe how they felt about responding to literature in public, one student enthused that "it made me feel good about myself. I can get my feelings down more on a computer." Another student wrote,

> I feel very happy about the class reading my writing because they can see how I write and what kind of style I use.... In a notebook you mostly read to yourself and get bored with it and in the computer your friends can read it.

Other students are ambivalent about sharing their work. "Usually, I don't feel comfortable sharing things [by reading aloud] with my class. So writing in the forums is a good way to share our writing with our classmates...sometimes students may like you for your opinions."

The practice of making student work public exists, to some degree, in every classroom in the use of activities such as school or classroom newspapers, research reports and projects, and publication celebrations. The TCF, however, codifies the practice of making work public into a daily routine that can be effectively sustained throughout the entire academic year.

The experience of three years of work with the Timilty Community Forum suggests three preliminary understandings. First, students are experiencing and building a community that supports good literacy practice. Students are writing, sharing, and reflecting not only with their teacher but also with one another. Students come to schools with their own rich funds of knowledge (Moje et al., 2004; Moll, 1992), which they draw upon when they read. When students are writing to peers with whom they have much in common, they seem to more naturally access these funds of knowledge and reference them in their reading. This seems to result in more authentic engagement with texts. Second, the electronic portfolio process allows students to generate and explore issues that are important to them as a group. For instance, one TCF class read and wrote to one another about a novel written from the perspective of a child living in an abusive home. Students researched the issue of child abuse, wrote to one another about the meaning of child abuse in their community, and connected these online discussions to other books they had read. The technology provided access to information on a high-interest topic, and it also provided a way for students to start and maintain in-depth conversation on a complex topic. Third, the TCF electronic process is generative. The more students write to one another and reflect about what they are reading, the more they want to write to one another, share other thoughts, and support one another's work.

Salem Education Forum: Implementation

The electronic portfolio and bulletin board work at Salem State College was built upon the work done at the Timilty Middle School and uses the same open source bulletin board and electronic portfolio technology. The Salem State initiative is also driven by the idea that when everyone in a classroom makes public all of their work all of the time and cares about everyone's learning, all learning is likely to be deeper and more robust.

At Salem State, students in a variety of undergraduate teacher preparation classes as well as graduate students in the education leadership program post all of their work—drafts and final products—on the Salem Education Forum (SEF) website, which is open to all members of the particular class in which students are enrolled. Since April, 2005, 385 students—graduate and undergraduate—have had access to the website. These students have posted more than 4,200 examples of their work in the five semesters in which the Salem Education Forum has been operating. In addition, from the period of April 2005 to March 2006, the website had an average of more than 43,900 hits a month.

The majority of the student postings are written work; however, students can also post pictures of classroom artifacts, student art, and even videos. In addition, the technology assembles the students' work into an electronic portfolio, which is periodically reviewed by the student, the professor, and members of the class. (Although this electronic portfolio can be used by the student to build the portfolio required for licensure as a teacher or administrator in the Commonwealth of Massachusetts, we consider this to be an entirely separate use of the technology and have not chosen to study it or report it for the purpose of this particular article.)

Salem Education Forum: Undergraduate Teacher Preparation Program

In a paper-based, teacher-preparation classroom, when, for example, students learn to craft lesson plans, they typically work individually or in small groups to learn about a planning process, practice drafting some plans, and get some guidance and feedback from their professor. As students become more skilled, they create a more finished product to become part of their portfolios, and, in the best situations, try the lesson plan out in a classroom and get yet more feedback from the professor. The Salem Education Forum expands this process in three ways. First, because everyone's work is always public, students get ideas and feedback not only from the professor but also from everyone in the class. But the SEF does more than give students feedback. It also provides a source of good ideas. In the same ways that inservice teachers are on the lookout for good teaching ideas as they browse the corridors and classrooms of their buildings or chat with their colleagues in the faculty room, preservice teachers in the Salem Education Forum classrooms can "scout" the SEF for good ideas from their peers. Tracking data tell us that every assignment posted in the fall of 2005 was downloaded by someone else in the class. Some assignments were downloaded by others as many as 15 times. We believe that this is one indication that the SEF affords students the opportunity to become members of a "community of practice," a context many believe leads to more effective teaching practice (Florio-Ruane & Raphael, 2001).

Second, using SMART Board technology (an interactive whiteboard connected to a computer), entire classes view, describe, and think together about examples of their own work. Teacher preparation candidates use a structured conversation—the Collaborative Assessment Conference (Allen, 1998)—to talk to one another in a rigorous way about the work they are doing. When students use this protocol rather than rushing to evaluate student work and teaching practice, they first are asked to describe this work without judgment. This simple first step encourages students to be more thoughtful and to see the complex nature of student learning and teaching practice. In the second step, students list the questions that arise from the work. Again, this step encourages students to be more thoughtful and allows presenting students to hear about their lesson plans without having to defend them. It is only after the class has described the work, asked questions, and speculated about the context that the presenting student presents some of the context of the lesson. Again the focus is on describing and building a shared understanding of a teacher's work. At the very end of the protocol, the group discuses the implications of these draft lesson or unit plans for their own teaching practice (Allen). This process is carried out both in the classroom and electronically on the forum.

Third, students publicly evaluate one another's work. In the SEF classes, students are asked to examine the work that is posted and to use a common set of rubrics, based on state and National Council for Accreditation of Teacher Education standards, to give one another feedback. The process of evaluating lessons and articulating and posting a response is valuable both for the student serving in the role of evaluator (who begins to build an understanding of state and national standards) and for the student receiving the critique (who gets feedback from a variety of perspectives).

After two years of work with undergraduates on the SEF, some patterns are becoming clear. First, students are taking advantage of the website to look at one another's work. Prior to the SEF, students rarely shared their work with anyone but the teacher. Now, on average, every post is viewed five times by someone else. Second, students are more committed to completing work and posting it in a timely manner because they are all responsible for one another. Instances of late, missing, or incomplete student work are rare. Third, students have a clearer understanding of the standards by which they are evaluated. Because students have seen many examples of student work and have publicly evaluated the work many times, there is little mystery left in the evaluation process. Finally, students frequently share their impressions that they write better. In a reflection session in the spring of 2006, one student commented, "Doing work in public was very interesting. It kept me focused and my writing was extremely purposeful." Another wrote, "Knowing that anyone could potentially view my thoughts through the writing assignments caused me to be more thoughtful about not only the purpose of my writing, but especially about how I expressed myself."

Salem Education Forum: Graduate Leadership Program

Graduate students preparing to be school administrators also participate in the SEF, which helps them assemble electronic portfolios that can be used in the licensure process. However, for the school leaders, participation in the SEF also models an important leadership idea: that effective leaders are able to do their work in public and as part of a professional community (Fullan, 2001; Heifetz & Linsky, 2002; Sergiovanni, 2001; Wagner & Kegan, 2006). Participation in the forum allows aspiring leaders to practice this important idea in three ways.

First, students post their work throughout their master's degree program on the SEF. During their course of study, they make public and share their work in such diverse areas as finance, community building, and professional development. One candidate reflected,

> Never having made my course work public [made doing so] very difficult to do at first. The idea of someone other than the instructor reading my materials and passing judgment made me anxious. As I worked through the process, however, I found my attention to detail became more sophisticated. It became a practice that I feel facilitates deeper leaning and understanding.

Second, the group uses a Consultancy Protocol (Allen, 1998)—another structured conversation—to ask one another clarifying and probing questions about their work, to raise questions, and to share thoughts about implications for leadership practice. The value of this protocol is that it allows a practitioner to present a problem of practice to a group of peers without feeling that he has to defend or justify his actions (Annenberg Institute for School Reform, 1996; Blythe, Allen, & Powell, 1999). The practitioner presents a problem, but then is required to listen for a substantial period of time while his or her colleagues talk about the dilemma. At the end of the session, the presenter can respond to any parts of the conversation that he or she felt were helpful or interesting. The goal is for the group to help the practitioner think more deeply or differently about the dilemma, not simply solve it (Annenberg Institute for School Reform). This process, done in class and on the SEF, allows for all of the expertise and learning of the group to be a resource for everyone.

Because the Consultancy Protocol is a regular feature of each group's work, student work is viewed by other members of the leadership program at a rate even higher than in the undergraduate program. One candidate summed up the experience by writing,

> It is interesting to me that the process of doing our work in public tends to draw out more thoughtful responses. When we sort through our ideas and dilemmas we write differently. I found this process much more beneficial and real compared to the isolated research papers we did in the past.

Third, the SEF also supports the creation of work groups that span a variety of school districts and school levels. Often students are asked to form work groups—much as "real" school leaders are—and collaborate to solve a dilemma of leadership or organizational practice. Both the group's deliberations and final product are shared on the SEF to get feedback from and act as a resource to other students.

Although significant work remains to be done to formally study the short- and long-term impact of the SEF, three promising ideas have surfaced. First, students in the educational leadership program use the SEF to look at one another's work at an even higher rate than the undergraduates. In the undergraduate classes, every piece of work is, on average, examined by someone else five times; in the graduate classes, the average is almost six. Second, although graduate students' initial rates of SEF use are lower than those of undergraduates, their participation exceeds the participation of undergraduates as they proceed through the program and become more comfortable with sharing work and giving one another feedback. Third, because much of the work that graduate students share is based on "real work" dilemmas of practice, students report that the suggestions, feedback, and learning that they get from their colleagues not only strengthens their thinking but also frequently changes some aspect of their practice. Students in the educational leadership program regularly report that they have tried out some idea or suggestion made on the SEF in their own school or classroom.

Final Thoughts

Commonly, electronic portfolios are perceived as a solution to the many problems of paper-based portfolios—a manageable system for collecting, organizing, storing, or displaying all of the writing, videos, presentations, project, and artwork students produce. Both the Timilty Community Forum (at www.timilty.org) and the Salem Education Forum (www.salemedforum.org) are electronic portfolio and bulletin board systems, and, as such, they are capable of addressing these needs. However, that is not what we set out to do when we began this work. Rather than change the ways teachers and students collect and organize data, we sought to change the ways teachers and students think about, talk about, and use data. In fact, we wanted to change the conversation of the classroom in significant and substantial ways—to make learning an ongoing process of collegial inquiry. In the case of adolescent learners, we posited that a classroom context of this type would contribute to higher levels of motivation and engagement, and as a consequence, improved opportunities for literacy learning. In the case of undergraduate and graduate students, we expected that these more collaborative classroom contexts would contribute to a deeper understanding of teaching and learning. To accomplish these goals, we made sharing, peer review, and peer evaluation an everyday occurrence—an expected, predictable, and inescapable routine. Although rigorous study of electronic portfolios remains to be done, we observed some consistent and promising patterns. First, everyone—middle school students and undergraduate and graduate students—shared and continue to share large amounts of their work. In each setting, students who had rarely submitted their work to anyone but their teachers quickly learned to make their work public to everyone in the class. Second, students who were rarely asked to give feedback learned to evaluate their classmates' work, share ideas, build on those ideas, and use the feedback to leverage further learning. In these forums, students not only shared work but also they used, reacted to, and learned from what others shared. Third, the forums encouraged students to generate and focus on ideas that were personally compelling. The Timilty Community Forum encouraged students to identify areas of personal interest and to explore those areas of interest with members of the class. The Salem Education Forum encouraged aspiring teachers and school leaders to make public the dilemmas of practice and to use the feedback they received to change their practice. Both forums encouraged students to connect their work to their own interests and passions.

Although the story of these forums is an optimistic one, it remains only a story. Many questions remain. One question relates to the nature of the sharing and feedback that occurs. It is clear that in these classrooms, students share and give feedback to one another at a much higher rate than ever before. However, we have not yet documented the effects of these interactions. Is the quality of student work better? Are their reflections increasingly insightful? Does feedback become more thoughtful? Are there downsides, especially to particular groups of students, to making work public, as suggested by Finders (1997) in her work with working class and less popular girls?

A second question relates to effects on teacher or leadership practice. Does participation in the forums build teachers' or leaders' understanding of collaborative, learning communities? Does it change teacher–student discourse? Does it change the final grading process?

Although the forums themselves are a rich source of data for answering some of these questions, others will require the collection of additional evidence, including achievement test scores, classroom observations, and transcripts of teacher and student talk.

References

Allen, D. (1998). *Assessing student learning: From grading to understanding.* New York: Teachers College Press.

Annenberg Institute for School Reform. (1996). *The consultancy protocol. Providence*, RI: Author.

Bandura, A., & Locke, E.A. (2003). Negative self-efficacy and goal effects revisited. *Journal of Applied Psychology, 88*(1), 87–99.

Beck, I., & McKeown, M.G. (2001). Inviting students into the pursuit of meaning. *Educational Psychology Review, 13*, 225–241.

Biancarosa, G., & Snow, C.E. (2004). *Reading next—A vision for action and research in middle and high school literacy: A report from Carnegie Corporation of New York.* Washington, DC: Alliance for Excellent Education.

Blythe, T., Allen, D., & Powell, B.S. (1999). *Looking together at student work: A companion guide to assessing student learning.* New York: Teachers College Press.

Calkins, L.M. (1994). *The art of teaching writing.* Portsmouth, NH: Heinemann.

Csikszentmihalyi, M. (1990). Literacy and intrinsic motivation. *Daedalus, 119*, 115–140.

Cuban, L. (1993). *How teachers taught: Constancy and change in American classrooms*, 1890–1980 (2nd ed.). New York: Teachers College Press.

Dufour, R., & Eaker, R.E. (1998). *Professional learning communities at work: Best practices for enhancing student achievement.* Bloomington, IN: National Education Service.

Eccles, J.S. (1999). The development of children ages 6 to 14. *Future of Children, 9*(2), 30–44.

Evans, R. (1996). *The human side of school change: Reform, resistance, and the real-life problems of innovation.* San Francisco: Jossey-Bass.

Finders, M.J. (1997). *Just girls: Hidden literacies and life in junior high.* New York: Teachers College Press.

Fisher, D., Lapp, D., & Flood, J. (2005). Consensus scoring and peer planning: Meeting literacy accountability demands one school at a time. *The Reading Teacher, 58*, 656–666.

Florio-Ruane, S., & Raphael, T.E. (2001). Reading lives: Creating and sustaining learning about literacy education in teacher study groups. In C.M. Clark (Ed.), *Talking shop: Authentic conversations in teacher learning* (pp. 64–81). New York: Teachers College Press.

Fullan, M. (2001). *Leading in a culture of change.* San Francisco: Jossey-Bass.

Fullan, M. (2005). *Leadership & sustainability: System thinkers in action.* Thousand Oaks, CA: Corwin.

Gee, J.P. (1996). *Social linguistics and literacies: Ideology in discourses.* London: Falmer.

Guthrie, J.T., & Wigfield, A. (2000). Engagement and motivation in reading. In M.L. Kamil, P.B. Mosenthal, P.D. Pearson, & R. Barr (Eds.), *Handbook of reading research* (Vol. 3, pp. 403–422). Mahwah, NJ: Erlbaum.

Harvey, S., & Goudvis, A. (2000). *Strategies that work: Teaching comprehension to enhance understanding.* York, ME: Stenhouse.

Heifetz, R.A., & Linsky, M. (2002). *Leadership on the line: Staying alive through the dangers of leading.* Boston: Harvard Business School Press.

Kamil, M.L. (2003). *Adolescents and literacy: Reading for the 21st century.* Washington, DC: Alliance for Excellent Education.

Langer, G.M., Colton, A.B., & Goff, L.S. (2003). *Collaborative analysis of student work: Improving teaching and learning.* Alexandria, VA: Association for Supervision and Curriculum Development.

Lewis, S., Ceperich, J., & Jepson, J.C. (2002). *Critical trends in urban education: Fifth biennial survey of America's great city schools.* Washington, DC: Council of the Great City Schools.

Little, J.W., & McLaughlin, M.W. (1993). *Teachers' work: Individuals, colleagues, and contexts.* New York: Teachers College Press.

Louis, K.S., & Kruse, S.D. (1995). *Professionalism and community perspectives on reforming urban schools.* Thousand Oaks, CA: Corwin.

McLaughlin, M.W., & Oberman, I. (1996). *Teacher learning: New policies, new practices.* New York: Teachers College Press.

McLaughlin, M.W., & Talbert, J.E. (2001). *Professional communities and the work of high school teaching.* Chicago: University of Chicago Press.

McLaughlin, M., & Talbert, J. (2002). Reforming districts. In A. Hightower, M. Knapp, J. Marsh, & M. McLaughlin (Eds.), *School districts and instructional renewal* (pp. 173–192). New York: Teachers College Press.

Moje, E.B., Ciechanowski, K.M., Kramer, K., Ellis, L., Carrillo, R., & Collazo, T. (2004). Working toward third space in content area literacy: An examination of everyday funds of knowledge and Discourse. *Reading Research Quarterly, 39*, 38–70.

Moll, L.C. (1992). Literacy research in community and classrooms: A sociocultural approach. In R. Beach, J.L. Green, M.L. Kamil, & T. Shanahan (Eds.), *Multidisciplinary perspectives on literacy research* (pp. 211–244). Urbana, IL: National Conference on Research in English and National Council of Teachers of English.

Nelson, B.S., & Sassi, A. (2005). *The effective principal: Instructional leadership for high-quality learning.* New York: Teachers College Press.

Newmann, F., & Wehlage, G. (1995). *Successful school restructuring: A report to the public and educators by the Center on Organization and Restructuring of Schools.* Madison, WI: Center on Organization and Restructuring Schools.

Pressley, M. (2006). *Reading instruction that works: The case for balanced teaching* (3rd ed.). New York: Guilford.

Public Agenda. (2001). *Trying to stay ahead of the game: Superintendents and principals talk about school leadership.* New York: Author.

Public Agenda. (2003). *Rolling up their sleeves: Superintendents and principals talk about what's needed to fix public schools.* New York: Author.

RAND Reading Study Group. (2004). A research agenda for improving reading comprehension. In R.B. Ruddell & N.J. Unrau (Eds.), *Theoretical models and processes of reading* (5th ed., pp. 720–754). Newark, DE: International Reading Association.

Rosenholtz, S.J. (1989). *Teachers' workplace: The social organization of schools.* New York: Longman.

Senge, P.M. (1990). *The fifth discipline: The art and practice of the learning organization.* New York: Doubleday.

Sergiovanni, T.J. (2001). *The principalship: A reflective practice perspective* (4th ed.). Boston: Allyn & Bacon.

Snow, C.E., Burns, M.S., & Griffin, P. (1998). *Preventing reading difficulties in young children.* Washington, DC: National Academy Press.

Vygotsky, L.S. (1978). *Mind in society: The development of higher psychological processes* (M. Cole, V.

John-Steiner, S. Scribner, & E. Souberman, Eds. & Trans.). Cambridge, MA: Harvard University Press. (Original work published 1934)

Wagner, T., & Kegan, R. (2006). *Change leadership: A practical guide to transforming our schools.* San Francisco: Jossey-Bass.

Questions for Reflection

- The authors explain that a difficult and persistent challenge in the use of electronic portfolios is establishing a safe environment in which students can publicly share personal connections and interpretations of literature. How would you explain to students the boundaries of respectful discussion? What guidelines would you set? How would you explain why these boundaries are essential for students to feel comfortable enough to share their thoughts and feelings?
- Examples in this article are drawn from experiences with middle school, undergraduate, and graduate students. How would experiences with electronic portfolios differ when used with high school students? Elementary students? How might the techniques in this article be adapted?